Men's Work, Women's Work

Feminist Perspectives
Series Editor: Michelle Stanworth

Published

Men's Work, Women's Work

A Sociological History of the Sexual Division of Labour in Employment

HARRIET BRADLEY

University of Minnesota Press, Minneapolis

Published by the University of Minnesota Press
2037 University Avenue Southeast, Minneapolis MN 55414.

Printed in Great Britain.

Library of Congress Catalog Card Number 89–051303

The University of Minnesota
is an equal-opportunity
educator and employer.

CONTENTS

ACKNOWLEDGEMENTS

Innumerable intellectual influences have gone into the making of this book. I should like to express my thanks particularly to the following: Lydia Morris and Pete Rushton, for assisting me with their bibliographic expertise and lending me their books; Pat Sykes, for help with information on the United States; Michelle Stanworth, for her patience and forbearance as an editor and helpful initial advice; numerous women at conferences around the country, whose faith and interest in the study of gender have kept mine from flagging, especially Anne Witz; all the third-year and evening-class students at Sunderland Polytechnic, male and female, who have shared with me their experiences of the world of employment and their ideas about it. Since one tends to give more space in a book to those with whom one disagrees, I should like here to record the fact that Sonia Rose has been working over much the same ground as myself and has reached very similar conclusions. Finally, my greatest debt is to Irving Velody both for his critical observations and for keeping me from despair through the lengthy period this book has been in the writing.

For Sandy, Sonia and Pat: working women

INTRODUCTION

Men's Work, Women's Work: the title of this book reflects current social priorities. All round the world women work, in the home, in the fields, in factories and workshops, alongside men or apart from them, growing food, making goods, rendering services. Yet the work that they do is habitually viewed as less important than the work performed by men, may not even be considered 'real' work. Moreover, in virtually every society of which we have knowledge men and women normally perform different types of work. This 'sex-typing' of jobs, the allocation of specific tasks to men and to women, has become so extensive and pervasive that the two sexes are rarely found doing exactly the same kind of work. Even when men and women are found obstensibly working side by side in the fields or in an office or factory, closer investigation may well reveal that they are actually doing different things: men are scything and women are gathering the cut corn, women are filing record cards and men are doing the accounts, men are stamping out parts and women are sewing and gluing them together. Men are controlling and women are obeying.

Which particular tasks and occupations are defined as 'men's' and which as 'women's' will vary according to time and place. Tasks which are now seen as men's tasks may historically have been performed by women or vice versa. For example, before the industrialisation of the cotton industry men habitually were weavers, while women did the spinning. The introduction of power-driven machinery brought a reversal of these roles. There are few tasks, even those that seem as typically 'masculine' to us in twentieth-century Britain as mining and forestry, which have not in some time and place been performed by women. The sex-typing of work may even vary from region to region in a country at any given time, as some of the case studies in this book will show. What remains constant, however, is the segregation of the sexes and the persistence of ideas of the suitability of some work for women, some for men, whatever the particular nature of the tasks involved.

There have recently been a great number of sociological and historical studies of women's work in Britain and elsewhere, including some general histories (for example, Lewenhak, 1980; Lewis, 1984; Walby, 1987). What makes this study different from most of these is its specific focus on the segregation of the sexes within employment and the sex-typing of jobs. It is chiefly concerned with developments since the Industrial Revolution in Britain, from approximately 1750 to the present day. Patterns of gender-based occupational segregation are traced back to their pre-industrial origins in order to explain how our current ideas of what constitutes 'men's work' and 'women's work' have come into being. This inevitably leads to some consideration of the sexual division of labour in pre-industrial societies. I have also tried to include, for comparative purposes, material on other industrial societies, particularly the USA, where I have been able to find it. Here I have found particularly useful three books which have covered some of the same ground: Baker's masterly empirical study, *Technology and Woman's Work* (1964), Matthaei's *Economic History of Women in America* (1982), which like my book is particularly focused on sex-typing, and Game and Pringle's similarly oriented survey of Australia, *Gender at Work* (1983).

Although this is now a flourishing area of research, the interest in gender segregation at work is relatively recent. Much of the research reported on in this book has emerged as a result of the upsurge of academic interest in what we might broadly categorise as women's studies. This has led to a new concern with women's history, the role of women in society and ways of thinking about and conceptualising the relation between the sexes. That academic interest was itself the direct product of the political regeneration of feminism in the late 1960s and 1970s. Since much of this work is new, and a great deal of it consists of specialised and detailed historical or ethnographic studies focusing on one particular place or time period, it is not always immediately accessible to the non-specialist. Part of the intention behind this book, therefore, is to pull together a number of disparate studies in sociology and history and present them to the reader in an easily digestible and summarised form.

The book is divided into three sections. The first attempts to draw together existing contributions to the study of sex-typing and to provide a general overview of the state of knowledge in this area. Chapter 1 presents empirical evidence of patterns of segregation and sex-typing in contemporary societies. Chapters 2 and 3 consider the causes and consequences of these patterns; the range of explanations for their evolution provided by historians and sociologists is set out and assessed. Debates and disputes about the conceptualising of gender relations and about historical trends are dealt with in this section.

The second part consists of ten case studies. These examine in much more detail the development of the sexual division of labour within a variety of industries and occupations. The case studies are drawn from all three sectors of employment, primary, secondary and tertiary, to illustrate both the range of employment areas in which women are currently found and the range of patterns of task segregation. In the mining industry, for example, women in Britain have been excluded almost completely from every task, while, at the other end of the spectrum, in the teaching profession women and men perform almost exactly the same tasks, although women are concentrated in the lower levels of the various teaching hierarchies. While each case displays unique features, it is hoped that they provide, when taken together, a clear indication of the major factors which have influenced current patterns of sex-typing. The case studies draw partly on published research material which I have tried to synthesise. Some of this is, as I have said, the product of the feminist revival, but older studies which have touched, however briefly, on the issues of gender segregation are also referred to. In this field, Alice Clark's *Working Life of Women in the Seventeenth Century* (originally published in 1919 and reprinted in 1982) and Ivy Pinchbeck's *Women Workers in the Industrial Revolution* (originally published in 1930 and reprinted in 1981), products of an earlier wave of feminist research, remain classic texts, although the interpretations they offer are coloured by views of gender relations rather different from those appertaining today. I have also included new material drawn from primary sources, where appropriate, particularly to show exactly what tasks within each area were assigned to men and women. Most of this material comes from the Parliamentary Papers, but I have used some other sources, mainly nineteenth-century texts and commentaries. The chapter on hosiery draws upon the research I carried out for my Ph.D., which involved a wide array of documentation, including union minute books. In most, though not all, of the case studies I have been able to include material for America and other societies. There is no attempt to give a comprehensive history of developments in these countries. Rather the material is used to point to interesting parallels or contrasts.

The third part presents some general conclusions about the origins of segregation and sex-typing and its perpetuation, on the basis of the case studies. It also deals with some implications both for further academic work and for policy-making. The broader consequences of sex-typing for relations between men and women and its relation to other forms of social inequality are also briefly considered.

This book was conceived of as a project in 'historical sociology' or 'sociological history'. While reading for it, I became aware of the fact that historians and sociologists seemed frequently to ignore each other's work, even when it related to similar topics. Initially this seemed odd, even irritating, but I realised as I worked on this book that it was not simply the result of ignorance or ill will. History and sociology have their own distinct languages and discourses, their own sets of dialogues, and this does pose a genuine problem for those of us who believe strongly that the two disciplines should draw closer to each other. This problem has its reflection in the style of my book. Whereas the empirical sections and case studies are written in a language which (I hope) anybody can understand, the parts dealing with historical and sociological debates assume some familiarity on the part of the reader with the basic concepts and concerns of each discipline, although I have tried where I could to give definitions of the more obscure pieces of disciplinary jargon. I hope that the reader does not find the result too positively schizophrenic! The attempt to make sociologists and historians familiar with each other's work still seems to me a vital one.

My study, of course, also has its political implications. In the last two decades, the reflorescence of feminism has led to increased demands and campaigns for the equality of women with men in all aspects of social life. Despite increased public awareness and despite new legal measures against sex discrimination, women remain in a disadvantaged position in most areas of paid employment in most, if not all, contemporary societies, as international studies such as the New Internationalist's *Women: A World Report* (1985) and Chapkis and Enloe's *Of Common Cloth* (1983) demonstrate. While gender-based occupational segregation remains strong, measures like the British Equal Pay Act of 1970 are likely to remain ineffective. To attack that segregation more effectively we must try to understand its roots and the reasons for its obstinate persistence once instituted. It is hoped that this book may make some contribution to that understanding.

Part I

THE SOCIOLOGICAL AND HISTORICAL CONTEXT

1

GENDER SEGREGATION AND THE SEX-TYPING OF JOBS

No more delightful wanderings ... Henceforth it must be work, woman's work, dreary and monotonous sometimes, yet pleasant withal, as it rewarded me with the proud consciousness that I was not only able to eat my daily bread but earn it.

Wills, Lays of Lowly Life

In these words Ruth Wills, Leicester working woman and poet, looked back in 1861 at her transition from childhood to womanly status, when at the age of ten or eleven she gained a job in the warehouse at Corah's hosiery factory where she was to work for the rest of her life. Her comment reveals to us some of the ambiguous and contradictory attitudes common to most people who have to work under the prevailing arrangements and conditions of industrial capitalism. But it also tells us interesting things about social perceptions of 'women's work' in the middle of the nineteenth century. During the succeeding decades, ideas about 'men's work' and 'women's work' were to stabilise into the forms familiar to us today, after the period of tumultuous change in the nature of working arrangements and relationships and in working people's daily lives, which marked the long, slow, painful transition from one type of society to another that we now know by the shorthand label of the 'Industrial Revolution'.

Women's work in Victorian England was indeed often 'dreary and monotonous', both inside and outside the home. Though we shall have cause within this book to consider domestic labour or 'housework', the focus of study here is employment outside the home, wage labour. Wage labour for Victorian women meant filling the less prestigious, more routinised, often less skilled tasks in both the new manufacturing and service industries and the traditional areas of agriculture and domestic service. While men's traditional trades and skills had often been challenged or destroyed by the new industrial system, they had succeeded in capturing for themselves the more responsible jobs and tasks which either were or could credibly be described as skilled. Women's work was low paid, often pitched at a level below subsistence needs, and few women, of any class, had expectations of anything better. Men were paid more and, while not yet attained, the 'breadwinner's' wage, sufficient to support a whole family, was their target, and claimed as their 'right' as head of a household. There was little sense that women's work was something that could be a source of pleasure and satisfaction in itself; it was undertaken solely out of necessity 'to earn one's daily bread'. The idea was gaining ground that all women, given the choice, would prefer to stay at home and devote themselves to things domestic. Few women had any real choice over the type of work they undertook, and the range of occupations open to them was limited. For men, however, a broader range of possibilities appeared, and for many middle-class and even some working-class men there was some prospect of a 'free' choice of trade and career. In any case men expected, if they did not always achieve it, some intrinsic satisfaction from their work, if only in the sense of the access it gave them to adult masculine status and the breadwinner role. Men's work offered an important source of social and personal identity, whereas for women the growing tendency was for their identity to be focused on their domestic roles as homemakers and mothers within the inturned, privatised family which was becoming the Victorian ideal. Finally, women's work was different in content from men's work: the characteristic features of women's and men's work as we know them today were becoming the norm in 1861.

As the case studies in this book will show, anthropological and historical evidence bears testimony to an almost infinite variety of forms of the sexual division of work. It would be hard to find any single activity which has not been, at some time or place, 'women's work'. Yet over time and space we can discern some general trends, some gender allocations that are more common than others. Murdock and Provost's wide survey of the sexual division of labour as recorded in 185 societies shows, for example, that hunting large animals, fishing, smelting ores, metalwork, mining and quarrying and lumberwork are almost everywhere male tasks. As we shall see throughout this book, female tasks tend to be less sharply distinguished. However, Murdock and Provost found that dairy production, cooking, carrying water and gathering vegetables were very commonly performed by women (Murdock and Provost, 1973). Virginia Novarra (1980) has argued, more generally, that six key tasks are performed mainly by women in the majority of societies: provision of food, care of the home, child care, nursing the sick, teaching and manufacture of clothing. These tasks are frequently performed by women in the home, as subsistence labour or unpaid housework. They can be linked to the association of women with 'domestic' activity and, in the later stages of social development, the ascription of women to a home-centred existence. But when women move into the wage labour sphere they often perform commercialised forms of these same activities which centre on the care and servicing of other people, 'production of people' to borrow a phrase from Murgatroyd (1985). Around the world today women in vast numbers work as teachers, nurses, cleaners and garment-makers.

As well as this personal care motif, typical 'woman's work' displays certain common features, as Game and Pringle (1983) have argued, at least in the ideal visions we have of it. It is usually indoor work, considered to be 'lighter' than men's work; it is clean, safe, physically undemanding, often repetitive and considered boring, requires dexterity rather than 'skill', often has domestic associations; it tends to lack mobility, being tied to a particular work station; it may well have associations and requirements of beauty and glamour. By contrast, if we visualise typical men's work, we tend to evoke images of the outdoors, of strength and physicality; 'men's work' may be heavy, dirty, dangerous, it is often highly mobile (men have a curious monopoly of jobs in the transport sectors), it requires 'skill' and training. It is frequently highly technical, based on mechanical knowledge or scientific expertise; at the highest level, it requires characteristics of creativity, innovation, intelligence, responsibility, authority and power. Such qualities are rarely ones we would associate with women's work!

These typical ascriptions were already being elaborated in 1861, and jobs were allocated to men and women in terms of matching up to some or other of these criteria. During the remaining decades of the nineteenth century, as the case studies in this book will, I hope, demonstrate, the familiar modern sexual division of labour in factories and offices, schools and hospitals evolved, and the related notions of fit work for the sexes became a commonplace of our culture. The object of this book is to investigate how and why this came about; and why, once jobs have become sex-typed, it is so hard to break down the patterns of segregation. It is a study, in sum, of the origins and persistence of sex-typing and gender segregation in the sphere of employment. Since I use these two terms so frequently throughout the text, it may be as well to define them at this point. By sex-typing, I mean the process by which jobs are 'gendered', ascribed to one sex or the other; while segregation refers to the way in which women and men are located in different types of jobs; in the words of Catherine Hakim: 'occupational segregation by gender exists when men and women do different kinds of work, so that one can speak of two separate labour forces, one male and one female, which are not in competition with each other for the same jobs' (Hakim, 1979, p. 1). This often involves the physical separation of the sexes in different spaces or locations. Sex-typing and segregation are thus analytically separable, although in practice they are almost always found in combination; in sociological terms, sex-typing can be seen as the ideological face of the structural process of segregation.

Since Ruth Wills wrote her autobiography in 1861 massive changes have occurred, which have affected women's social position and the relations between the sexes. Women have gained legal and political rights. The evolution of the welfare state has freed them from total dependence on fathers and husbands and the development of effective contraception has freed them from the burden of perpetual pregnancy and childbearing. Two important political waves of feminism have generated energetic campaigns for equal rights and opportunities and pushed women's view of their own disadvantages into public consciousness; partly as a result, higher education and many professional areas have opened up for women; two world wars have provided them with an opportunity to try their hand at almost every type of work deemed socially necessary; most recently, legislation has been passed outlawing discrimination in the field of employment. Yet, in spite of all this, the prevalence of sex-typing and segregation in paid work has diminished very little since 1861. In the words of one researcher: 'the most striking difference between men and women on the labor market is the work they do. Men and women are, to a great extent, found in different spheres of economic activity and occupations, and within most occupations they are employed at different levels and with different work tasks' (Jonung, 1984, p. 44). Surveys and statistical information reveal that Britain in the 1980s retains a structure of sexual differentiation at work which has apparently resisted all the persistent campaigning for equality.

Sex-typing and Gender Segregation in the 1970s and 1980s

More women in Britain are currently in paid employment than at any time this century, 9.6 million in 1987. According to the 1981 Census, 71 per cent of single women and 60 per cent of married women were economically active. Women then made up 42 per cent of the work force (64 per cent of these being married), and by 1987 this had risen to 45 per cent. However, while men's share of jobs has diminished they have kept their dominance over full-time work. Figures from the 1984 Labour Force Survey show that 88 per cent of part-time workers are women. In fact nearly half of employed women are in part-time jobs (45 per cent, as opposed to 4 per cent of men) and 55 per cent of married women work part-time (Beechey, 1986). The number of women in part-time jobs has increased from 784,000 in 1951 to 3,543,329 in 1981, the bulk of these jobs being in the service sector. Indeed, this has been the major growth area in the British economy since the recession of the 1970s. Areas like retailing, fast food and hotel work have provided a new crop of low-paid, low-status jobs for women; 96 per cent of the new part-time jobs in the 1970s were in service work (Sharpe, 1984).

Despite the Equal Pay and Sex Discrimination Acts, there are still clear pay differentials between women and men. In 1987 the average gross weekly earnings of women were equal to 66 per cent of men's. As we shall see, this two-thirds differential has assumed an almost magical quality for over a hundred years. However, part of the discrepancy arises from the fact that women work fewer hours than men, even when working full-time, so that they receive fewer bonus payments and fewer payments for overtime and shiftwork. It has therefore been customary, in order to get a fairer comparison, to consider hourly rather than weekly earnings. Figures derived from the New Earnings Survey 1970–87 show an immediate improvement in the level of women's wages following the passing of the Equal Pay Act in 1970 and its full implementation in 1975. But subsequently women have fallen back a little so that no move towards full equalisation has been sustained. Thus the average hourly earnings of full-time women employees as a proportion of men's (overtime excluded) in 1970 were 63.1%; in 1974 67.4%; in 1977 75.5%; in 1980 73.5%; in 1984 73.5%; and in 1987 73.6%.

This differential may partly reflect the fact that some women may (still) be doing virtually the same work as men for less pay, but without doubt gender segregation is the major cause of pay disparities. In her important and influential study, published in 1979, Catherine Hakim distinguished between two different aspects of segregation: horizontal segregation refers to the concentration of women and men in different types of work; vertical segregation to the concentration of men in higher grades, women in lower grades, both within and between occupations and industries. Taken together, these account for women's lower levels of pay and face us with a substantial picture of inequality.

Figures gathered by the Equal Opportunities Commission (EOC) for its Annual Reports reveal the strength of horizontal segregation. Many occupations and industries are heavily dominated by men. In 1981 men were 95 per cent of the work force in mining and quarrying, 91 per cent in shipbuilding and in construction, 88 per cent in vehicle construction and in metal manufacture, and 89 per cent in farming and fishing. Such 'heavy' industries maintain their traditional image as 'men's work'. Women, by contrast, are less markedly dominant in any given industry or occupation, as these are classified by the collectors of official statistics. However, in 1981 they constituted 76 per cent of clerical workers and of workers in catering, cleaning and personal services and 74 per cent of clothing and footwear workers (Huws, 1982). Hakim argues, on the basis of such figures, that men are more likely to find themselves working in a job where their own sex is numerically dominant.

However, within each industry and occupation there is a tendency to the sex-typing of particular jobs, which is not revealed by statistics based on such broad categories. Jonung argues, rightly, that 'segregation is higher the more detailed the occupational level studied' (Jonung, 1984, p. 53). Accordingly, over 90 per cent of secretaries, typists and receptionists, of cashiers, of nurses, of canteen assistants and of maids are women, for example, and over 75 per cent of chars, office cleaners, sewing machinists, laundry workers and kitchen maids (Lockwood and Knowles, 1984; Dex, 1985). The case studies in this book will provide further examples of jobs ascribed to one sex or another and suggest the likelihood that a majority of workers of *both* sexes will find themselves in working groups of their own sex. This is confirmed by the recent survey of women's employment carried out by Martin and Roberts (1984). This substantial survey of over 3000 women workers found that 63 per cent of those who worked among others doing the same job worked only among women; the figure for men working only among men was 81 per cent, although this was based on a much smaller sample.

In another sense, women's employment can be seen as *more* concentrated than men's, in that the range of occupations and industries in which they are found is more restricted. Thus 85 per cent of female manual workers are found in three of the occupational categories used by government statisticians: catering, cleaning and other personal services; painting, repetitive assembly, inspecting, packaging and related activities; making and repairing (excluding electrical and metal goods.) Among non-manual women concentration is even starker, as 91 per cent are to be found in three categories: selling; clerical work; professional work in education, welfare and health (Cockburn, 1985). Ursula Huws' useful profile of women's activity in one geographical area (West Yorkshire) reflects such a pattern. For every 100 women of all ages 32 are in employment; of these nine are in clerical work, eight in factories, seven in cleaning and catering, four in the teaching, nursing and social work professions, three in sales and only one in other occupations (Huws, 1982, p. 15).

The case studies which follow demonstrate extensive vertical segregation in each area studied. In every sector of the economy women are relegated to the lowest levels of the job hierarchy and grossly under-represented in top jobs. In 1983 they held only 9 per cent of managerial jobs (Beechey, 1986). The entry of women into higher-status professional work has been concentrated in certain areas, notably the lower-paid public sector jobs. Thus while women are 65 per cent of health, education and welfare professionals, they are only 7 per cent of scientific, technological and engineering professionals and 23 per cent of professionals supporting management and administration. Moreover, as the case studies of teaching and medicine will show, women are concentrated in the lowest ranks (for example as infant teachers and nurses) and are progressively less represented at each level of the hierarchy; only a tiny minority reach posts with a substantial element of administrative or managerial functions. At the other end of the spectrum, women in manufacturing industry are under-represented in supervisory posts (it is not uncommon to find an all-women work group headed by a man) and are found mainly in jobs labelled as unskilled or semi-skilled. Hakim's historical survey revealed that between 1911 and 1974 the percentage of women among skilled manual workers fell from 24 per cent to 13 per cent, while among the unskilled they rose from 16 per cent to 37 per cent (Hakim, 1979).

The pattern of segregation has been largely undisturbed by the changes and upheavals in the economy which have resulted from the introduction of computers and information technology, from the restructuring of jobs and the shakeout of workers brought about by the recent recession, and the other changes which some have seen as a 'second industrial revolution'. Figures from the Labour Force Survey of 1985 (table 1.1a) show continuity with the 1981 figures quoted above, which themselves were little different from similar data for the 1970s.

TABLE 1.1a Proportions of men and women (aged over 16) within selected occupations, 1985.

	Percentages	
Occupation	*Men*	*Women*
Construction, mining and related	99.5	0.5
Processing, making, repairing and related (metals and electrical)	96.4	3.6
Transport operation, materials moving and related	96.4	3.6
Professional and related in science, engineering and technology	93.3	6.7
Farming, fishing and related	83.1	16.9
Professional and related supplying management and administration	77.1	22.9
Managerial	74.9	25.1
Professional and related in education, welfare and health	34.8	65.2
Clerical and related	22.8	77.2
Catering, cleaning, hairdressing and other personal services	20.8	79.2

Source: *Labour Force Survey, 1985*

Indeed, Hakim's historical investigation revealed an extraordinary stability of patterns of segregation over the whole of this century. Examining data for the period between 1811 and 1871, she concluded that

TABLE 1.1b Proportions of men and women within selected industries, 1986.

| | Percentages | |
Industry	Men	Women
Retail distribution	37.3	62.7
Hotels and catering	33.5	66.5
Education services	32.4	67.6
Footwear and clothing	25.8	74.2
Medical and health services	20.1	79.9

Source: *Eurostat, Employment and Unemployment, 1988*

while there had been a decrease in the number of occupations which completely excluded one sex or the other, the likelihood of a man working in an occupation where his sex predominated has actually increased over the period. In 1971 50 per cent of men worked in occupations where they outnumbered women by nine to one, and two-thirds in occupations where the ratio was four to one. Where horizontal segregation was weakened over the period it was related to male inroads into 'female' occupations. There was little compensatory expansion of women into male areas. Moreover, she argues that vertical segregation also increased over the period: the exclusion of women from skilled manual jobs has cancelled out the slight increase of women in top managerial and professional posts. In a second article examining 1981 data, she argued that there had been no significant change in the intervening decade. Mallier and Rosser's later study (1987) slightly challenges this verdict, suggesting that in contrast to the earlier period women have recently been making some inroads into male-dominated occupations. This, however, they consider insufficient to change established notions of what is 'women's work', and since men are not entering female-dominated occupations in any numbers they conclude that the general pattern of segregation has been little disturbed. We can see that, by and large, the structure of segregation has persisted obstinately throughout the twentieth century.

Although this study is concerned with gender differences and not with ethnic disadvantage, it should be acknowledged that many have discerned a pattern of segregation within segregation when looking at the position of black women in Britain. Parmar (1982) argues that, while, as indicated above, all women face a restricted set of labour market opportunities, racism and discrimination ensure that the position of black women is even more restricted. West Indian women, for example, tend to be concentrated in unskilled jobs of very low status which white women are unwilling to take on, such as hotel and catering work, hospital domestic work and the lowest grades of nursing. Moreover, while many women's jobs are based on ideas of feminine attractiveness and charm in handling clients (secretaries, receptionists, bank clerks, shop assistants, hostesses), racial discrimination and stereotyping act to keep black women out of such 'visible' jobs and confine them to the backstage areas, such as kitchens and laundries. This social invisibility of black women means that their contribution to the economy and to the welfare of the community is obscured and unappreciated. West Indian women are also grossly under-represented in top jobs, only 2 per cent of them being in managerial and professional work as opposed to 17 per cent of white women and 20 per cent of Asian women. Asian women, however, are more likely than West Indian or white women not to enter the labour market at all (Beechey, 1986). Traditional family relations may compel many married women to remain at home. Language difficulties also make it hard for some of the older women to enter non-manual work, and in fact Asian women are quite heavily concentrated in unskilled factory work, especially in Yorkshire and the Midlands. They are also often found as homeworkers, which partly reflects the hostility of some Asian men to the idea of their wives leaving the home and exposing themselves to an alien culture with its threat of sexual temptation, which challenges traditional notions of *izzat* (family pride and male honour) (Wilson, 1978). But, as Allen and Wolkowitz (1987) point out, women tend to do homework only when they fail to find opportunities outside the home, and the discrimination which black women face in the labour market may also force them into this low-paid form of employment.

Homework is seen by many as epitomising the devaluation of women's work. Although it is hard to make an accurate assessment of the numbers currently employed as homeworkers, Allen and Wolkowitz suggest that this is not only a long-established form of female employment but also, in the context of the restructuring of the economy, a potentially growing trend. Often done for appalling pay (as little as 50 pence an hour), in unpleasant conditions, unprotected by union organisation and isolated from the companionship which for many women is a major attraction of work outside the home, it symbolises the subjugation of women to domestic obligations, which, as we shall see, has been such an important factor in promoting sex-typing and segregation.

Some International Comparisons

Reports and data from other industrialised societies indicate similar, if not identical, patterns of segregation and sex-typing. The occupations and industries that are largely occupied by women may vary from country to country, but in each case women are likely to be found in the lower status, less highly rewarded jobs. All countries show marked levels of vertical segregation, although in some countries, such as Sweden, Norway, Denmark and Canada, women have made greater advances into the professions, and in the USA and Canada they have gained greater access to management.

In America, as in Britain, the proportion of women in the labour force has risen considerably over the century, from 14 per cent in 1901 to 28 per cent in 1947 to 38 per cent in 1985 (Lapidus, 1978; New Internationalist, 1985). Between 1970 and 1980 the percentage of economically active women rose from 49 per cent to 59 per cent (Schmid and Weitzel, 1984). They are less likely to work part-time; only 21 per cent of adult women do so, although the majority of teenage workers of both sexes are part-timers (Mallier and Rosser, 1987). But they have moved into a circumscribed labour market. Hakim in her study found a broadly similar pattern of segregation in Britain and the USA. The difference was that, whereas at the beginning of the century segregation was *more* pronounced in America (as the case studies will suggest), since the 1960s this tendency has been reversed and there has been some reduction of segregation (a finding confirmed by the later research carried out by Jonung). However, Hakim also noted that the proportion of women among professionals had actually declined between 1940 and 1970, from 42 per cent to 39 per cent, a period in which there was a considerable expansion of women in clerical and sales jobs. Where America scores more strongly is in the greater proportion of women among managers. This rose from 11 per cent to 16 per cent over the same period and has climbed steadily to 28 per cent in 1982; today nearly 4 per cent of all women workers in the USA are in managerial and administrative posts (Hakim, 1979; United States Bureau of the Census, 1984; New Internationalist, 1985).

Other commentators have noted the limited successes of women in the professions (Rohrlich-Leavitt, 1975). In 1973 women were only 7 per cent of doctors, 3 per cent of lawyers and 2 per cent of dentists and pharmacists. The proportion of women academics in the 1960s was less than before World War II (Saffioti, 1975; Dodge, 1978). Since the mid-1970s, however, the position of women has improved considerably, partly as a result of feminist campaigning and because of the early implementation of equal opportunities legislation: the Equal Pay Act was passed in 1963 and Title VII of the Civil Rights Bill of 1964 covered sex discrimination in various areas (Beller, 1982). According to Dex and Shaw (1986), this has helped to improve access to managerial and top professional posts, but it has made much less impact in the lower-status sectors of the labour market. Mallier and Rosser in their comparative study of Britain and America are a little more sanguine, concluding that in the 1970s in the USA there have been large increases in women's share of certain professional and managerial occupations. This is confirmed by the Census Bureau figures: women are now 18 per cent of doctors and lawyers, 4 per cent of dentists. There is a long way to go, but this is a considerable advance on the 1973 figures quoted earlier. Nevertheless, Mallier and Rosser conclude that, as in Britain,

> Overall progress has been slow. Although female entry into some occupations, such as the professions, has been quite rapid, the overall employment distribution has only been marginally affected by these changes. Most women work in occupations that have been traditionally female-dominated, and, as relatively few men have entered these occupations, sex inequalities in occupational distribution remain substantial. (Mallier and Rosser, 1987, p. 58)

If we turn to these sectors, the 'crowding' of women into specific occupations is notable, as in Britain; 76 per cent of women are in the service sector (73 per cent in Britain) (Mallier and Rosser, 1987). In the 1970s 73 per cent worked in occupations where women are heavily over-represented, 59 per cent in occupations that are 70 per cent or more female (Lapidus, 1978). In 1977 women were 99 per cent of kindergarten and nursery teachers and 97 per cent of registered nurses: in the early 1980s they were 99 per cent of typists, secretaries and telephone operators, 97 per cent of household service workers, 94 per cent of keypunchers, 80 per cent of clerical workers and 63 per cent of textile workers. Notably, while being 63 per cent of computer operators they made up only 39 per cent of computer specialists; and they were in 1982 only 4 per cent of electrical and electronic engineers. In traditional blue-collar areas women are particularly poorly represented, being in 1982 less than 2 per cent of carpenters, masons, plumbers, electricians, truck drivers and automobile mechanics, 7 per cent of police workers and 9 per cent of transport operators (United States Bureau of the Census, 1984; Larwood and Gutek, 1984; Mallier and Rosser, 1987). Beller (1982) in her survey concludes that a majority of occupations are male dominated, very few are integrated and women are found clustered in less than a third of all occupations.

As we would predict, occupational segregation affects pay. In the 1970s, professional women averaged 66 per cent of their male counterparts' earnings, while for female sales clerks the figure was 40 per cent! This does not arise from women being less qualified, for Saffioti shows that women's pay levels are 60 per cent of men's where the amount of schooling is equivalent. On the basis of such figures, American researchers have been led to conclude that sexual segregation is more firmly established than racial segregation; whereas in 1939 white workers of either sex earned on average more than black workers of either sex, in 1969 black males fared better than women of both races (Gross, 1968; Rohrlich-Leavitt, 1975). Rohrlich-Leavitt concludes that 'the lessening of economic racism has been offset by the rise of economic sexism' (Rohrlich-Leavitt, 1975, p. 279).

Broadly speaking, we can say that there are strong similarities between Britain and the USA in terms of the extent and persistence of segregation and sex-typing, although, as the case studies will show, there are some national variations in the gender ascription of particular jobs. For example, hosiery is more definitely 'women's work' in America, and schoolteaching is more feminised, while in Britain women have done better in medicine and have retained midwifery as a specialist female profession. However, the similarities are more marked than the differences, and we may concur with Saffioti that 'the professions and other occupations, as well as the various positions within each of these, have been stereotyped as "masculine" or "feminine"' (Saffioti, 1975, p. 72).

Indeed, Hakim's survey suggests that similar patterns exist in most advanced industrial societies. In all of them, women are concentrated into what we now think of as 'typical' women's jobs, such as nursing, teaching, office and shop work, and routinised unskilled assembly-line work. The internationalisation of the world economy has surely helped to further this, both through the international development of industry, with multi-national companies spreading their systems of work organisation around the globe, and because of the diffusion of the culture of industrial capitalism, particularly through the media of mass communication, with their standardised images of gender activities and ideals. Nevertheless, as Hakim points out, there are still cultural divergences, both in the specific nature of sex-typing and in the degree of segregation. For example, the proportion of women in various professions shows a certain amount of national variation as the list demonstrates in the case of women doctors.

USSR	75.0%
Finland	23.4%
West Germany	20.05%
Italy	18.8%
Great Britain	18.0%
Sweden	17.4%
Denmark	16.4%
Switzerland	13.6%
France	12.8%
USA	6.7%

(Figures for 1965, except for Finland (1960), Soviet Union (1963) and Britain (1966))
Source: *adapted from Hakim, 1979, p. 39, table 25*

There are also considerable variations in the earnings differentials between men and women: in Japan women earn less than half men's wages, in America the figure is 58.6 per cent, with the gap vastly reduced in Scandinavia and Swedish women achieving an impressive 88.6 per cent (New Internationalist, 1985; Wolf, 1985).

All in all, however, the similarities are striking. Taking up arguments from Boserup (1970), who considers that these gender hierarchies are typical of the modern urban economy, and are less marked in domestic economies, whether of a subsistence or a market type, Hakim speculates as to whether the prevalence of segregation and sex-typing is a specific product of advanced industrialism: 'the question needs to be asked whether the current level and form of occupational segregation on the basis of sex, and the prejudice and stereotyping that go with it, are in fact a product of urban industrial society. If so, they are likely to be found in their most extreme and institutionalised form in those countries where industrial urban social structures are longest established' (Hakim, 1979, p. 42). If this were so we should expect segregation to be most marked in Britain and America. Immense difficulties of measuring total levels of segregation would make such a proposition difficult to establish, but we may immediately note the counter-example of Japan, a late industrialiser, where women's work is extremely restricted and very heavily sex-typed; this suggests that the influence of traditional culture has also to be taken into account. Careful investigation of the assumption that sex hierarchies were less pronounced in pre-industrial societies is also needed. This question will be explored in the next chapter and in the case studies.

Hakim's question is couched in terms of the distinction between industrial and non-industrial societies, rather than capitalist and non-capitalist. Others, however, have claimed explicitly that segregation is a product of capitalism, or at least of class-divided societies (Larguia, 1975; Coontz and Henderson, 1986). This issue will also be explored in chapter 2. But it is worth looking briefly at one example of a non-capitalist industrialised society, the Soviet Union.

As the list of figures for women doctors in various countries suggests, the pattern of segregation and sex-typing in the USSR, although these are not absent, is markedly different from the industrialised norm. This is partly because the percentage of women working outside the home is particularly high, partly because of official political commitment to sex equality in the economy and partly due to the historic lack of manpower faced by Russia after the Revolution and two catastrophic world wars. In 1982 women made up over half the work force (51 per cent), while constituting 53 per cent of the population; 82 per cent of women of appropriate age work, as compared to 88 per cent of men, and another 8 per cent are in full-time study (Attwood and McAndrew, 1984). Attwood and McAndrew comment that female participation is essentially at its demographic maximum. Thus women are an important numerical presence in each sector of the economy, and this includes the professions. In sharp contrast to the American figures quoted earlier, women in the 1970s predominated in many professions. They were 75 per cent of doctors, 77 per cent of dentists, 95 per cent of pharmacists, 36 per cent of lawyers and 72 per cent of teachers. Perhaps most notable of all, women are 44 per cent of engineers (the US figure is 6 per cent), showing that the strong negative association between women and technology, which we shall find to be one of the strongest features of sex-typing in most societies, is absent (Lapidus, 1978; Rohrlich-Leavitt, 1975).

However, this apparent appearance of female success is considered by most commentators to be misleading. Although women have done very well in the professions, this is chiefly in public health and education (85 per cent and 73 per cent respectively), where they have also made most ground in the West (see table 1.1a). It could be argued that these are the least prestigious professions. In any case, in the Soviet Union professions are not so sharply distinguished from other work in terms of status, power and financial reward. Moreover, women do not rise to the top posts. For example, in 1975 women made up over 70 per cent of all schoolteachers of grades one to eleven, were 83 per cent of primary school heads, but only 29 per cent of secondary heads, a picture not too remote from that in Britain, as we shall see in chapter 13. Although women do better in the field of science than in Western societies, making up 50 per cent of junior researchers, they are only 10 per cent of top academicians and professors. Nor do women make it to top management posts as easily as men, whether in business or services. Only 9 per cent of directors of industrial enterprises in 1973 were women. The position is better in the health service, where women have been ministers and vice-ministers and have headed local departments (Dodge, 1978; Lapidus, 1978).

In the other sectors, the situation is closer to that in capitalist societies, as Lapidus' useful study *Women in Soviet Society* reveals. In agriculture women do particularly badly, although their participation is very high: 'a peculiar division of labour has arisen between men and women: the sphere of mechanised work is a male privilege, and that of manual labor is reserved to women' (Zinaida Monich, quoted Lapidus, 1978, p. 176). As in Britain, men monopolise skilled farm work, drive tractors and operate all types of machinery. Women are left with the brunt of routine work, planting, cultivating, harvesting and picking, milking, tending pigs and rearing poultry. They provide over 90 per cent of the labour in these last three tasks. Vertical segregation is also extreme. In 1975 women were the directors in less than 2 per cent of state and collective farms. Lapidus quotes the surely ironic comment of Nikita Khrushchev: 'it turns out that it is men who do the administrating and the women who do the work' (Lapidus, 1978, p. 179).

In the industrial sphere women have slightly more access to skilled work, but nevertheless predominate at the lower level. Lapidus reports one study of Moscow factory workers which showed women outnumbering men five to one in the bottom two grades, while in the top grades the ratio was reversed. Moreover, although horizontal segregation is less complete than in Britain and America, women are concentrated in the same kind of industries, such as textiles, clothing and food processing, while their participation is much lower in construction (29 per cent) and transport (5 per cent) (compare with table 1.1a). Women figure as strongly as in capitalist industrial societies in the lower-status service occupations, being 99 per cent of typists, 98 per cent of nurses, 95 per cent of librarians and 94 per cent of cashiers.

In sum, horizontal segregation is somewhat less marked that in the West and in that respect Russia is more egalitarian than the capitalist nations: but it is still considerable, and vertical segregation is nearly as pronounced. In Russia, as in Britain, there are clear ideas of 'men's work and 'women's work'. McAuley (1981) has argued that segregation has actually increased since the war. The failure of women to achieve promotion and rise to the top of hierarchies can be partly ascribed to the survival of traditional social attitudes, especially among men, and to family relationships; the responsibility for housework apparently falls even more heavily on women than in Britain and America. The persistence of vertical segregation ensures that in general women's economic position is not as favourable as men's in this purportedly egalitarian society. A recent survey estimated that women earn on average 70 per cent of men's wages, which is better than the American figure of 58.6 per cent but far below the remarkable Swedish figure quoted earlier. One of the positive achievements of the Soviet Union, however, is that it is considered as natural for women to go out to work as for men. Nor do women withdraw from the labour market after childbirth as much as in the West, partly because of more extensive collective child-care provision. Ironically, the liberalising climate of *perestroika* may threaten this. Public discussion in recent months has focused on the burden of women undertaking child care as well as work outside the home, but the solution is *not* seen as greater male involvement with domestic work, but the withdrawal of married women from the labour force. Such a development would almost certainly result in higher levels of vertical segregation; Russian women would then lose the advantage they currently have over their sisters in the capitalist West.

The Russian case, then, suggests the importance of traditional gender relations. As another illustration of this we may look, finally, at a less developed socialist society, China, where traditional family values are even more strongly pronounced. In China, some 80 per cent of the population live in the countryside. By the late 1970s, it was estimated that 40 per cent of the collective farm work force was female, but working outside the family is much less the norm in these conservative peasant communities than in the cities. Wolf (1985) reports that only about one-third of rural women work full-time. Croll (1983) considers the likely effects of recent changes in government policy: the growth of private family production of crops and livestock for the market and of agricultural 'sidelines' (such as knitting, plaiting, making bamboo implements), both of which are especially the province of women, may serve to confine peasant women further to the home and subject them more fully to dependence on the household unit. As elsewhere, 'tradition' has it that women do not do 'heavy' or skilled work; men are responsible for tractor driving, operating machinery, ploughing and managing large animals like carthorses and water buffalo. Women do the routine, unskilled work, tending crops and smaller livestock such as poultry and pigs, and most carrying and fetching, of water, bricks and cement, for example. As Wolf points out, this work is actually much heavier than driving a cart! But women's work is lower valued both socially and financially: women earn less and are given fewer work points, even when doing the same work. A comment made by a female farm worker to Wolf seems to epitomise the paradoxical position of women in agriculture in China, and in other traditional peasant societies: 'It used to be that the men did the heavy work and the women did the light work, but now there are more women workers than men workers, so the women do it all and the men just supervise them' (quoted Wolf, 1985, p. 79).

Urban women, by contrast, expect to work outside the home, just as in Russia. It is estimated that over 90 per cent of those aged 20 to 49 do so. But segregation, both horizontal and vertical, is pronounced. There is the familiar crowding of women into certain industries (cotton textiles, silk weaving, electrical assembly). Women are also crowded into the co-operative workshop sector, working under what we would think of as sweated conditions. According to Croll, 90 per cent of these workers are women. Despite the belief that women are not fit for heavy work or for highly technical tasks, they do seem to have advanced further into these areas than in Britain, making up 18 per cent of labour in mining, 14 per cent in metallurgy. However, they do badly in the professions, apart from medicine. This is a major difference from Russia; in China women are only 25 per cent of teachers in higher education and 26 per cent of scientific and engineering professionals (Croll, 1983). A nurse told Wolf how her aspirations to be an architect were quashed as it was not 'suitable for women' (Wolf, 1985, p. 56). This seems to reflect strong ideas about masculine and feminine capacities which ensure that vertical segregation is particularly pronounced. Again one of Wolf's interviewees (a textile worker) says it all: 'It is simple. The managers are all men; half the foremen are men, half are women; the workers are all women. It's always that way' (quoted Wolf, 1985, p. 71).

And, indeed, as we have seen, it appears to be 'always that way' around the world. International surveys of women in both industrialised and industrially developing societies (for example, Schmid and Weitzel, 1984; Davidson and Cooper, 1984; New Internationalist, 1985) reveal a striking consistency in the overall pattern: women concentrated into certain occupations and sectors; the extensive sex-typing of jobs as 'mens' or 'womens' work'; some variation in what particular jobs are assigned to women, but a tendency for certain work to emerge as 'women's' all over the world (nursing, school teaching, cleaning, typing, operating sewing machines); the concentration of women in lower grades; and, above all, the exclusion of all but a rare handful of women from posts of power and authority. Around the world, women work. Men give orders.

Explanations of and 'Orientations' to Segregation and Sex-typing

How, then, can we start to explain the origins of segregation and sex-typing of work, and their remarkable persistence? Discussion has focused on a number of historical and sociological factors, which will be examined in the course of this book: the dynamics of capitalist industrial development and in particular the confrontations and negotiations between employers and male workers which have characterised it; the sexual division of labour within the household; women's childbearing role; authority relations in the family; prevailing ideologies and social attitudes of both men and women, and in particular the role of the 'domestic ideology' elaborated by the Victorian middle classes, as described, for example, in the work of Catherine Hall and Leonore Davidoff (Hall, 1979, 1980; Davidoff and Hall, 1987); the attitudes of employers to women workers; processes of socialisation in the home, at school and in later life; and the role of the state in fostering certain social definitions of male and female activities.

Attempts to explain sex-typing and segregation within various broader theoretical perspectives will also be considered. But I should say at this point that, in my opinion, there is currently no completely satisfactory sociological theory of gender divisions. It may be tempting to attribute this to the relative youth of feminist social analysis, the sexual division of labour having been a neglected topic within sociology (and especially within industrial sociology) until the late 1960s. Certainly this is implied in the work of many feminist sociologists, such as Michele Barrett and Sylvia Walby, who see themselves as laying the groundwork for a complete reconceptualisation of gender relations. My own belief is that sociologists should no longer aspire to *any* comprehensive and totalising theory of society; no single model which explains each and every aspect of social life can be constructed. The challenge posed by postmodern theory, like that of Lyotard (1984), to structural forms of explanation should, at the least, make us wary of over-ambitious claims in our attempts to understand and depict social reality. This is indeed one of the significant challenges that feminism has made to the more rigid forms of Marxist structuralism with which it first tended to engage. While exposing the limitations of an approach which wishes to subsume all social divisions into the category of class and the analysis of surplus and value, feminists should be alert to the danger of falling into the same kind of error themselves, as I shall argue in chapter 3, when considering the extremely important contributions of Sylvia Walby.

The belief that sociological analysis is necessarily incomplete and partial, that no single theory can explain everything, is not, of course, to reject theoretical work or the task of perpetual redefinitions of existing theories and concepts. One of the key features of sociological work is its 'essential contestability' (we shall *never* agree exactly what social reality *is*, let alone how to go about studying and analysing it). The quest for understanding proceeds through debates and it is through this very contestation that insights are gained. Feminism, in its debate with existing forms of sociological analysis, has opened up whole new areas of investigation: new topics and issues, new problems and agendas, new concepts and theories emerge from the process of argument. For this reason I have chosen to organise the next two chapters, which deal with the existing literature on gender and work, by focusing on a series of debates and disagreements within historical and sociological studies. My argument is that these disputes provide us with enlightening material and that we can draw on all of them in our attempts to comprehend the processes of sexual division.

Before I proceed to these more specific issues I wish to look briefly at the attempts to develop a general analysis of gender differentiation in terms of existing sociological perspectives or, as I prefer to term them, orientations. We can discern three such orientations, or rough groupings or clusterings of ideas, within the existing debates on the sexual division of labour.

The first orientation, which we can call the 'production orientation', examines gender differences within existing frameworks for analysing other social divisions; it subsumes, as it were, the *sexual* division of labour into the *social* division of labour. This approach is particularly associated with Marxism, but has also been adopted by others, including Weberians or pluralists, who espouse a basically materialist approach. The focus of analysis here is firmly on the sphere of *work* or of *production* and it proceeds by *adding gender in*, adapting existing economic concepts to explain women's specific position. As we shall see in chapter 3, this has undoubtedly generated some of the most influential thinking about sex divisions at work. For example, Marxists have made use of the idea of the reserve army of labour or related women's position to the process of 'deskilling' (see Braverman, 1974; Beechey, 1977). An alternative conceptual frame, closer to the Weberian tradition, has drawn on the notion of dual or segmented labour markets (for example, Barron and Norris, 1976; Kreckel, 1980; Rubery, 1980). Economists have considered working women within the prevailing frameworks of the discipline of economics, those of calculative choice and consumer preference; for example, segregation is explained in terms of discrimination (that is, the preferences of employers for particular types of labour) (Becker, 1957). These theories will be considered in chapter 3; but the point to be made here is that in general they fail to take account of the specific nature of gender divisions, which are seen as no different in kind from class, ethnic or other kinds of social division. Moreover, the almost exclusive focus on the work sphere leads to a neglect of family relationships, which are seen merely as a precondition for the exploitation of women by employers and/or male workers.

The second or 'reproduction orientation' reverses this order of priority. Here the causes of gender divisions are sought within the *domestic* sphere. The key concepts are culture, ideology and reproduction. Many different theoretical strands feed in to this orientation. Conventional mainstream sociology, especially American functionalism, with its stress on socialisation and sex roles, has been an influence, even where writers like Ann Oakley have rejected the slippage into biological determination which is often discernible in the work of sociologists such as Parsons and Murdock. Yet such a slippage may also be evident in the writings of those feminists often labelled as 'radical' who consider reproductive relations or constructions of sexuality to be the root of the sexual divisions and male power (for example Firestone, 1979; de Beauvoir, 1953). To avoid this problem, many feminist anthropologists, whose work is discussed in chapter 2, have concentrated on the symbolic opposition of nature and culture seen as virtually universal in all societies, and the way that the linking of women with nature may serve to downgrade their economic contributions (Rosaldo, 1974; Ortner, 1974; Ardener, 1975). Marxism, too, can feed into this orientation: some Marxist feminists have argued for the existence of a mode of reproduction separate from any mode of production but interacting with it (Mitchell, 1975; Mackintosh, 1977). Alternatively others (Dalla Costa and James, 1972; Delphy, 1977) have seen domestic labour as itself constituting a distinct mode of production which generates sexual inequalities. The major problem with these approaches is exactly the reverse of those in the first orientation: inequalities in the economic sphere are assumed to be a simple reflection of inequalities produced in the family or the domestic sphere, or to arise from social attitudes learned through socialisation or generated by patriarchal ideology or culture. The way in which the economy itself breeds sexual divisions is ignored. As Mies (1986) has argued, these approaches are more useful in explaining why segregation at work persists than why it developed in the first place.

The third orientation (and the reader may perhaps have already guessed that it is one to which the writer is most sympathetic!) is based on the argument that an understanding of sexual divisions must embrace both work and home, production and reproduction. We might call it the 'joint orientation'. It involves an explicit claim that concepts drawn from Marxism, structuralism, functionalist sociology or cultural studies are insufficient to that understanding, and that new concepts, based on the specificity of gender divisions, must be elaborated. The key concepts here have been patriarchy and male dominance. These are seen to transcend the familiar sociological distinctions between production and reproduction, private and public, even perhaps, more controversially, structure and culture, material and ideological. Thus, for example, Walby has defined patriarchy as a set of interlinking institutions that cut across all sectors of society:

> ... a system of interrelated social structures through which men exploit women ... The key sets of patriarchal relations are to be found in domestic work, paid work, the state and male violence and sexuality, while other practices in civil society have a limited significance. (Walby, 1986, pp. 50–1)

Although, as I shall argue in chapter 3, there are many problems as yet not overcome within the 'joint orientation', its comprehensiveness seems to me to be its great strength. Neither structural nor cultural, material or ideological factors *alone* can explain the origins and persistence of segregation and sex-typing. That is why I argue that we need the insights from all these orientations to further our understanding of the processes of sexual differentiation. The next two chapters, therefore, deal with some of the key debates, first within anthropological and historical literature concerned with the evolution and development of the sexual division of labour, then within sociological work which has attempted to provide frameworks for analysing sex divisions.

2

THE HISTORICAL DEBATES

In the last two decades many researchers, both female and male, have turned their attention to the history of women's work, both reinterpreting existing data and studies and locating new sources of data and interpreting them. As a result we now know a great deal more about the sexual division of labour and women's share of it than we used to: a wealth of material covering a wide range of activities, epochs and societies is now available. But the accumulation of data does not, of course, preclude ambiguities and disagreements about a phenomenon and its significance. In this chapter two major areas of debate and four more minor ones will be explored.

In the Beginning ...

One area which has attracted considerable speculation is the origin of the division of labour. When exactly did women and men start to perform different social tasks? In what circumstances did this come about? Feminist (and other) anthropologists have written quite extensively on these issues. Inevitably, their answers remain speculative, in view of the lack of any real 'hard facts' about prehistoric human societies, even though ingenious attempts have been made to utilise fossil evidence or to derive theories from the study of primate behaviour (Zihlman, 1981; Leibowitz, 1986). As Coontz and Henderson admit 'the search for origins will never be definitively settled' (Coontz and Henderson, 1986, p. 27). We may ask, in that case, whether there is any point in continuing to debate the question? Coontz and Henderson argue that we must, in order to counter the continuing popular assertion that male dominance is a 'natural' state of affairs. Mies' (1986) answer, too, is yes, because only in this way can we begin to develop a coherent theoretical framework for explaining the continuing history of sexual divisions and the subjugation of women by men. Others would respond that no such universal framework can ever be developed and thus the whole endeavour is fruitless (Elshtain, 1987). Nevertheless human intellectual curiosity about the origins and causes of things remains insatiable, and as people are unlikely ever to stop asking 'why?' it seems worth reviewing this material here, at least briefly.

We may distinguish a series of interlinked questions over which there has been disagreement. First, have all societies at all historical times been characterised by sexual differentiation, or can we find evidence of societies where the sexes shared all activities equally? Secondly, why does the sexual division of labour develop and (if the existence of egalitarian societies is accepted) when and in what circumstances? Finally, does the mere existence of the sexual division of labour imply sexual inequality or can we distinguish societies which are sexually differentiated but where the status of the sexes is equal and their different work equally valued?

In an extremely influential paper Ortner has argued that all societies of which we have any real evidence are sexually differentiated. She rejects all attempts to identify a sexually egalitarian society or a society marked by matriarchal power. Furthermore, she argues that the work done by women, socially necessary as it may be, is universally devalued: 'the secondary status of women in society is one of the true universals, a pan-cultural fact' (Ortner, 1974, p. 67). Ortner has surely been influenced here, like many others, by the doyen of cultural anthropologists, Lévi-Strauss, who sees the exchange of women as brides by men as *the* basic and primal act which defines human activity as social and cultural. Thus, from the beginning of anything worthy of being called 'society' men dominated women and this is reflected in the universally lower status of female activities (Lévi-Strauss, 1969).

In opposition to this a number of writers have claimed the existence of egalitarian societies, along the lines of the primitive communism as described by Engels, where if there is any sexual division of tasks it is rudimentary and not institutionalised into a line of permanent cleavage (Chevillard and Leconte, 1986). Leibowitz (1986) and Zihlman (1981) both argue, on the basis of fossil evidence, primate behaviour and knowledge of existing hunting and gathering tribes, that in early hominid societies the sexual division of labour is likely to have been minimal, as group members worked jointly to find food and to perpetuate the species. Leibowitz argues that the major task division would have been on the basis of age, as young individuals learned the tricks of survival from adults. She speculates that only when groups began to exchange any surplus food between groups did any specialisation develop. Zihlman believes that the prevailing interpretations which portray man as hunter and woman as gatherer are back projections of contemporary assumptions about human nature. Like many other anthropologists, she argues that gathering rather than hunting was the primal activity, and the most important one, in which both sexes must have participated. Evidence from contemporary hunting and gathering societies confirms that gathering provides for the bulk of subsistence needs; hunting only contributes 20 to 30 per cent of food and tends to cater for luxury rather than staple foodstuffs (Mies, 1986).

Although the above accounts can be no more than speculative modelling, other anthropologists argue for egalitarian examples among existing societies, usually of hunter-gatherers (or should we say gatherer-hunters?) Dahlberg (1981) points to the Agta tribe of the Philippines, where both men and women hunt and gather, and Leacock (1975) has argued similarly that many foraging societies, such as North American Indian tribes, have a flexible and egalitarian division of labour. This view appeals particularly to adherents of Marx and Engels' model of social development, as reflected, for example, in this view of non-settled foraging societies: 'organised into bands that are essentially non-territorial and bilocal, gatherer-hunters reject warfare and group oppression, and value above all cooperation, egalitarianism and personal autonomy. In such societies women and men are equal partners in communally-based subsistence and social activities' (Rohrlich-Leavitt, 1975, p. 621).

Many answers have been offered to the second question (why and how the sexual division of labour originated); these answers reflect the way prehistoric and tribal societies are conceptualised. Many accounts still reflect the traditional primacy given to biology. For some, the sexual division of labour is built into all human societies because of sexual dimorphism (the different physical forms of the two sexes); even leaving aside female reproductive functions, men's larger frames are said to predispose them to longer-range foraging and more muscular activities (McGrew, 1981). Others put even more stress on physique and aggression, portraying hunting as the primal activity and the driving force behind human evolution: the bonding of males in hunting (and warfare) is the basis of universal male domination (Tiger and Fox, 1971). Sociobiologists also see genetic and biological difference as the cause of the asymmetrical division of labour; in the words of one of the discipline's founders:

> In hunter-gatherer societies, men hunt and women stay at home. This strong bias persists in most agricultural and industrial societies and, on that ground alone, appears to have a genetic origin ... My own guess is that the genetic bias is intense enough to cause a substantial division of labour in the most free and most egalitarian societies ... Even with identical education and equal access to all professions, men are likely to continue to play a disproportionate role in political life, business and science. (Wilson, quoted Coontz and Henderson, 1986, p. 5)

Most feminists and many sociologists would reject such biologistic explanations, claiming that the link between genes, hormones, instincts, physique and sex differences and behavioural patterns has never been satisfactorily proved and that reliance on biology ignores the extent to which all forms of human behaviour are cultural and variable. However, as noted, feminists and other commentators who see culture as the main determinant of human behaviour may, paradoxically, also prescribe to a universalistic view of sexual differentiation, whereby women's reproductive role takes on a symbolic significance so great that in practice such accounts are hard to distinguish from those of the biological determinists. Indeed MacCormack argues that this group of theorists (including Ortner, Rosaldo, Firestone, Ardener and de Beauvoir) 'root femaleness in biology and maleness in the social domain' (MacCormack, 1980, p. 18).

For Ortner and Rosaldo, a key factor is the symbolisation of women as closer to nature and the identification of men with culture which they see as nearly universal. Whatever men do then becomes the high-status activity. Even where economic activities are less differentiated, men's control of political and religious activities (a point often ignored in accounts influenced by Marx and Engels) ensures their social dominance. In Rosaldo's words 'male, as opposed to female activities, are always recognised as predominantly important and cultural systems give authority and value to the roles and activities of men' (Rosaldo, 1974, p. 19). For her, it is above all the domestic orientation of women which lies at the basis of sexual division and this arises from the demands of pregnancy, childbearing and childrearing. The restrictions these place on women are frequently cited as a major determinant of their limited economic activity (for example, Humphries, 1987). But this position is hard to sustain in the face of evidence from societies, such as those of the aborigines, where women do participate in hunting and long-range foraging despite pregnancy and responsibility for childrearing. Moreover, while this argument might help explain the exclusion of women from certain long-distance and heavy activities (fishing and mining, for example) it cannot explain the extent of sexual segregation in less demanding tasks, nor the common devaluation of most 'women's work'. Ortner's broader cultural perspective may seem preferable here and this is supported by Ardener's claim that men have the power to impose their systems of social categorisation upon their womenfolk; women's versions of social reality become, in his term, a 'muted structure', a story that is not told, and by this means their power of actualising their own visions is blocked. On these grounds he argues that in most societies men do have domination over women (Ardener, 1975).

Marxists, however, prefer to see male power as economically rather than culturally rooted. The essayists in Coontz and Henderson's collection, *Women's Work, Men's Property*, work towards materialist explanations of 'the origins of gender and class', taking primitive equality as a starting point and arguing that economic developments, of one sort or another, led to male dominance and sexual differentiation. In their own account, which they base on studies of existing lineage societies, Coontz and Henderson (1986) argue that the unequal sexual division of labour emerges gradually along with the development of settled societies which are patrilocal (where wives and children live with the husband and his parents). The growth of competitive exchange between lineage groups organised on a patrilocal basis led to men controlling the labour of women in order to procure surplus goods for exchange. Thus the growth of male dominance is inextricably involved with the development of class hierarchies.

Other Marxist accounts rest on the notion of a 'sudden break', some moment in history when men actively seize power from women. This goes back to the ideas of Bachofen and Engels, who both suggested that the earliest societies were matriarchal, based on a 'mother-right' derived from women's reproductive power, which was then ousted by patriarchy. Rosaldo finds this idea of the sudden break 'implausible' and it is hard to disagree. Moreover, Bamberger's arguments against Bachofen's original formulations are persuasive; she points out that he founded his theory on myths which feature a primeval state of women's power, from which they were ejected either by guile or force. Bamberger considers it dangerous to assume that myths represent some previous reality; it is more plausible to interpret them as an ideological justification for the existing reality of male social power (Bamberger, 1974). Nevertheless, Chevillard and Leconte (1986) and Saliou (1986) argue that, while matriarchy in its pure form may, indeed, never have existed, in matrilocal societies (where husbands and children live with the wife and her family) sexual equality does appear to be greater. For them the 'sudden break' involves the shift to patrilocality which consolidates power on the male side of the family and initiates sex oppression; this, for Chevillard and Leconte, is prior to class oppression and can in fact be seen as the original form from which all subsequent class divisions evolve.

These Marxist accounts avoid some of the universalism of the theories previously discussed, but fail to provide a totally convincing account of how exactly sexual inequality originated. Indeed there is some ambiguity as to whether sexual inequality is simply synonymous with the sexual division of labour. Coontz and Henderson do, in fact, argue that there is no logical link between the two. By contrast Ortner, as we have seen, sees inequality as well as differentiation as universal. But others would argue for the possibility of a society where men and women perform different tasks but are seen as making a contribution of equal value. Rohrlich-Leavitt (1975) argues, for example, that in some African societies sexual roles are sharply segregated but are also socially evaluated as complementary and balanced. In such societies women as well as men make decisions; nor are they constrained by their reproductive functions. The universalistic views of male dominance ignore anthropological and historical evidence of female power.

These arguments are taken even further by the contributors to the collection of essays edited by MacCormack and Strathern (1980), who stress the variability of the sexual division of labour and the relativity of meanings attached to it and to other gender categorising systems. They reject all attempts, whether by Marxists or cultural structuralists, to develop universal models of gender relations. Even to generalise is seen as dangerous. For Strathern, power arises from human interactive processes and cannot be taken for granted. Each society requires separate empirical investigation. Power relations between men and women are seen as characteristically complex and ambiguous and any overall narrative of 'oppression' is rejected. While this stress on cultural variability is to be saluted, like many accounts which centre on the relativity of meanings, there seems to me to be here an almost neurotic fear of reaching general conclusions. Thus, the society in which male and female power is truly 'balanced' seems to me as empirically elusive as Bachofen's matriarchy. Indeed the empirical studies in the collection (for example, those by Jordanova of the eighteenth-century Enlightenment and by Strathern of the Gimi people of New Guinea) could easily lend themselves to reinterpretation in terms of Ardener's muted structures. Both reveal the power of men to impose their definitions of gender on women.

I hope here to have given to readers less familiar with this material something of the flavour of these debates which, as stated at the outset, must remain ultimately irresolvable. What we can say, looking at evidence from all types of documented societies, is that the sexual division of labour is extremely variable, which should make us suspicious of overly universalistic explanations, especially those hinging on biology. Nevertheless, looking at contemporary societies, we shall see that economic arrangements reflecting male authority over women's labour, cultural definitions of gender roles, and the restraints placed on women by childbearing do *all* still have a major influencing role. We should accept that all of them may have had a part in the origination of sexual divisions, however elusive final explanations may be. Moreover, we shall see some of the same debates and dilemmas (generalisations versus variability, male dominance versus complementarity of power) as we turn to look at pre-industrial and industrialising societies.

'Before and After': Women's Status in Pre-industrial and Industrial Societies

Despite the disagreements noted above, most of the authors I have discussed seem to share the assumption that the development of state societies leads to a deterioration of women's position, making them more powerless. Coontz and Henderson, for example, assert that 'women's social status was undermined by the separation of public and private spheres' (Coontz and Henderson, 1986, p. 152). Yet historians have found this issue less clear-cut. A considerable debate has developed about the economic and social status of women in the centuries before industrial capitalism developed. Some interpreters see a position of near equality in marriage in traditional European societies, while others see women as prisoners of patriarchy, waiting to be freed by the onset of industrialism. This debate is usually linked to an account of how the position changed when industrial capitalism brought its transforming power to men and women's public and private lives. On the one hand, accounts which see this change as derogatory to women's status have been described by Middleton (1985) as constituting a 'critical-pessimistic tradition'; others, often writing within the tradition of modernisation theory, take an optimistic view, emphasising the expansion of opportunities for women.

Paramount among the pessimistic accounts is Alice Clark's classic study *Working Life of Women in the Seventeenth Century*, first published in 1919. Clark argues for the egalitarian view of marriage in pre-industrial societies which were founded on household subsistence production or on family-based production for the market. Marriage was a partnership, the private and public spheres were not sharply divided, while men and women both shared in productive work and what we would now call 'domestic' work (household maintenance and caring for children). Although there was a sexual division of labour, women's contribution was as socially valued as men's and gave them the potential for an independent existence. The onset of capitalist methods of production, marked by wage labour, the individual rather than the household wage, and the separation of home and workplace, eroded women's economic role and with it their social status. Peasant women were forced into low-paid wage labour at pay levels making it impossible for them to survive without male support; artisans' wives lost their access to the craft skills they had formerly learned working side by side with their husbands in the home, and upper-class women suffered worst of all, losing their partner role in the management of estate or business and becoming decorative status symbols, their social function limited to household matters and motherhood. Lowered social status, dependency and impaired psychological functioning were the gloomy results.

As Middleton says, this kind of view became for a time unchallenged orthodoxy for the new wave of feminists, appearing, for example, in the sociohistorical studies of Lewenhak (1980), Oakley (1976a) and Hamilton (1978). However, other historians have challenged some aspects of the 'critical-pessimist' tradition, notably the view of the egalitarian nature of marriage in pre-industrial societies; they argue, by contrast, that patriarchal family relations had already relegated women to a secondary place in the division of labour. Perhaps the most concerted attack on Clark and the pessimists has come from Edward Shorter. Basing his arguments on his study of pre-industrial France and Germany, he asserts that women's work in traditional peasant societies was clearly segregated from men's; they were largely confined to the home and universally took responsibility for what he calls the three big Cs: cooking, cleaning and child care. Although this economic role was clearly important, he argues that in traditional societies status did not derive from economic activity. Women's general social status was determined by their husbands ('femmes couvertes' in the fullest sense). Industrial capitalism, by contrast, raised the possibility of women attaining economic independence and achieving social standing in their own right. Essentially, the market liberated women from the cage of the patriarchal home: he concludes 'it was in the traditional "moral" economy that women suffered the most serious lack of status, and it was under capitalism that working women advanced to within at least shouting distance of social equality with men' (Shorter, 1976, p. 513).

Disagreements between the two sides hinge, therefore, on two main issues. What exactly was women's economic role and status in pre-industrial societies; was the division of labour more egalitarian than what followed? And, secondly, did industrial capitalism restrict or broaden women's opportunities? I will deal with each in turn. From the outset, however, we should bear in mind that, as some recent contributors to the debate have noted (Middleton, 1985; Charles, 1985; Gittins, 1985), these processes of change are immensely complicated; national and regional variations in women's roles 'before' and 'after' and the ambiguities of status and power make it difficult to characterise this change as a simple trajectory, in one direction or the other.

Shorter's arguments about the inferior economic role of women appear to gain support, on the surface at least, from a number of more detailed historical studies. For example, Martine Segalen's study of French peasant households, although she espouses the view of complementary power relations rather than male dominance, confirms the link of women to the home, in France at least. While the detailed assignment of tasks to, the sexes is extraordinarily variable, not just from region to region but from village to village, in general woman's place is the house, the barn, the farmyard, the garden; she much less frequently works in the fields and ventures much more rarely into the village and public life except for marketing (Segalen, 1983). Hanawalt's study of English medieval society also locates women's work as primarily in a domestic environment, skills being learned and carried out inside the home: 'in the country, women's space was the home and men's the fields. In the city, women worked in the home or shop along with men, but they did not perform the same tasks and they did not take finished products to the marketplace' (Hanawalt, 1986, p. x). Middleton's work (1979) on the sexual division of labour in feudal England indicates that while women, both in the home and as wage labour, might perform a wide variety of agricultural tasks, the key activities such as ploughing were performed by men and it was this that brought them into the political arena of feudal services and obligations, emphasising their public role as representative of the household.

In the urban context, too, studies indicate that women were confined to the lower-status types of work. Where men were specialists, women were more likely to be generalists. Although, as Clark and Oakley have shown, women could be found in almost every trade and occupation, the work they carried out was strongly linked to their marital status and their position in the life cycle. Women often got access to work through fathers and husbands. Their work histories, as Kowaleski (1986) shows in her study of medieval Exeter, were more likely to be varied and intermittent, whereas men stuck steadily to their chosen craft. Indeed, the Statute of Labourers of 1363 gave legal sanction to this distinction, requiring men to restrict themselves to a single trade while women were permitted to combine several. For Hanawalt, this indicates that for women work was often a matter of 'makeshift', in modern terms, 'making do', 'getting by'. Women's working lives, in fact, had the fragmented quality that is so familiar today.

Although women participated in guilds, as Oakley (1976a) among others has demonstrated, on the whole they did so on the basis of family connections, as wives and daughters of guildsmen, rather than in their own right as independent craftswomen. Widows were allowed to continue as guild members in their husband's place, but some guilds forbade other women to practise their crafts. There are some cases of all-female guilds (in Paris and Cologne, for example), but it is highly indicative that these were administered and run by men (Howell, 1986). Once again we see women excluded from the political processes by which economic activity is made to confer high social standing. While individual women could be found in almost every craft, nevertheless in most areas (clothing and retailing were the exceptions) they formed a tiny minority, so that most major crafts and trades can be described as male dominated (Power, 1975; Wright, 1985; Hutton, 1985). Indeed, in medieval cities we can discern exactly the 'crowding' of women into certain activities (spinning, brewing, nursing) that we have already seen to be typical of the twentieth century.

So far the evidence has all been on Shorter's side, but we can also find evidence to set against him. At the least it seems that his position is overstated, perhaps because of his reliance on the example of France. As Macfarlane has brilliantly argued in *The Origins of English Individualism* (1978), Britain can be seen as standing apart from the continent, displaying a distinct pattern of social behaviour which made it apt to become the 'first industrial nation'. People in Britain were more mobile, geographically and socially, more independent, less constrained by blood ties and community controls, more prepared to innovate in order to improve their financial position; women, too, shared in this greater mobility and freedom from traditional restraint. There is ample evidence that in Britain women were heavily involved in trade and retailing, and in that sense gained access to the public sphere (along, on occasions, with the legal status of 'femme sole', independent from husbands, as opposed to the 'femme couverte', whose legal identity was merged into her husband's, barring her from involvement in legal action in her own right). Reyerson's study (1986) of medieval Montpellier shows that even in France in some places women could take on important public roles; they were active in the grain market and in real estate, even if they were not so involved in long-distance trading as were men. Once more we see how locally variable women's position was and how difficult it is to generalise about societies which were still heavily influenced by local and community (rather than national) cultures. For example, evidence shows that women were involved in a much wider range of trades in fourteenth-century London than in fourteenth-century Shrewsbury (Lacey, 1985; Hutton, 1985).

Shorter's conclusions are challenged by two impressive studies which espouse the pessimistic view. Boserup's research into women's role in economic development in non-European societies shows how important women have been in traditional agriculture. She distinguishes two types of farming system, in one of which (based on shifting cultivation and common throughout Africa) women do virtually all the work. Her study reveals the range of agricultural tasks performed by women around the world, and the widespread employment of women in tasks conventionally seen as 'too heavy' or 'unsuitable' for them, such as mining and construction. Like Clark, she argues that in family systems of production, whether for subsistence or for exchange, although there is a division of labour it is a 'horizontal' one. Women may help men, but men may also be assistants to women. The formation of work hierarchies (apart from those of age) and of strict sex-role segregation is, in her opinion, the product of urbanisation and economic growth. However, her comparative study of developing societies again reveals national and regional variations. In Islamic societies, for example, patriarchy is at its strongest and confinement of women so extreme that in some Arab countries they may not even venture out shopping. In these societies 'the idea of female participation in trade is an abomination' (Boserup, 1970, p. 87).

More recently, some powerful support for Clark has come from Keith Snell's fine study of eighteenth-century England. Using information from parish indentures and inland revenue payments on apprenticeships, he argues that women and girls in the seventeenth and eighteenth centuries could still be found working as apprentices and craftswomen (some as independent mistresses) in a very extensive range of crafts, from blacksmith to wheelwright, from barber-surgeon to clockmaker, from bricklayer to musician. He argues that the growth of industry was accompanied by a hardening of the sexual division of labour and a narrowing of women's options, with, for example, the sharp decline of women's participation in agriculture: 'the general picture of relatively more equal and sexually shared labour before the nineteenth century is supported by evidence on female apprenticeship and artisan activity' (Snell, 1985, p. 309). We may note, however, that he makes no claim that women and men were numerically equal in the trades more familiarly associated with men.

Unlike Pinchbeck and Clark, Snell does not so much link these changes to the decline of family industry and the spread of capitalist organisation as to demographic change, population pressure and male unemployment, the latter leading men to become fearful of women's competition for the first time and thus to campaign actively for their exclusion from crafts and occupations.

Finally, as already pointed out, sex-role segregation need not necessarily imply inequalities of power. Some historians, indeed, suggest that the medieval peasant marriage was founded on complementary power; Hanawalt describes it as a 'classic partnership' to which each contributed valuable necessities and skills. Scott and Tilly have a similar view of pre-industrial gender relations: 'separate spheres and separate roles do not imply discrimination or hierarchy. It appears, on the contrary, that neither sphere was subordinate to the other' (Scott and Tilly, 1975, pp. 44-5). If men dominated outside the home and acted for the household in all public, legal and political affairs, within the home women ruled the roost, often controlling the household budget and making important decisions about provisions and household enterprises.

However, other interpreters suggest that men did hold the ultimate power in the family, ensuring that women took more marginalised and subsidiary work roles. Charles sums up:

> Overall, women's labour is seen as determined by, and subordinate to, the demands of husband, household and family. On the whole they were also legally subordinate to their husbands and their economic activity was in theory closely confined by legal incapacity, which affected, among other things, their right to own and dispose of property. This, however, was not as incapacitating as the legal subordination of women in the nineteenth century. (Charles, 1985, p. 7)

In particular, this power discrepancy was reflected in the lower status which men accorded to women's work. Thus Gullickson writes of the eighteenth-century proto-industrial French community she studied, 'the evidence reveals a culture that valued male work more highly than female work and provided more leisure and status consumption for men than for women, despite the importance of women's earnings' (Gullickson, 1986, p. 85). Even Boserup concedes this point: 'men usually despise occupations manned (*sic*) predominantly by women, be it agricultural or trade, and they will normally hesitate to take part in such work' (Boserup, 1970, p. 92).

These studies, then, present quite a confusing and sometimes contradictory picture of women in pre-industrial societies; but I will suggest a few tentative conclusions. First, all traditional societies, European and non-European, feudal, monarchic, peasant, proto-industrial or whatever, display some kind of sexual division of labour with women either limited to a narrower range of occupations than men, or carrying out tasks more firmly centred on the home; but specific patterns of the division of labour are extremely variable, by country, region, even by community, so that it is hard for the historian to reach general conclusions about sex-roles. This contrasts with contemporary industrialised societies which display, as Boserup argues and as we have seen in chapter 1, quite striking consistencies in the patterns of sex-typing and segregation. Secondly, the sexual division of labour is much more flexible; while there are clear social expectations about gender roles and while social rules usually assign women to the more marginal and subordinate tasks, these expectations and rules are often infringed by individual women (and, to a lesser extent one suspects, men). I would suggest that this flexibility is related to two factors; first the uncertainty of existence in pre-industrial societies, which forces households to be extremely adaptable in order to survive. Thus, as Snell argues, a more rigid adherence to sexual segregation and sterotyping is found to emanate from the higher, more economically secure, social strata. The other factor is the family or household system of production, in which members co-operate to perform tasks, juggling their labour supply to fit varying economic demands. As this breaks down with the spread of wage labour, first on feudal estates (Middleton, 1979) and then as part of the general capitalist development, the sexual division of labour slowly rigidifies.

It is more difficult to adjudicate on the issue of male dominance or power complementarity because of the lack of qualitative evidence about the internal dynamics of the family. But both legal and literary evidence suggest that pre-industrial societies were patriarchal, marked by male dominance, both in the sense of the women's loss of legal rights on marriage and in terms of male authority within the household. This patriarchal power was consolidated, most significantly, by the male's virtual monopoly of access to political institutions and processes. Men took political roles by virtue of their position (unchallenged where there was a husband) of head of household (Hartmann, 1976). Only widows and spinsters had a comparable position. However, as Power suggests, 'the position of women is one thing in theory, another in legal position, yet another in everyday life' (Power, 1975, p. 9). While I am not convinced by her assertion that everyday life in medieval England was characterised by a 'rough and ready equality' of the sexes, it seems feasible that the flexibility of the division of labour referred to above offered *some* women (although these would have been a minority) the chance to challenge and resist 'theoretical' and 'legal' patriarchy, thus being enabled to sustain an independent economic existence which was to be denied to women in the nineteenth century. Several researchers suggest that a progressive diminution of this potential for independence and a consequent tightening of patriarchy made itself felt between the fourteenth and sixteenth centuries (Zemon Davis, 1986; Howell, 1986). This trend was consolidated in the nineteenth century.

Having said this, however, we should note the danger of generalising about women's situation from the achievements of those few outstanding women who are strong and persistent enough to buck the system in any given society; it would be a great mistake to read off the position of women in Britain of the 1980s from the examples of Margaret Thatcher and Edwina Currie! The mass of women in medieval society, I submit, would be found in work sex-typed as 'women's work' and limited in their opportunities by obligations to fathers and husbands.

We may deal in rather less detail with the issue of the impact of capitalist industry, as this forms much of the subject matter of the case studies in this book. But a few general arguments need addressing. First we must note that the pessimistic accounts are often ambiguous as to exactly when the decline in women's status occurred (early eighteenth century? late eighteenth century? early 1800s?) and also as to exactly what caused the change. Middleton rightly criticises the confusion in Clark's account as to whether it was industrialism (machine production, the factory system) or capitalism (private ownership, wage labour) which caused the decline. As he notes, the onset of capitalist organisation long precedes the separation of home and work, which Clark makes so central to her argument. Evidence certainly seems to confirm that the deterioration predates both the factory system and the widespread use of powered machinery (Middleton, 1979; Snell, 1985). The link may more correctly be made between changes in the division of labour and the capitalisation of production, with consequent alterations in work organisation (often involving the breaking up of the labour process into fragmented tasks) and increased class antagonism and conflicts over work. This, in turn, may be linked to the decline of family-based work systems. However, as Snell suggests, there is no firm evidence as to the causal sequence. As the case studies in this book will show, both capitalisation and the breakup of family production systems do seem to be intimately connected with changes in the sexual division of labour and with sex-typing of jobs. But technology is also implicated, and, as we shall see, technological developments in the later part of the nineteenth century certainly helped to increase job segregation. What we *can* be certain about is that any major change in work organisation is likely to have its effect on the sexual division of labour.

As we have seen, Shorter has argued that the introduction of the 'free' market of industrial capitalism maximised women's choices and opportunities and broke down patriarchy. This extreme version of the optimistic theory is hard to sustain, because evidence clearly shows that the immediate impact of industrial development, in the period 1750 – 1850 before new women's occupations (clerical and shop work, the professions) had opened up, was one of diminishing opportunities and worsening conditions for women. However, the ambiguities of the situation are revealed, for example, in the more balanced account by Ivy Pinchbeck (1981). She provides us with a classic account of the exploitation of women and children in the early mills and factories; but she also argues that *in the long term* capitalism did benefit women. The very fact of the restriction of work opportunities for middle-class women led to the growth of the emancipationist movement and thence to the opening up of higher education and professional careers to women. Working-class women too benefited in the long term, as rising living standards and wages offered them the chance of well-paid factory jobs and escape from patriarchal and parental control.

Pinchbeck, like Shorter, makes much of the fact that capitalism, by its power to generate social prosperity, provided women with a totally new option: the choice *not* to work (or we, should more accurately say, to become a full-time domestic worker!). The positive features of the new homemaker's role of middle-class women are also explored in Branca's interesting study *Silent Sisterhood* (1975), which emphasises women's important social contribution as pioneers of modern household management, child-care methods and consumption. For Branca, the new society's demands create a new complementarity between man the producer and women the consumer, both necessary for successful modernisation.

Others, of course, would take a much more jaundiced view of the position of the full-time housewife! An opposing view comes from Hall (1979, 1980). She describes the evolution of the Victorian 'ideology of domesticity' developed by the middle classes and strongly influenced by Evangelical Christianity. This saw the world as divided into two distinct spheres, with women taking the purely domestic role. Women and men were allocated to their separate spheres on the basis of differences in their natures: 'nature decreed all women were first and foremost wives and mothers' (1979, p. 31). The very qualities that fitted them for this, tenderness, nurturance, fragility, moral purity, disqualified them from the tough and ruthless world of work and public office, for which the man's spirit was considered to be framed. The moral mission of the woman was to provide support for her menfolk and to preserve a domestic retreat untouched by the cares of the public sphere (see also, Davidoff et al., 1976; Davidoff and Hall, 1987). Ideally, this meant that women should have no contact at all with the world of work. Such ideas lent a moral dignity to the growing campaign to withdraw women from waged labour: 'no taint of market forces should corrupt the love-service relationships within the domestic citadel' (Davidoff et al., 1976, p. 153). Arguably the effect of this pressurising of women into the housewife role was dependency on a husband and acceptance of secondary status, which in turn promoted the marginalisation of women when they did involve themselves in wage labour (Oakley, 1976a).

It is also worth pointing out that the expansion of 'choices' for women referred to by Shorter and Pinchbeck was not really experienced by any class of women until the twentieth century and that the range of 'choices' has continued to be restricted, especially for working-class women, by the growing rigidity of the sexual division of labour. While the range of choices may indeed have increased in *absolute* terms (and pay levels certainly have), the expansion of economic opportunities for women *relative to men* is much less impressive! Moreover, while some middle-class women can now, in the 1980s, be found equalling and surpassing the prosperity and independence of the medieval businesswomen of Montpellier, many working-class women do not share their good fortune. Rather, they find themselves faced with 'choices' among a limited range of 'women's' jobs which pay less than subsistence wages, thereby forcing them into economic dependence on husbands (or the state) in exactly the way described by Clark.

We may conclude by referring to the work of two authors who stress the ambiguous effects of the changes we have reviewed. For Ehrenreich and English (1979), the onset of industrial capitalism did, as Shorter claims, bring an end to family patriarchalism; but, as it freed women from the home, at the same time it subjugated them to the exploitative control of capitalist employers, who, in a world structured round the needs and priorities of men, were happy to use women as a source of cheap labour, confining them to unfulfilling, mechanised and monotonous jobs. Moreover, industrialism took from women the traditional female skills (brewing, baking, medicine, spinning and weaving) which they had learned in the home and which were a means of gaining social standing and respect in the community.

Overall the effects of capitalism are complex, contradictory and ambiguous; it has improved standards of living for many women, offered them various forms of choice and freedom, while simultaneously, up till the 1980s at least, engendering a division of labour (as the case studies will show) which traps them in a limited range of socially acceptable roles and activities.

Men, Women and the Maintenance of Segregation and Sex-typing

In this final section I shall make some comments on four areas which historians have seen as significant in maintaining or weakening sexual segregation: the separation of home and work, the family wage, protective legislation and the effect of the two world wars.

As we have seen, Clark makes the separation of home and work a key factor in her account of the decline in women's economic activity, and this is affirmed even more strongly in the work of Hamilton (1978). The moving of work out of the home into factories and offices is seen as the basis for the redefinition of sex roles, assigning men as producers to the public sphere and women as domestic specialists, housewives, to the private sphere. Men's social range remains broad as they move between the two spheres at will but women's social role is narrowed and becomes secondary: there must be production before there can be consumption. In consequence women were quite literally trapped within the home, enmeshed in a life given over to purely domestic activity. On the face of it, this account seems accurate. Certainly the notion that capitalism and industrialisation led to a sharp split between the private sphere of the home and the public sphere of work and politics has for long been part of sociological orthodoxy, being central to the work of Talcott Parsons, and a core assumption of both functionalist and Marxist accounts of the family.

However, recent work, by Gittins (1985), Bradley (1986b), Rose (1986) and Allen and Wolkowitz (1987) among others, brings into question the extent to which this separation has really occurred. For a start, the considerable number of women who are employed (as women always have been) as outworkers or homeworkers poses a challenge to the thesis. In addition, many studies show that the family-based work system continued well into the nineteenth century in some occupations (see the chapters on hosiery and shoemaking in this book). Even when the majority of industries and services had been moved into factories, shops and offices, a small but significant number of people continued to work from their home: farmers, small shopkeepers and business owners, hoteliers and publicans, among others.

Moreover, in a more general way, the family remains linked to the world of work, performing some important functions for it, especially those of training and recruitment. In many occupations (from acting to mining, medicine to shipbuilding) there is a strong tradition of children following their mothers and fathers into work. In the nineteenth century, and among poorer families right up until World War II, it was still commonplace for parents to decide what work their children should take up (see Burnett, 1984; Sarsby, 1988). Even now, attitudes and skills learned in the home are probably the single most important influence on choice of career or occupation. As Finch (1983) has shown, many wives are involved in, in her phrase 'incorporated' into, their husbands' jobs, providing help, support and essential back-up services. In times of recession the family is especially likely to become involved in co-ordinating and monitoring the work and activities of its members, as joint decisions and strategies are adopted to ensure the best economic future for the family unit. Pahl (1984), who has documented the importance of household strategies during the 1980s recession, has even suggested that the postwar epoch when work was seen as a matter of personal individual choice may have been an historical aberration: the norm, he suggests, may well be that work lives are mediated by the family, that work is a 'family concern'.

All in all, then, the links between work and family have not been totally severed, so we may feel some doubt as to the extent to which home/work separation is really the cause of women being channelled into inferior work. Moreover, the example of Russia (see chapter 1) suggests that responsibilities for running a home and for child care, while they may hamper a woman's chances of reaching the higher echelons, do not in themselves prevent women going out to work or taking on a wide range of types of job. It is social attitudes about 'woman's place', rather than the realities of work location, which act as a block to economic participation.

We may alo note that, if the separation of home and work was indeed the cause of job segregation, the return of work into the home should be a way of breaking it down. Such certainly was the Utopian vision of Clark; and many of the more optimistic observers of the contemporary scene, noting the growth of the 'home office', 'teleworking' and the 'electronic cottage', have made similar suggestions for the future in which men and women might work together in creative and fulfilling work of their own individual choosing. However Allen and Wolkowitz's study, among others, gives a bleak view of homeworking. Under the prevailing conditions of capitalist work organisation, homeworking is a convenient and profitable way of shifting some of the costs of production from employer to employee. Homeworkers are at the bottom of the pyramid in each occupation, in terms of pay, fringe benefits, promotion changes and status – and are mainly women. All this suggests that, whatever the original effect of the move out of the home, this is no longer the major cause of segregation. It would be possible, theoretically at least, to achieve sexual equality in a world where people 'went out' to work. Nevertheless, consideration of this issue remains important, as it points to the way in which home and work are linked together, so that both must be taken into account in explaining work relationships: this, of course, is one of the key assumptions of the 'joint orientation' outlined in chapter 1, which also questions the absolute nature of the traditional home/work and private/public distinctions.

The family wage has similarly been seen as a prop to women's inferior work status, as well as helping to perpetuate the association between women and domesticity. For most commentators, the family wage remains an ideal, rather than an actuality. Only a minority of working-class men (the labour 'aristocrats') have ever really earned enough to support a family without contributions from other family members; and in the 1980s even 'yuppie' couples find it necessary for both to go out to work to maintain the standard of living thought proper to their class. Nevertheless, that ideal of the family wage has had a constraining effect on women. Indeed, for Heidi Hartmann it is 'the cornerstone of the present sexual division of labour' (Hartmann, 1981, p. 25).

The notion of the family wage helps to sustain the idea that men are breadwinners and women dependent housewives, an idea which has been particularly influential in the past in framing state welfare provision and family policy. The assumption of most social security provision, until the last few years, has been that women are dependent on men rather than independent wage-earners with rights to independent state support (Land, 1976; Barrett and MacIntosh, 1980). Historically, the campaign for the family wage, which was espoused by many trade unions from the 1840s onward, has been linked to moves to exclude women from factory work and either confine them to the home or channel them into work seen as 'fitting' for women, such as domestic service or laundry work. Such a movement found enthusiastic support among men, both middle-class reformers and philanthropists and working-class trade unionists.It is less clear how working women responded, though Lewis (1984) suggests that by the end of the nineteenth century they had come to share the view that it was better for wives to stay at home. Yet this did not stop numerous married women from working.

Almost alone among feminist researchers, Humphries (1977) has written in favour of the family wage. She sees it as part of the repertoire of strategies used by the working-class family as it historically struggled to maintain its independence from capitalist employers. The family (or household) wage was a mechanism whereby the family could maintain its own responsibility for its members who could not be self-sufficient (children, the sick, the old) without having to rely on the handouts of the state, generally viewed as inadequate and demeaning. Also, it reflected a collectivist orientation, in which the wellbeing of the group is seen as more important than the striving of the individual. This can be traced back to the pre-industrial family production system and is to be preferred to the ethic of competitive individualism intrinsic to the notion of the 'individual wage'.

All these arguments are seductive; but the weakness of Humphries' account is that it presents the family as a unified, homogeneous collectivity, ignoring the uneven distribution of power within it. Nobody has ever campaigned for a 'family wage' to be paid to working wives! While the family wage remains linked to an ideal vision of a breadwinning man supporting a non-earning dependent wife and children, it must be seen as a prop to sexual sterotyping and the defining of women's work as secondary. The notion of a decent individual 'living' wage may have undesirable ideological connotations, but it alone offers women the chance of independence, while the family wage has become part of the symbolic apparatus which maintains segregation and sex-typing. As Hartmann (1981) points out, the concept is used by trade unions to justify sex differences in wages; men actively collude in keeping women low paid; this, in turn, acts to keep women dependent on men, and their inferior wage-earning potential pushes them into taking responsibility for housework. Thus the vicious circle is perpetuated.

Contemporaneous with the family wage campaign was the passing of legislation regulating hours and conditions of women's work. The 1842 Mines Act was the first to deal with women, prohibiting them from underground work, and all subsequent Factory Acts covered women as well as children. Since its inception this protective legislation has provoked controversy, and indeed it was a source of division between the Victorian feminists of the first wave (Banks, 1981). Some believed that the legislation did truly 'protect' women, preserving them from super-exploitation by unscrupulous employers. Others argued that it deprived women of the freedom and rights attendant upon adulthood, reducing them to the same minor status as children and confirming the social definition of women as dependents, incapable of defending their own interests; moreover, it acted to push women out of the best-paid factory jobs into the female ghettoes of sweatshops, laundries and domestic service where nobody seemed bothered about controlling hours and conditions.

Hutchins and Harrison's classic history of the Factory Acts (1911) sets out the former position: they argue that feminist opponents were blinded by their middle-class concern with the exclusion of women from high-status professions and were ignorant of the realities of working-class life. Working women wanted and needed protection. They also claim that male workers who campaigned for the legislation were not discriminating against women. Rather, they were 'fighting behind the petticoats of women'; since they knew that regulation of the hours of adult males would never be acceptable to governments and employers, they used the issue of women and children as a device to get their own working day reduced. A similar sympathy to the tactics of working-class men is shown by Humphries (1981); her account of the Mines Act, further discussed in chapter 6, sees it as representing the wishes of the female mineworkers and being a progressive development.

I am not the only one to find these arguments unconvincing. In a recent re-interpretation of the Factory Acts, Walby (1986) has argued powerfully for patriarchal motives in their imposition: male operatives were frightened of women's competition and consequent downward pressure on their wages and, she believes, they also wished to re-establish their authority in the home and ensure themselves of home comforts. These latter concerns tallied with those of the reformers, the 'bourgeois philanthropists' as she calls them, who had become obsessed with sexual morality, with the breakup of the family and the rise in infant mortality. As she rightly says, the evidence of patriarchal motives among the reformers is overwhelming. Among the operatives, my own reading is that economic considerations were foremost, but the argument that the campaign about women was a smokescreen is hard to sustain; the men clearly wanted their wives to stay out of competition for jobs they believed were theirs by right and the union movement threw its weight solidly behind the notion that a non-working wife was best. From the 1840s onwards union leaders and bodies representing union interests such as the TUC have clung to the idea that the 'woman's place is in the home' as many historical studies have shown (Boston, 1980; Braybon and Summerfield, 1987). Only the feminist reawakening of the 1960s has led to the (reluctant?) abandoning of this part of TUC policy.

The argument over legislation continues today, as women's work remains subject to restrictions: the ban from underground work and certain other dangerous processes, the ban on night work in factories. In America, too, feminists have argued that protective legislation encourages gender segregation. In 1969 46 states had laws limiting women's working hours (Madden, 1975: Gates, 1976). In Britain the Equal Opportunities Commission (EOC) has campaigned for the scrapping of existing legislation, while the TUC wishes to retain it. In an interesting article Coyle (1980) argues that, although it represents 'a conglomeration of reactionary interests' the legislation does limit the exploitation of women's labour: the substitution of free collective bargaining could work against women when they lack power within the political system and are still seen as a source of cheap labour.

What concerns us here is the effect of the legislation on segregation and sex-typing. In the nineteenth century it played a part in pushing women into certain types of work and confirmed the view that women were unfit for 'heavy' and 'dangerous' work. Today most people are unaware of the existence of the legislation, which, anyway, is often disregarded by employers, who may also be able to obtain exemption orders. However, arguably it still has a restricting influence; for example, it keeps women out of 'men's work' in the hosiery industry, where knitting machines are operated on a three-shift system (see chapter 8); in pottery, too, employers give it as a reason for not employing women in certain jobs reserved for males (Sarsby, 1988). The importance of this is that it gives the state an official role in maintaining the structure of segregation, which is often overlooked or even denied: Charles (1983b) and Dahlerup (1987) are examples of commentaries which see protective legislation as irrelevant to the maintenance of segregation. As Madden says, writing about the position in America, 'the government has made itself a partner in the establishment of sexual power through the enactment and enforcement of protective labor legislation' (Madden, 1975, p. 157). In the manufacturing sector at least, this places limits on women's options which are not faced by men; and its existence has a symbolic role in maintaining the view of women as weak, vulnerable and in need of paternal protection, from husband or state.

Finally, by contrast an important challenge to sex segregation in this century is seen to have been provided by the events of two world wars. The conventional interpretation is that in both wars women were able to prove their worth in taking over the full range of jobs performed by the men who were absent at the front, from constructing aircraft to driving buses, from managing offices to maintaining railways. Although the effect of the depression after World War I was to push back women into the female ghettoes or into the home, their contribution had been acknowledged and they were rewarded by getting the vote. After World War II, despite some calls for the return of women to the home and social anxiety about latchkey children, maternal deprivation and juvenile delinquency, the expansion of the economy and the consumer boom created a demand for labour which ensured that women stayed on in the labour market. In short, the war was a liberating experience for women.

This optimistic scenario can be challenged in a variety of ways. First, while women may indeed have demonstrated their capacity to fulfil all sorts of tasks, including the heaviest and most responsible, the return of men from the forces was quickly followed by, in one case, a total return to the prewar division of labour, and even a reinforcement of segregation as many employers introduced the marriage bar; while after World War II, women may have stayed on in the labour force, but they were quickly channelled into new types of 'women's work' in the service sector. Except for the progress of women in the professions (which was partly the result of earlier struggle) wartime experience had little long-term impact on the structure of segregation, as Hakim's study discussed in chapter 1 has revealed.

Moreover, recent studies by Thom (1978), Braybon (1981) and Summerfield (1984), among others, have suggested that the takeover of men's tasks was less complete than is popularly supposed. Many employers (for example in engineering and in hosiery) took advantage of the situation to develop new forms of work organisation, often involving new machinery or a further elaboration of the division of labour; the least skilled components of the reorganised work process were given to the women brought in to replace the men. Alternatively, a group of women might work under a male foreman, co-ordinator or mechanic, who took overall responsibility and performed the hardest parts of the work, such as setting up or altering machinery; or again several women might do what one man had formerly done. Arrangements like this also enabled employers to justify paying women less than men and establishing 'women's rates'. It is significant that the differential between men and women's average wages only decreased by 5 per cent during World War II (Braybon and Summerfield, 1987).

Although women did fill a much greater range of jobs than before the wars, the process of female substitution or 'dilution' was overseen by male trade unionists in such a way that the *authority* of men within the workplace was not challenged. Indeed, while the wars may have improved women's position, they improved the position of the trade unions even more! The heightened power of the unions, derived both from remarkable increases in membership and from the social recognition and political influence accorded to them by the government (and more reluctantly by employers), allowed them to reassert their own priorities after the war. They were able to negotiate a return to the prewar gender status quo with their employers. In the hosiery industry, the union succeeded in ending the longstanding attempts of employers to feminise the industry, so that segregation actually became more marked after 1945. The case studies in the book will provide more examples of this kind of process.

Wartime experience is significant because it reveals to us the extent to which the sexual division of labour is an artificial construct and not a 'natural' effect of sex differences in physique and personality. It also provides a salutary example of how rapidly change can occur if the 'national will' and governmental power is behind it. We may contrast this with the limp progress of the current anti-discrimination legislation half-heartedly enacted by the British government under pressure from the EEC. But the dispiriting aspect of the wartime experience is the evidence it provides of the pertinacity of social attitudes. Men never seem to have given up their negative views of women's competence. Braybon and Summerfield conclude

> The belief that men and women naturally occupy separate spheres within which they pursue quite different tasks was not shaken during either war: men were not expected to take an equal share of domestic responsibilities . . . Although there were many changes, there was an undertow pulling women back during both world wars, by emphasising that change was temporary, that women were 'really' wives and mothers and their place was at home,

and that they were doing skilled important jobs and earning relatively high wages on sufferance. (Braybon and Summerfield, 1987, pp. 2, 281)

Once the emergency was over both men and women relapsed to an acceptance of the old definitions of gender roles at home and at work. The power of these social definitions and the symbolic apparatus which incorporates them is only just gaining due recognition in the writing of feminists on women's work (for example, Matthaei, 1982; Scott, 1986; Beechey and Perkins, 1987; Sarsby, 1988). It will be a continuing theme in this book.

3

THE SOCIOLOGICAL DEBATES

In chapter 1 some of the sociological concepts used to explain gender segregation at work, such as labour market segmentation or the reserve army of labour, were briefly mentioned. This chapter will examine these more fully. However, the use of these various concepts has to be considered within the context of a wider debate which has preoccupied feminist sociologists since the early 1970s, the debate as to whether it is capitalism or patriarchy that is the root cause of sexual inequality or, to use the term preferred by most of the participants in the debate, the oppression of women. Can the sexual division of labour be satisfactorily explained in terms of the workings of the capitalist economy? Or is it necessary to turn to the analysis of some pre-existing and theoretically distinct structure of patriarchy for a proper understanding of gender inequality? This in turn begs the question of what exactly is meant by 'patriarchy'. In this chapter I shall start by considering these wider issues before looking more specifically at sociological theories of segregation and sex-typing. I shall begin by considering the debates over the basis of patriarchy and whether it can be seen as a valid sociological concept; I will then review the capitalism versus patriarchy debate, and conclude by discussing the range of concepts used to explain sexual divisions in employment.

Defining Patriarchy

Our society, like all other historical civilisations, is a patriarchy ... The military, industry, technology, universities, science, political office, finances – in short, every avenue of power within the society, including the coercive force of the police, is entirely in male hands. (Millett, 1971, p. 25)

The characteristic relation of human reproduction is patriarchy, that is control of women, especially of their sexuality and fertility, by men. (Mackintosh, 1977, p. 122).

The material base upon which patriarchy rests lies most fundamentally in men's control over women's labor power. (Hartmann, 1981, p. 15)

The quotations above illustrate the spectrum of meanings given by feminists to patriarchy: the universal social domination of men by women, family relationships where men police women's childbearing and sexuality, economic relationships whereby men exploit women's labour. Without doubt, patriarchy has been the key concept used in the feminist critique of other types of social, political and cultural theorising. Yet there is considerable disagreement over its meaning, except at the most general level, and some feminists have come to feel considerable doubt as to its usefulness as a concept. Much has been written on this topic, and the debates have been particularly well surveyed by Barrett (1980) and Walby (1987), who provide useful and full accounts of the various individual contributions. Here, I shall simply make some general points about the dispute.

As the quotations indicate, patriarchy has proved quite hard to define. This is partly due to disagreements as to where it is based (in production relations, in the family, in discourse, in psychic structures) but it is also true to say that it is often used in a vague and universalistic way to refer to male dominance in every form. Thus it can (and has) been used to account for almost any aspect of difference between men and women at any stage in history. In contrast to the Marxist concept of capitalism which involves a detailed, comprehensive, logical account of a particular set of relationships at a particular stage of economic development, the term patriarchy seems hopelessly imprecise and intrinsically descriptive. It may give us an accurate account of the picture on the screen, but it doesn't tell us how the cathode ray and the circuitry work. Moreover, not being rooted like the concept of capitalism in a theory of historical change, it lays itself open to the charge (sometimes merited) of being intrinsically ahistorical and resting upon unwarrantable assumptions of universality. Thus, even were it true to say that *all* societies at *all* times have been patriarchal, that men have *always* oppressed and exploited women, such a statement tells us very little about the precise nature of power relations between men and women in different historical epochs and societies. Men and women relate to each other very differently in America, in China and in India, for example, just as there are stark differences in women's position in medieval, Victorian and contemporary English society. To describe all these societies as patriarchal is unhelpful unless we can go on to describe the specific mechanisms by which patriarchy is maintained in each of them.

It has been difficult for feminists to take this further step because of the lack of consensus as to exactly *where* the base of patriarchy should be sought. Marxist feminists (like Beechey, Hartmann and Delphy) have tried to find a 'material' base for patriarchy as part of a system of production and/or reproduction. Taking as a starting point the idea developed by Engels in *The Origin of the Family, Private Property and the State* (first published in 1884) that the material base has a 'twofold character', involving the production and reproduction on the one hand of *things*, the means of existence, and on the other of *people*, the propagation of the species, they have attempted to uncover the base of male dominance through the analysis of labour power or of domestic labour. Radical feminists, and those influenced by psychoanalytic theory, have rejected this focus on production and have seen patriarchy as rooted in biology and the family (Firestone), in psychological structures of personality linked to childrearing practices (Mitchell, Harding) or in the realm of discourse, symbol and ideology (Coward). Others again argue that patriarchy is all-pervasive, rooted in all aspects of society, material, familial, ideological and psychological (Barratt, Walby). Like other key sociological concepts, patriarchy must be seen as 'essentially contested' (Lukes, 1974). The theoretical assumptions with which these various feminists start (reflecting the three different orientations discussed in chapter 1) will inevitably influence the way they derive their definitions. This need not in itself invalidate the concept; after all the indispensable sociological terms 'class' and 'power' are equally contestable. But it does compound the problems of vagueness and imprecision referred to above.

Other object to the use of patriarchy on the grounds that it is, anyway, used inaccurately by feminists, who have, as it were, hijacked the term from its original sociological context. For example, for Weber patriarchy or 'patriarchalism' referred to a particular type of authority relationship, associated with traditional societies:

> 'Patriarchalism' is the situation where, within a group which is usually organised on both an economic and a kinship base, as a household, authority is exercised by a particular individual who is designated by a definite rule of inheritance ... The authority of the patriarch carries strict obligations to obedience only within his own household. (Weber, 1964, p. 346)

Hartmann (1981) has pointed out that these relations, as described by Weber and others (and often linked with feudal societies), were basically arrangements between man and man, involving the specification of reciprocal rights and duties within a male social hierarchy, a fact which she has tried to incorporate into her own definition of patriarchy. But it has also been used to describe gender relations, notably by historians, such as Lawrence Stone, although in the context of a particular institution (the family) rather than of society as a whole. In Stone's account (1979), the patriarchal family is one based on the power of the father, with the older man taking precedence over the younger, the males taking precedence over the women. He argues that this type of family structure began to break down in the seventeenth century, giving way to the 'companionate' marriage in which spouses viewed each other as partners in an egalitarian alliance. In both these usages, though, patriarchy is seen as a thing of the past. This idea is typified by the pronouncement of Marx and Engels in the *Communist Manifesto* that 'modern industry has converted the little workshop of the patriarchal master into the great factory of the industrial capitalist' (Marx and Engels, 1967, p. 87): while, as Ehrenreich and English put it, 'the decline of patriarchal authority in the family was a constant theme of early twentieth century sociological writing' (Ehrenreich and English, 1979, p. 11).

In response to these problems, some writers, such as Rowbotham (1981) have rejected the use of the term altogether. Some prefer to substitute the less loaded terms 'male dominance' or 'male supremacy', although these do not get round the problems of impreciseness and the assumption of universality. Rubin (1975) has suggested the use of the term 'sex-gender system'. This has the great advantage of allowing for the (theoretical) possibility of egalitarian gender arrangements, possibly even of female dominance. Thus, it avoids the universalistic assumption of male dominance which characterises the work of some radical feminists (Brownmiller, 1976; Firestone, 1979) and the tendency to have to explain that universality in terms of biology (male brute muscle power, female incapacity through childbearing). It is then possible to argue that certain types of sex-gender system are indeed patriarchal, using the term in the stricter sense.

Barrett (1980), too, sees the concept as problematic, being uneasy about its transhistorical and universal tendencies, and rejects the idea that capitalist society is correctly described as 'a patriarchy' although it may well have patriarchal elements within it (and everywhere does, as I shall argue). In particular, she points to the persistence of patriarchal ideology identifying differing social roles for men and for women. While she does not reject the term altogether, she suggests limiting its use to instances where the 'rule of the father' can clearly be discerned. For her, patriarchy is only one historical type of male dominance, which may take many different forms.

Ehrenreich and English also consider patriarchy a thing of the past. What they call the 'Old Order' of pre-industrial societies was patriarchal, although paradoxically 'gynocentric' in that within the home everything centred round the skills, knowledge and activities of the woman. But the authority rested with men. Contemporary societies they consider more correctly described as 'masculinist'. Although the power of the father has crumbled in the face of the 'free' market, male dominance has taken a new form, in a world in which social arrangements and ideologies are 'cast in a realm apart from women' (Ehrenreich and English, 1979, p. 16).

The alternative path, taken for example by Hartmann and Walby, is to work towards a more satisfactory definition of patriarchy, one that is historically grounded and precise. Hartmann has defined patriarchy as

> A set of social relationships between men, which have a material base, and which, though hierarchical, establish or create interdependence and solidarity among men that enable them to dominate women ... The material base upon which patriarchy rests lies most fundamentally in men's control over women's labour power. (Hartmann, 1981, pp. 14–15)

Such a definition acknowledges the existing conceptual history of the term as used by Weber and others, while incorporating it into a Marxist framework which can take account both of class (and ethnic) hierarchies and of gender hierarchies. It avoids both what she calls the 'sex-blindness' of traditional Marxism and the blindness to historical development which she ascribes to radical feminist theories of patriarchy: the latter can be overcome through identifying the 'material base' of patriarchy, as she believes she has done. Then it will be possible to trace out the different forms taken by 'men's control over women's labour power' in different historical stages. Thus Hartmann's definition opens the way for a more precise account of patriarchal relations, firmly grounded in history.

These achievements should be recognised. However, there are still problems with this approach. Hartmann's position appears curiously and paradoxically sexist in defining patriarchy in terms of relations between *men*, thus relegating relations between men and women to a secondary position. Surely this mirrors the gender bias inherent in nineteenth-century social thinking where the sociological usage of the term originated, when it was taken for granted that social arrangements and institutions were formed by men alone? Similarly, the location of the material base in the analysis of 'labour power' gives privilege to the theorising of production, ignoring other aspects of the relations between men and women that go on in the family and elsewhere: the dominant role of men in sexuality for example. As Harding (1981) and Ehrlich (1981) argue in response to Hartmann, she has improved on orthodox Marxism by extending the analysis of economic domination from the sphere of industry into the family; but that still gives a limited, economistic account of male/female relations. Consequently, as I shall argue in the next section, gender domination is reduced once again to being a by-product of class relations.

Walby in a later discussion credits Hartmann with having produced the best account to date of patriarchy, but tries to surpass it in an analysis which does not tend to reduce gender relations to an aspect of class:

I define patriarchy as a system of interrelated structures through which men exploit women ... The model I shall construct here will be composed of a limited number of relatively autonomous structures with the relative importance of each specified. The key sets of patriarchal relations are to be found in domestic work, paid work, the state, male violence and sexuality; while other practices in civil society have a limited significance. (Walby, 1986, pp. 51–2)

Unlike Hartmann, she argues that patriarchy should be seen as a distinct mode of production; this, she claims is based in domestic work. However in capitalist societies, structures of patriarchy in paid work assume a special importance, and patriarchy also operates in the other areas mentioned.

The great strength of all Walby's work on patriarchy (as opposed to almost everybody else's) is that it correctly emphasises the important presence of patriarchal structures in wage labour, especially in postwar industrial capitalism, and does not rest on the assumption that all women are primarily housewives (as is the case, for example, with Delphy and the various contributors to the debate on the social significance of domestic labour). But the attempt to characterise patriarchy as *both* a domestic mode of production *and* a set of structures external to it seems to me theoretically dubious. If patriarchy really is a mode of production, all those elements must surely be included within it? This seems a clear attempt to have your cake and eat it. Apart from that, the problem of her approach is that by including almost every manifestation of male dominance in the definition it loses the sharp focus achieved by Hartmann and reverts to the imprecision so characteristic of writing about patriarchy. In the end, her definition looks quite similar to that of Millett with which this section started! Much of the discussion which follows her definition is essentially descriptive and does not seem to offer the potential for systematic historical analysis that Hartmann's definition does. This is not to say that what Walby says is invalid; it merely illustrates the tendency of analysis of patriarchy to slide into description. The reasons why this seems to me inevitable will be discussed in the next sections of this chapter.

While believing that the definitions given by Hartmann and Walby are the best on offer, patriarchy seems to me to be a flawed concept. As long as it is used, the danger of a slippage into an ahistorical universalism, or a reduction to Marxism (because of the greater power of the Marxist analysis of capitalism), or conversely into a descriptive generalism, cannot be avoided. My own sympathies are with Rowbotham and Barrett; it would seem preferable to develop an analysis of male dominance confining the use of patriarchy to pre-industrial societies characterised by 'father rule' and to use some term such as 'androcentric' (following Ehrenreich and English) for contemporary capitalist societies. I shall say more about this in chapter 14; in the case studies that follow I have tried to use the term only where it appeared to me applicable in the stricter sense.

However, having said this, I believe we have to go on talking about patriarchy, if only on the grounds of conventional usage. This has become the key concept in the new history and sociology of women and cannot be rejected. *De facto*, it has become indispensable. As Mies (1986) has argued, its link with the feminist reawakening of the 1960s gives it a political and symbolic power which rival terms like 'sex-gender systems' simply do not have. Moreover, all the alternatives are cumbersome and awkward to use, apart from having no resonance in popular speech. Cockburn is therefore right to say that most feminists use the term knowing that it is not ideal but for lack of a better; indeed, she argues that the more neutral term 'sex-gender system' is implicit within the theoretical parameters of the word: 'behind its use has always been the idea of a *sex-gender system* that has been and could be different from what it is today' (Cockburn, 1986, p. 82). Nor need it worry us that the word now means something rather different from what it meant to Weber. Like the words of everyday speech, academic concepts change in meaning with new contexts, as Weber himself recognised. The ideas now linked to patriarchy were not available when Weber was writing but they have now become part of its current symbolic resonance. Therefore, in spite of the difficulties, we must persevere with the analysis of patriarchy in trying to develop further insights into gender relations.

Capitalism versus Patriarchy

The debate about the relative power of capitalism and patriarchy as frameworks for explaining sexual divisions, and about the precise nature of the link between the two systems, has been going on since the early 1970s and volumes (literally) have been written on this topic. Some of this writing is couched in the dense and demanding language of Althusserian structuralism, which was the Marxist orthodoxy current at the time of this outburst of feminist theorising. It would be impossible to do justice to the intricacies of this debate within a few pages; readers who wish to delve more deeply into it are referred to the excellent surveys by Barrett (1980) and Walby (1986) and to two of the key texts *Feminism and Materialism* (Kuhn and Wolpe, 1978) and *Women in Revolution: The Unhappy Marriage of Marxism and Feminism* (Sargent, 1981). All that I shall do here is to provide a schematic account of the various possible positions.

For traditional Marxism, gender divisions can be explained within a theory of class. For example, Engels believed that the social subordination of women emerged at the same time as the institution of private property; the control of women by men was part of their attempt to secure their control of the surplus and hand it on to their heirs. The implication is that in a classless (that is, socialist) society gender divisions would disappear and so women are urged to join in the common struggle for the overthrow of capitalist domination (despite the clear evidence, dealt with in chapter 1, that existing socialist revolutions have not destroyed male supremacy). Thus Marxists (for example Zaretsky, 1976) have tried to explain the position of women in contemporary societies in terms of their relation to capitalism, seeing no need for any separate theory of the relations between women and men. In Ehrlich's phrase, male dominance is seen as 'a disfiguring but localised excrescence on the skin of capitalism, to be cured by the strong medicine of state socialism' (Ehrlich, 1981, p. 110). In an extreme and crude version this could lead to the view that gender inequality was actually *initiated* by capitalism, a view given some credence by the exaggerated accounts of family and work equality in pre-industrial society which were reviewed in chapter 2.

Few feminists take quite this position, though it is still commonly held by many socialist activists (and not only males). Most Marxist feminists came to the conclusion that traditional Marxist categories are, indeed 'sex-blind' as Hartmann argues, providing only a theory of 'empty places' in a system of production and not telling us 'who will fill the empty places' (Hartmann, 1981, p. 10). It was necessary to add gender in to the traditional analysis. But some believed it was possible to do this within the basic framework of class theory. Marxism needed rewriting rather than transforming. Thus women's position was analysed in terms of their specific role within capitalism, employing the existing vocabulary of 'labour power', 'the reserve army', 'reproduction' and so forth. The series of papers known as the 'domestic labour debate' is the most eminent example of this; here women's subordination was explained in terms of what capital gained from the unpaid work of women in the home (for example, Dalla Costa and James, 1972; Seccombe, 1974; Gardiner, 1976).

Such approaches continued to see women's position solely in terms of the needs of capital. There was insufficient recognition that men, as a social group, might also profit from the inferior position of women in employment or their assignment to domestic duties. The contribution of organised male workers in bringing these about was conveniently ignored. Moreover, there was a tendency to look only at working-class women; the way women of the bourgeoisie themselves were disadvantaged could not be explained in a framework which really ended by seeing gender subordination as an aspect of labour's subordination to capital.

At the other extreme were the radical feminists who were interested only in the analysis of patriarchy, seeing gender as the primary form of social inequality from which all others sprang and rejecting Marxism and the concentration on production. In this view all societies are characterised by male dominance which is seen as rooted in the family and in particular in women's reproductive role. In contemporary societies sex inequality is seen to be perpetuated by the institutions of monogamous marriage and heterosexuality, by ideologies of sex differences and masculine superiority, by psychological differences arising from childrearing practices within the nuclear family. Many radical feminists, especially in America, drew on Freudian theory or other forms of psychoanalysis as an alternative theoretical framework to Marxism, although conceding the need to rework it to remove what were seen as sex biases (for example the idea that women are inherently psychologically inferior because of their lack of a penis and the resulting 'Electra complex'). The work of Chodorow (1978) on mother and child relationships was particularly influential here.

We have already noted the tendency for this kind of account of patriarchy to become unwarrantably universalistic and ahistorical, glossing over all sorts of variations in gender relations. This is exemplified by the work of Firestone (1979) which, despite its power and sophistication, cannot ultimately escape from perceiving women's biology as their destiny. A woman who bears a child within her body is doomed to be subordinate to men. The psychoanalytic analyses, too, tended to a deterministic view, women's passivity and men's dominance emerging as the inevitable product of the way they differentiate themselves as subjective beings from their mothers. Most importantly, this approach neglected other sources of division (class, race, age) which matter because they intersect with gender. Discussion of gender alone could not explain the differences in the family and work experience, for example, of women of different classes and ethnic groups. The tendency to shy away from materialist accounts and see patriarchy as an ideology, a set of psychic structures, ignored the way gender divisions are actually created in the economic sphere. Thus the view of sex oppression as primary was as limiting as seeing class oppression as primary.

Few academic feminists would now subscribe to either of these polar positions. Most would recognise the contributions made by both original perspectives, but accept that neither an account of patriarchy nor of capitalism alone will adequately explain sexual divisions and that an analysis in terms of both gender and class is needed. Within this third group, however, there are two subdivisions. Some call for a unified theory, integrating class and gender analysis into a totalistic theory of capitalist patriarchy or patriarchal capitalism (for example, McDonough and Harrison, 1978; Eisenstein, 1979; Young, 1981). Others believe the two must be analysed separately, conceiving patriarchy and capitalism as two separate but interrelated (or interacting, symbiotic) systems (for example, Hamilton, 1978; Hartmann, 1981; Cockburn, 1986).

The first group see their objective as going beyond both Marxism and feminism. For example, Vogel (1981) and Hicks (1981) believe that a more sophisticated type of Marxism, taking account of political, cultural and ideological dimensions of society, could incorporate a satisfactory account of gender divisions: while Harding (1981) considers that Marxism is inherently incapable of dealing with non-economic relationships and that its undoubted insights on class should be abstracted and incorporated into an improved theory of patriarchy based on psychoanalytic concepts. This should illustrate the persistent problem with the search for unification. In every case it involves a slippage back into either Marxism or radical feminism (usually the former: Stanley and Wise (1983), have not unjustly portrayed all this as an attempt to 'save' Marxism). In such attempts, gender is reduced to class or class to gender.

The other approach is known as the 'dual-systems' approach. This holds that class cannot be reduced to gender or gender to class. Each must be theorised separately, although at any given historical moment they are found interacting (often in combination with other dynamics, such as that of race). Theories of this type can again be subdivided into two groups. In one, class relations and gender relations are seen as founded in different spheres of the social totality, for example class arising from the economy and patriarchy founded in the domestic sphere. Some versions employ the Marxian distinction between production and reproduction. Mitchell's work provides a classic statement of this kind: 'in analysing contemporary Western society we are (as elsewhere) dealing with two autonomous areas: the economic mode of capitalism and the ideological mode of patriarchy' (Mitchell, 1975, p. 412). The danger of this position, as Mies argues (1986), is its exaggerated account of duality, the identification of reproduction/the family/the private domain/patriarchy on one side and production/work/the public domain/capitalism on the other. In fact gender and class relations not only spill over between work and the family but are both embedded and developed in both dimensions (so that, for example, authority relations and housework arrangements will vary greatly between middle-class and working-class families). This insight informs the work of the other group who believe that both class and gender systems should be seen working at all levels of society. This is the approach of Hartmann and Walby.

This is the most coherent position as yet, but, as I have already argued, there is still a danger, exemplified by Hartmann's work, of allowing the original Marxian framework to dominate so that 'in the last instance' class becomes logically prior. The reason for this, as I have implied, is that the explanatory framework of Marxism, and in particular the account of the capitalist economy and its dynamic possibilities, is so coherent, systematic and powerful, that all the attempts to develop an historical and explanatory account of patriarchy to match it seem puny by comparison. This is the problem which Walby's work, sympathetic as I am to it, cannot overcome (and I mean cannot overcome rather than fails to overcome). In attempting to define patriarchy as a 'mode of production' comparable to the capitalist mode of production she is comparing two intrinsically dissimilar things. Put more theoretically, it is not possible to conceive of patriarchy as a structure homologous to capitalism (or indeed to the more general structure of a 'mode of production' in the Marxian sense). Marxian class theory can be firmly grounded in a specific set of relations, the social division of labour for the production of goods and services, and is then built up from there. But gender relations cannot legitimately be confined to a single social activity (even the family) or even be said to originate in one level and spread into others. Gender activities pervade all aspects of social existence and so no satisfactory base/superstructure account can be produced. Without this, it is hard to develop a logical dynamic of change. Walby has struggled to get round this by her idea of a domestically grounded base plus other sets of relations; but the result appears vague, unbounded, all-inclusive, fuzzy and ultimately descriptive rather than explanatory.

Middleton (1988) has developed a somewhat similar critique of dual systems theory, emphasising the point that the term patriarchy is merely descriptive, not part of an explanatory framework; but his conclusion appears to be that we must return to the search for a unified theory, essentially an elaborated form of Marxism. I am not convinced. Gender is not the product of class! It must be theorised separately. However, if gender relations are to be conceived as a system they are not a system of the same type as that which Marxism has modelled. This problem bedevils the best work in this area, like that of Hartmann and Walby. Is there a way round it?

Beyond Capitalism versus Patriarchy ... ?

Before trying to answer that question, we should note that not all attempts to understand sexual divisions, especially in employment, have been couched in the terms of this debate. Many sociologists have found it quite acceptable to take a 'middle range' approach, employing specific sociological concepts (such as socialisation, division of labour or labour market segmentation) to explain sexual inequalities, without explicitly using them in the context of any overarching perspective. These aspects will be dealt with in the final section of the chapter. However, there also exist more theoretical challenges to the prevailing orthodoxies, which typify alternative strands in sociology. I will examine two of these.

Stanley and Wise, in *Breaking Out* (1983), offer an ethnomethodological approach to the study of gender. They are fiercely critical of what they see as the dominance of Marxism in feminism but also attack all forms of causal and structural analysis, which they see as embodying a positivistic view of reality, as something 'out there' separate from the lived experience of individual women and men. Rather, they argue, feminism should take seriously the idea that 'the personal is political' and work towards a new type of feminist theory founded in women's consciousness and everyday experience. Instead of taking sexism as a 'resource', as evidence on which structural causal explanations are founded, it should become the 'topic' of feminist theory, with researchers examining the way that they themselves experience, interpret and handle sexism in their daily lives. This would involve a respect for the different ways in which different women interpret the world. In later work, they have also argued for a greater appreciation of the complexities of power between the sexes and a rejection of a simplistic dichotomous view of 'oppressor' and 'oppressed' (Wise and Stanley, 1987).

Stanley and Wise see their theorising as part of feminist practice, which, indeed, is for them its prime objective. A very different view is taken by Elshtain (1987) who wishes to free the academic study of women from what she sees as the distorting influence of 'feminist rhetoric'. Her call for a more objective sociology comes from a position which appears to be a mixture of traditional liberal pluralism and postmodernist theory (what these two have in common is the view of society as fragmented by the diverse experience of groups and individuals). Words like 'oppression' are anathema to Elshtain who, like Stanley and Wise, deplores the dominance of Marxist and structural accounts in the discussion of gender, though on slightly different grounds. All such accounts, she argues, embody a rhetorical narrative based on false and teleological assumptions (that is they specify an assumed primal position and a given end towards which history is moving). What she calls the 'sex neutrality' narrative (essentially Marxism) rests on the belief of an original equality (and androgyny); oppression (whether of sex or class) was then created by man. Through critique of the 'structures of oppression', history may be moved towards a final state of restored equality. Conversely she identifies a rhetoric of 'sex polarity' (radical feminism) which stresses the biological differences between men and women and therefore sees them as irrevocably divided. Instead of these Elshtain proposes a view of 'sex complementarity' (different but equal?) which will deal with the complexity and variety of gender relations without any unwarrantable assumptions. This is all associated with the postmodernist rejection of 'meta-narratives' (her term is 'narratives of closure'): views of history resting on the notion of 'progress', a logical development towards a given end (a classless society, sex equality). This also involves rejection of any universalist view of human action and experience (for example, that all the working class are exploited, all women are oppressed). In Elshtain's case she wants an open-ended account of the variability of power relations between men and women.

The stress on variability and complexity in these two approaches provides a useful corrective to the sometimes oversimplistic general-isations of structural theories, but both carry in them the usual problems of anti-structuralist theories. There is the danger of falling into a kind of liberal voluntarism whereby the notion of gender divisions and inequalities of a systematic kind are denied, despite the firm evidence for them provided, for example, in chapter 1. There is also the danger of reading too much from the examples of individual women who fight back, beat the system and rise to the top and so forth (Thatcher and Currie again!) We have already seen this tendency in the historical debates discussed in chapter 2; historians' use of the narrative method may lead them to overemphasise differences at the expense of clearly discernible regularities. Moreover, if structural analysis is rejected, the work that can be done within the kind of framework proposed by Stanley and Wise, though quite legitimate and interesting, is limited. While we do need to know *how* sexism is sustained we also want to know *why* and we know from our own experience that there are 'whys' as well as 'hows'. So much is that the case, that hidden structural accounts often creep into anti-structuralist theorising. Thus Stanley and Wise cling to the idea of 'men as oppressors' (which itself implies a structured regularity) and use a kind of psychological structural theory to explain why (the power of the penis combined with the fear of the 'other'). Unless 'theory' is confined to simple narrative description of individual experiences and events (and that is a thing much harder to achieve than most people realise) elements of structural explanation will inevitably enter by the back door. The fact remains that there exists systematic evidence of sexual divisions and inequalities, of male power and female lack of it (however powerful some individual women may be) and that still has to be explained. Unlike Elshtain, I see no logical reason why structural accounts should be teleological, though I would hope that they would be informed by a moral concern for a more just and equal world.

This returns us to the thorny issue of how a structural theory of gender should proceed without falling either into universalism or class reductionism. It seems to me that the whole root of the problem is the sociological notion of 'system'. I would tentatively suggest that the way ahead is a form of structural theory that abandons the notion of system or at least operates with a severely modified version of it. This is dangerous ground, I know, but I would like briefly to indicate why and how this should be done.

If system is conceived, in the classic functionalist way, as a set of self-sufficient, self-maintaining unified parts (the plumbing system, the combustion engine) whereby a regular input consistently produces the same output, then it seems to me a hopeless metaphor for society. Any society contains far too many elements all interacting frantically under highly localised conditions, has far too many highly contingent inputs, to be conceived of in this way. That is quite apart from the well-known point that the elements *think*! If the metaphor is used more modestly to refer to some particular aspect of society which is made up of interrelated sets of relationships (the education system, the economic system), and if it is also recognised that other sets of relationships may impinge on to and interact with it, then it seems to me viable. To be more concrete, when Marxism explores society using the system metaphor in the second way, as in its analysis of the statics and dynamics of the capitalist production for profit (an analysis which has not been surpassed), it is working in the right way. It is when it tries to extend itself to use the system metaphor in the functionalist way and claims that the analysis of the economy can be extended to explain every aspect of human activity that it goes wrong. The critiques of feminists (and work in other fields such as race relations) have, it seems to me, exposed the futility of trying to explain absolutely anything and everything in terms of a single set of relationships; the study of gender and of race has revealed the limitations of the system metaphor (whether the system be capitalism or patriarchy).

The way ahead, it seems to me, is to conceive social structure in terms of many sets of interconnected relationships (class, gender, ethnicity, politics, culture, etc.) and to analyse these within the context of their historical development. Each set of relations can be theorised in isolation, though a complete understanding of each will not be gained unless their interaction with the others, both at any given time and through their history, is also taken into account. This may seem a tall order, but in fact I believe it can be done by concentrating on some particular aspect, and an example of this will be offered in the next section. It does mean acknowledging that our explanations will inevitably be limited and incomplete, although sufficient at least to be a good basis for thinking about how to change society.

It should be emphasised that I do not see this as abandoning either Marxism or feminist concern with patriarchy. What I am advocating, perhaps, is using those types of structural analysis within an approach which sees social reality and the endeavour to comprehend, understand and explain it in terms more in line with the methodological prescriptions of Weber. As an example of how this could work in practice, Walby's concrete accounts of class and gender relations in *Patriarchy at Work* seem to me exemplary. What she is actually doing is right! What she claims to be doing is misguided.

Explaining Gender Segregation at Work

Having surveyed the general theoretical frameworks for understanding gender inequalities, we must now turn to the more specific explanations for gender segregation in employment which sociologists have developed. Many of these, in fact, involve concepts drawn from economic theory. Again my discussion must be brief, and readers who wish to consider any particular position in more detail are recommended to the very useful surveys provided by Beechey (1986), Beechey and Perkins (1987) and Thompson (1983).

Economists have considered sex segregation within the orthodox frameworks of supply and demand and individual preference. One concept they have employed is that of human capital. It is argued that employers select labour on the base of the human capital which is accrued by each worker, in the form of education, qualifications, training, experience and skills; the worker with the least human capital goes to the back of the queue and gets paid least. Women are seen typically to possess less human capital, largely because of the interruption of their work careers when they have children.

However, studies such as those of England (1982) and Beller (1982) suggest that the evidence does not support human capital theory, in a number of ways. For example, women who work continuously without breaks are still found in low-paid female jobs, despite the human capital they have accumulated. Where men and women start with equal qualifications (as in medicine and teaching), women quickly fall behind in the promotion race, even before taking time off for childbirth, as the case studies will show. Women who leave the labour market and return characteristically have to enter at a lower level (a skilled secretary doing routine filing or barwork, for example) their 'human capital' disregarded. Moreover, while this might explain vertical forms of segregation, why women do not get to the top, it tells us nothing as to why whole occupations, at every level (like nursing) are staffed by women; nor can it explain the sex-typing of jobs.

An alternative approach, which does recognise that female and male workers might actually be treated differently *from the outset* (like black and white) and are not equal starters in the queue for jobs, employs the concept of a taste for discrimination which employers may exercise, thereby making what would conventionally be considered 'non-rational' economic decisions (that is, not choosing the best equipped or most suitable worker for the job). This is because, rather than maximising profits, they may prefer to minimise their contact with certain groups (women, black people) (Becker, 1957). This in turn leads women to 'crowd' into sectors where employers are not exercising their discriminatory taste, and which male workers reject; as these areas are overstocked with workers (supply outstripping demand) the result is that women can only command low wages.

Much of this seems little more than descriptive and begs the sociological question of how employers acquire such a 'taste', especially if it is clearly spread through whole sectors of employers! But, in any case it is erroneous to assume that employers necessarily shrink from employing women (although the theory may apply more accurately in the case of ethnic minority groups). Rather, as the case studies will show, in certain circumstances employers will show a positive taste for employing women to replace men, although the power of male workers may prevent them from getting their way! Indeed, Lloyd argues that the whole framework of 'taste' and 'preference' fails to engage with the realities of male power (Lloyd, 1975). Although the 'crowding' concept accords more recognition to horizontal segregation than human capital theory does, it is based on some dubious assumptions: rather than overstocking of labour, many of these typical female jobs have been marked by severe shortages at many times in their history (see, for example, the case studies of nursing, teaching and hosiery). Such shortages led neither to increased wages nor to men taking up the jobs, even in times of male unemployment. It seems that purely economic frameworks will not get us far in understanding segregation.

Radical economists critical of such conventional approaches developed in response the concept of segmented labour markets. This idea has been taken up by many sociologists as it moves beyond the economistic framework of individual attributes and preferences to consider the motivations of social groups, conceiving labour in terms of different social categories. It has been eleborated in a number of versions, but the basic idea is that the labour market is in fact divided into two or more separate sectors between which it is very difficult for workers to pass. Market sectors described as 'primary' are characterised by well-paid, high-status jobs and good career chances, markets which are 'secondary' by dead-end, low-paid jobs, bad work conditions, tight supervision and little chance of promotion. Various groups may be confined to secondary markets (ethnic groups, migrants, the young, the old), but Barron and Norris (1976) have suggested that women are an ideal source, because of their characteristics of low economism, lack of training, low levels of trade union organisation and so forth. Also their visibility makes them easy to recruit. In some versions it is argued that segmentation arises from the need of employers for two types of labour, a stable core of committed skilled workers and marginal groups which can be taken on and laid off as the economy expands and contracts. This also conveniently serves to split the work force and inhibit class solidarity and concerted industrial action (Edwards, 1979). Others have stressed the role of male workers and trade unions in seizing hold of the primary jobs for themselves (Rubery, 1980).

On the face of it, this seems a reasonable explanation of women's labour market position as many women do work in jobs which display 'secondary' characteristics. But not all do. Many characteristic 'women's jobs' (such as teaching, nursing, knitwear) are clearly not of the secondary kind: they require training, experience, skill, and many women do have careers within them, some working for years for a single employer and taking on a 'core' role. Moreover some kinds of casualised secondary work (for example in construction or agriculture) may be filled by men. Although segmented labour theory illuminates some aspects of women's work it does not go very far in explaining segregation especially of the horizontal kind. Moreover, the explanations in terms of capitalist employers' motivations and union responses ignore the fact that segregation predates capitalist industry and cannot tell us why it was socially acceptable to allocate women to secondary jobs in the first place.

The idea of secondary labour has been used by Marxists but they have perhaps more commonly turned to the rather similar idea of the reserve army of labour or surplus population. The reserve army is seen as a crucial part of the capitalist structure. Capital requires a pool of labour (agricultural workers, immigrants, the old and the very young, women) which it can draw upon in times of market expansion, throw out in time of slump. The existence of the reserve army serves as a disciplinary threat to those in work who fear being replaced by unemployed members of the pool if they step out of line. Again, women are seen as a particularly useful labour reserve as they can be returned to the home when their labour is no longer needed with the minimum of social disruption or protest, and without any drain on government resources in the form of unemployment benefits (witness the continued history of the reluctance of the British government to pay benefit to married women). Thus capital feeds off and reinforces the dependency of women on fathers and husbands.

Again, this seems superficially persuasive; it fits particularly well with the use made of women's labour in the two world wars and the attempt to return them to domesticity afterwards. Capital may well look upon women as a pool or reserve of labour. However, once again, the concept has problems. If it is correct, it should mean that women are the first to be laid off in times of recession. This gained guarded support from a study by Bruegel (1979), which, however, suggested that women should not be seen as necessarily part of the reserve army; whether they are or not depends on particular historical circumstances. Humphries' work (1983) throws considerable doubt as to whether this has been the case in the 1980s depression. On the contrary the pattern has been for full-time male jobs to be lost and part-time female employment to expand. Moreover, the assumption of the reserve army hypothesis is that men and women are doing the same kind of jobs. We know that is not the case. Also, women who have been pulled in to substitute for men have often not been pushed out again but remain there permanently, in clerical work for example. The reserve army thesis largely overlooks the existence of sexual segregation and thus cannot be seen as an adequate explanation of sexual inequality at work.

Humphries used her material on unemployment to suggest an alternative hypothesis: that women, because their labour was cheaper than men's, were in fact the 'ideal proletariat' and that what we have witnessed since industrialisation is a process of 'female substitution' or 'female proletarianisation'. The preference of the first factory masters for women and children is well known, and many instances of female substitution will be reviewed in this book. Humphries' hypothesis, therefore, seems more convincing than the reserve army thesis. But there are many problems with it. Why is women's labour cheaper? If female proletarianisation proceeded far enough would not the power relations between the sexes be reversed? And would not then male labour become cheaper? One reason why this does not happen is that, as More (1980) and Braybon and Summerfield (1987) among others have shown, employers have historically preferred to keep men in certain jobs, while using women in others. The gender dimension is essentially missing from Humphries' account, which is as blind as the reserve army thesis to the persistent fact of segregation.

All these approaches suffer from the same failing. Drawing on existing economic theories, researchers have been content merely to 'add women in'. In Hartmann's phrase, they are all theories of empty places. Women are then seen as suited to fit the empty places for a variety of more or less contingent reasons. But this seriously understates the extent of gender divisions and the way in which they are involved in any type of social and economic transformation. Gender cannot be reduced to an afterthought. What is needed is a much more radical approach which recognises that historically the places have been 'gendered' from the start.

Walby has made a beginning in trying to move beyond the economism of the other positions and seeing patriarchal motivations as having their own dynamic as well as capitalist motivations. Thus she describes the use of women's labour in the nineteenth and twentieth centuries in terms of a conflict between the desire of capitalists for cheap labour (pulling women into jobs) and the motives of capitalists as men and, particularly, of male workers to keep women under patriarchal control in the family (pulling them back into the home). This is not just a matter of fear of female competition, as assumed in segmented labour market theory, but of a wish for a comfortable home with a full-time domestic worker catering to her husband's needs, along with a desire that women should not challenge the authority of the male breadwinner by gaining full economic independence. This Walby argues, accounts for the ebbs and flows of women's labour market participation. Yeandle (1984) has distinguished similar conflicts between 'economic' and 'traditional' motives affecting the choices of families in the 1980s: families want the additional earnings of wives, but at the same time they still tend to adhere to the traditional view of the ideal family as male breadwinner with wife as full-time mother. Walby is correct, I believe, and the case studies that follow will provide plenty of the examples of these complex sets of motivation at play. However, even this does not go far enough, in that it fails still to give sufficient recognition to the segregated nature of work.

One way to do this is by reworking the body of ideas known as the 'labour process debate'. This derives from Harry Braverman's reformulation of some of the ideas from Marx's *Capital*. Braverman (1974) argues that the struggle for control of the labour process between capitalists and workers has led to a progressive 'degradation' of tasks as new technology is adopted and work processes reorganised: a process which has been popularly known as 'deskilling'. In his own account Braverman noted the link between degradation and the use of female labour (Braverman, 1974). But it is possible to provide a more complete account if we accept that from the *beginning* of industrial development the labour process was not only 'capitalist' but also 'gendered'. That is, that as capitalists introduced new techniques and reorganised the process of production they in fact created 'men's' and 'women's' jobs, utilising the characteristics that were socially ascribed to men and women as workers: the 'skill' and 'technological expertise' of men, the 'cheapness' and 'adaptability' of women. Matthaei (1982) argues that jobs which involve 'social homemaking' (teaching, social work) present another example of the gendering of new forms of work from the outset. The attempts of men to resist change and retain traditional forms of skill and work practices only served to entrench this kind of segregation. Thus a dualisation occurred not within the labour *market* but in the labour *process* itself. The subsequent operation of the market reflects that fact.

My own study of hosiery workers (Bradley, 1987) provided one clear example of these developments. These have also been explored in an excellent series of books and papers by Cynthia Cockburn (1983, 1985, 1986). Cockburn rightly gives special emphasis to technology and notions of skill. Women and men have always had a different relation to technology. Men are seen as technically competent, creative; women are seen as incompetent, suited only for the minding of machines which have been constructed, maintained and set up by men. Notions of skill, too, are founded on gender distinctions. Men capture skilled jobs (that is those involving training, expertise, knowledge) for themselves; moreover all jobs done by men, simply by virtue of that fact, are seen as more skilled than those done by women. Similarly women are pushed into unskilled jobs, and the skills that they do have are seen as 'natural' (cooking, caring for people, sewing) and therefore devalued (see also Westwood, 1984).

This version of the labour process theory, I would argue, is an example of the type of approach I advocated above. It involves investigating the way different sets of relations (gender, class) interact within a particular historical context and how they develop together. However, even this remains an insufficient explanation of segregation as it is still too narrowly focused on work and market issues. We need also to look at how gender and class operate in the family.

Although the family no longer directly assigns its members to specific jobs outside the home, it still has a crucial role in preparing young people for segregated work through processes of differential socialisation (Oakley, 1981). Within it children take in ideas about proper behaviour of girls and boys, women and men, and develop expectations about their own adult futures. This process is then carried on in schools and other educational establishments; research has shown that the expectations of teachers, parents and other pupils all tend to push boys and girls towards jobs considered suitable for their sex (Sharpe, 1976; Oakley, 1981; Wainwright, 1984).

Feminists have often criticised sociologists' use of the concept of socialisation for the danger it holds of a too deterministic view of these influences in early life: young people are sent out into the world preprogrammed to be lorry drivers or nurses! What we need to remember is that the individual's exposure to social definitions and redefinitions of sex roles goes on all through adult life. Recent research by women who have studied in detail the relationships in particular factories or workplaces has revealed the crucial role of the work environment as a site for these processes. In Westwood's words:

> Girls arrive in the factory and they become women on the shopfloor ... The family and school have a major part to play, but it is at work that adulthood is acknowledged and made through the wage that itself generates a class identity and through the way that women workers are always situated in the capitalist labour process and the labour market. (Westwood, 1984, pp. 10–11)

The key idea here is that of a 'gendered work environment' or 'work culture'. The studies by Pollert (1981), Cockburn (1983) and Westwood (1984) among others have shown how in factories segregated workgroups of women and men develop their own highly specific and mutually excluding cultures. Women's cultures centre on their home lives, on families and domesticity: conversation, rituals and symbols are concerned with homes, romance, marriage, children, clothes, food and the feminine lifestyle. Cakes and recipes are exchanged, clothing catalogues circulated, advice on how to handle husbands and boyfriends passed on. By contrast men's cultures are more work-centred, and also emphasise exaggerated versions of masculinity (sometimes symbolised by aggressive initiation rituals): talk features sport, heavy drinking, sexual bravado, anecdotes stress strength, audacity, resistance to authority, physical exploits of various kinds (see for example Tunstall, 1962; Sykes, 1969; Willis, 1977; Cockburn, 1983).

Although white-collar and professional workers tend to work in mixed sex groups, studies show that friendship patterns and group relations still emphasise sex boundaries. For example the paper by Barker and Downing (1980) on office workers shows how the 'boss' characteristically adopts the role of a patriarchal father, whereby in return for the women's total obedience and commitment to him they are allowed to develop their own gender-based rituals and activities. Women 'feminise' the office with photos and pot plants, developing their own homely patterns of social contact. In this way, Barker and Downing argue, patriarchal control is subtly maintained. By contrast, the papers collected by Spencer and Podmore (1987) about women entering male-dominated professions show how women have to struggle to fit into male work environments and cultures, often finding themselves excluded from male friendship groups and social activities crucial in making contacts and furthering careers: the gatherings at pubs and clubs, the chats on the golf course or at the firm's sports teams' matches.

The importance of these gendered work cultures has not yet been sufficiently recognised. Reflecting *and* enhancing segregation, they serve to divide the work force and to set women and men apart as rivals, if not downright competitors. They help to preserve conventional views of proper masculine and feminine behaviour both inside and outside of work. They 'domesticise' or 'masculinise' capitalist work conditions, making them more human and tolerable, but also ensuring that people are less likely to challenge them or to seek reform. They perpetuate views of sexuality which portray men as aggressive and predatory, women as seductive and flirtatious, so that sexual relations are conceived as a game or even a war, rather than a free merging of equals. As much as any other social institution gendered work cultures maintain the idea that the sexes are inherently different; in so doing they ensure that men's and women's work experience does indeed stay different and jobs stay sex-typed.

We shall see evidence of this in the case studies which follow. These are presented in a descriptive, narrative fashion, but many themes from these two chapters will reappear: family work and authority relations; labour process development and the struggles between employers and workers; technology and skill; ideologies of masculinity and femininity; and the gendering of work cultures. All these factors are at play in the creation of 'women's' and 'men's' jobs.

Part II

CASE STUDIES

A

Primary Production: Food and Raw Materials

---

*Look at me! Look at my arm! I have ploughed, and planted, and gathered into barns,
and no man could head me. And ain't I a woman?*

Thus thundered Sojourner Truth, the black American female emancipist,
in a declaration which encapsulates some of the ambiguities and
complexities of women's place in agriculture.

In non-industrial societies, the bulk of social productive activity is
devoted to obtaining or growing food and other raw materials. In almost
all such societies women have had an essential economic role, sometimes
even the predominant one. Boserup's study (1970) shows the continuing
importance of women's contribution to primary production in many
countries in Africa, Asia and South America. Although in more developed
countries this contribution has diminished, our current sexual division of
labour has its roots in the social arrangements made in these societies. For,
though the allocation of tasks to men and women differed greatly between
societies, in the majority of them some specific division of labour between
the sexes did occur. The patterns which slowly began to emerge are still
reflected in social assumptions about sex roles today. For this reason, more
than usual space is given over in these chapters to discussion of women's
pre-industrial roles.

Technological advance and capitalist development in primary production
had an even more drastic effect on women's lives than on men's. Indeed, it
is plausible to argue, as do Ehrenreich and English (1979), that these
changes brought into being what was referred to in the nineteenth
century as the 'Woman Question', by depriving woman of her economic
role as household manager within the household system of production,
and leaving her poised uncertainly and ambiguously between the new roles

of wage-labourer and unpaid full-time housewife. It is ironic that in the majority of industrial societies the three activities studied in this sector, agriculture, fishing and mining, in all of which women have in the past performed essential tasks, are now marked either by a near total absence of women, or by their restriction to an extremely limited range of tasks.

These chapters explore how this change came about, in terms particularly of the factors identified as central in chapter 3: the development of productive forces and relations, altering patterns of behaviour within the family, redefinitions of masculinity and femininity of what is proper behaviour for both sexes; as we have noted, these social changes have an economic, a familial and an ideological dimension. All of these have served to render women in the industrialised West if not absent at least curiously invisible in spheres of productive activity which are now seen as constituting 'a man's world'.

4

AGRICULTURE

Agriculture is the most basic and primal of human productive activities, and wherever it is undertaken women have a hand in it. It is estimated that the labour of women today produces half the world's stock of food. Three-quarters of agricultural work in Africa is currently done by women, and half the work in Asia (New Internationalist 1985, p. 16). Their labour is hard, back-breaking, time-consuming and almost all done by hand, using traditional tools and methods. Where mechanisation and modernisation have occurred, and where there is a switch to cash crop rather than subsistence farming, men often, although not always, take over (Boserup, 1970). We have seen an example of this in Russia (chapter 1). In the highly industrialised societies of the West, commercialised farming has become large-scale and highly capital-intensive. One can drive through the rich farming area of East Anglia for miles without ever seeing a human being at work on the land. In Britain, at least, this has led to a diminution of women's contribution, as the remaining jobs become more specialised, more technological, often involving the operation of machinery. Nevertheless, in 1981 women still constituted 20 per cent of the British agricultural work force (including farm workers, horticultural and gardening workers, operators of agricultural machinery and other related workers).

In tribal societies the agricultural work of women was crucial to survival, and they performed an extensive range of tasks. In hunting and gathering societies the work of gathering often fell to women, while men concentrated on hunting tasks; but, as discussed in chapter 2, the image of man the hunter and woman the gatherer should not be overstated. In some cases both sexes would share in both pursuits, and women sometimes bore sole responsibility for hunting smaller types of animal.

Some such societies today are marked by a sharp sexual division of labour, while in others it is minimal: but whatever the precise allocation of tasks, women have a major role to play in foraging for food and preparing it. Women's contributions remained vital as societies took to settled agricultural production. Lewenhak argues that women were responsible for initiating many gardening and farming techniques, such as hoe cultivation, domestication of poultry and small animals like pigs, and the pounding and milling of grains and roots for flour (Lewenhak, 1980). Certainly women have been largely involved in hoe cultivation (Boserup, 1970; Brown, 1970; Murdock and Provost, 1973). Murdock and Provost's survey of the sexual division of labour in 185 societies indicates that round the world today farming tasks are largely carried out by both sexes. Only lumbering, land clearance and tending large animals emerge from their analysis as predominantly masculine tasks. Crop planting, harvesting and tending, along with milking, are as likely to be carried out by women as men, while care of small animals and dairy production are predominantly women's tasks.

An almost infinite variety of arrangements for sharing farm work is possible in non-industrial societies. The following examples demonstrate the range of possibilities. Among the Agta people of the Philippines, women are involved in all subsistence activities: they help hunt pig and deer, spear fish and collect shrimps, gather roots and procure palm flour starch (Estioko-Griffin and Griffin, 1981). Both women and men of the New Guinea Kaulong are involved in gardening, pig-keeping, planting and harvesting bananas, taro and tobacco, as well as gathering foodstuffs in the forest (Goodale, 1980). Another New Guinea tribe, the Gimi, exhibit a more conventional division of labour: men hunt in the forest and grow bananas and sugar cane, while women's activities are centred on the gardens, growing maize and vegetables and rearing pigs (Gillison, 1980). Among the Laymi people of the Bolivian Andes, men and women jointly cultivate roots and cereals, and the women tend herds of sheep and goats while the men care for the llamas (Harris, 1980).

In the developing societies of the Third World, women have, if anything, a more significant role in farming, especially in the production of food crops. In many cases men obtain jobs in manufacturing industry or in the service sector, sometimes moving into the towns, and leave responsibility for farming to the women; this is largely the case in Kenya, for example. In producing food crops women perform tasks which, as we shall see, have elsewhere become female specialisms: planting, weeding, harvesting, processing and storage. In Java women harvest rice with sharp knives; in Kenya women carry baskets of tea weighing up to 80 lbs on their backs; in India women raise wheat, milk and tend water buffalo (Harrison, 1979; New Internationalist, 1985). Harrison points out that almost universally women have responsibility for the essential tasks of fetching water, procuring fuel and fodder and milling and pounding flour, a finding confirmed by Murdock and Provost.

United Nations figures show that in Africa women carry out 85 per cent of food storage and processing, 70 per cent of weeding, 60 per cent of harvesting and 50 per cent of planting and tending livestock: they also perform 30 per cent of ploughing, a task which in other societies has been considered an exclusively male task (New Internationalist, 1985, p. 17). It is fair to say that there are *no* tasks in agriculture, however heavy, skilled or responsible, which women have not undertaken at some place, at some time.

The roles of women and men in pre-industrial European societies were rather different, where there was no industrialised sector to draw away menfolk as in the 'dual societies' of the Third World today. In pre-industrial Britain men and women were, in the main, working side by side within the family or household enterprise, whatever it might be. In agriculture there were three main roles for women (Pinchbeck, 1981; Clark, 1982). Farmers' wives shared in the activities and management of the farm. Their actions tended to centre on the house, and the domestic management of an often large household, but they were also involved in many aspects of farm work, such as cultivation of gardens, fruit and vegetable growing, poultry keeping and care of smaller livestock, and in particular the management of the dairy. As well as being engaged in this wide range of household and farming tasks, such women were often involved in the financial and business management of the farm (Clark, 1982). In this they seem to have differed from their French counterparts, as a French farming manual of 1600 claimed that 'buying and selling and paying of wages belongs to the men' (quoted Fussell and Fussell, 1985, p. 54). As argued in chapter 2, this difference may be related to the greater amount of individual freedom and mobility which characterised English society; even women were able to acquire considerable property rights (Macfarlane, 1978). Certainly English farm women were extensively involved in marketing, especially of dairy goods and eggs.

The wives of peasants and cottagers were also active in household management and farm work; gardens, poultry and pigs were their special responsibility, but, unlike the richer farmers' wives, they also undertook field work, especially if their husbands were away on business. Finally, many women were engaged as farm servants (on a live-in basis) and, in growing numbers from the mid-eighteenth century, as wage labourers. Again, these women carried out a wide range of tasks in the home and on the farm; female wage labourers in particular often put in heavy effort in the fields.

The debate over the status of women in pre-industrial society has already been dealt with in chapter 2. I have argued that women were not considered equal to men, although their economic contribution was of great importance to the household: they carried out a wide range of tasks but often under the direction or control of men; women and men sometimes shared work but more commonly there was a clear delineation between men's and women's work, with women's tasks centred on the house. This division of labour was eulogised in the sixteenth-century manual of Thomas Tusser who saw 'husbandrie with huswiferie as cock and hen':

> Good husband men must moile and toile,
> To laie to live by laboured feeld:
> Their wives at home must keepe such coile,
> As their like actes may profit yeeld.
>   (Tusser, 1984, pp. 7, 9)

The range of women's work was certainly formidable by modern standards. The farmer's wife in the Elizabethan period, for example, was responsible for feeding the household, baking, brewing, textile production, dairy work, feeding pigs and poultry, sewing flax and hemp, gardening, planting, winnowing and caring for the medical needs of the household. If necessary she helped with the more characteristically male tasks: haymaking, harvesting, manuring and driving the plough. In France in the same period among the tasks specified for the wife by Estienne and Liebault in *The Country Farm* were clipping sheep, tending the cellar and kitchen garden and keeping bees. A farm servant's duties, too, reflected this wide range of skills. Nicholas Breton in *Court and Country* in 1618 described the 'lazy hylding's' work: 'I must serve the olde woman, I must lerne to spinne, to reele, to carde, to knit, to wash buckes, and by hande, brew, bake, make Mault, reap, bind sheaves, weede in the Garden, milke, serve Hogges ...' (quoted Fussell and Fussell, 1985, pp. 31–45, 54, 66).

Much of this work was highly skilled and depended on the possession of considerable knowledge. Dairying in particular was seen as a woman's craft, the knowledge of which was passed down from woman to woman. Pinchbeck quotes the wry comment of a man who dared compile a manual on dairywork in anticipation of a hostile reception for his book: 'what does he know of Dairying, or how should a Man know anything of Cheese making?' (Pinchbeck, 1981; p. 13). But there was growing anxiety as to whether women were fitted for the heavy work of lifting cheeses, which might weigh up to a hundredweight, and gradually in the eighteenth century employment of men in dairies to carry out the heavier work became more common.

If we turn to field work, it appears that by the fourteenth or fifteenth century certain farm tasks were already being labelled as 'men's work', notably ploughing, hedging and ditching and scything. Specialist jobs, such as those of shepherd, horseman, stockman and carter, were also associated with men (perhaps because they involved long absences from home) and this became more pronounced over the centuries. This left many jobs which women undertook, either alone or jointly with men: haymaking, reaping with sickles, hoeing, harrowing, winnowing, planting, pulse and fruit picking and spreading manure were commonly done by women. It was customary for two women to assist a man at thatching, one attending him and making bands, the other selecting and assembling straws. From the eighteenth century female labourers were particularly in demand to fulfil new types of job associated with the new root crops like turnips, beet and swedes; such jobs included planting, thinning, singling, transplanting and hoeing. Right up to the late nineteenth century an important occupation for women, along with children, was 'leasing' or gleaning (the traditional right of working people to gather scraps left by the harvesters). With luck a family might collect five or six bushels of grain and of peas, the yearly complement for one man (Fussell and Fussell, 1985, p. 154).

Everitt argues that many of the tasks which were assigned to women and children, such as stone gathering, weeding, rush cutting, raking and fruit picking 'required little skill', merely laborious effort (Everitt, 1967, p. 432). Although this was true of many jobs, not all women's work was unskilled, even if the skills involved were undervalued. Green argues, for example, that an inexperienced and clumsy hoer could do untold damage to a root crop (Green, 1927). In addition, women certainly on occasion carried out the more skilled 'male' tasks. Rodney Hilton argues for this position in his study of the English peasantry; for example, in Leicestershire in 1400 women were paid to mow, drive oxen and break stones (Hilton, 1975, p. 102). Women also worked occasionally as shepherds and sheepshearers, especially in Scotland. In some areas women's work had become much more constricted by the eighteenth century, when, for example, it was recorded that in Oxfordshire women were not required to 'exert their strength and skill in husbandry' as they had done formerly, when they had been known to handle manure, drive teams at plough and ride horses to market. Yet elsewhere they continued with the heavier tasks: in 1794 Arthur Pringle reported that in Westmoreland women were driving teams of three or four horses with harrows and ploughs and 'it is not uncommon to see, sweating at the dung-cart, a girl, whose elegant features and delicate nicely-proportioned limbs, seemingly but ill accord with such rough employment' (quoted Hill, 1984, p. 186).

There is disagreement as to whether women's and men's labour was rated equal in terms of the wages they received. Hilton cites examples of women in the medieval period receiving male rates, but much evidence suggests that women were normally paid less than men, although this might, of course, relate to the performance of different tasks. Everitt argues that such differentials were well established by the sixteenth century. State legislation on agricultural wages supports this view. A statute of 1388 fixed wages of shepherds and carters at 10 shillings a year, ploughmen at 7 shillings and swineherds at 6 shillings, while women labourers and dairymaids were to receive 6 shillings. This differential is not great, but by 1444 the gap had widened. The statutory wage for male farm servants was 18 shillings and 4 pence plus food, shepherds receiving 24 shillings, while women were paid considerably less, 14 shillings plus food (Tickner, 1923). As Middleton (1985) points out, women (except dairymaids) were usually employed as generalist not specialist workers, which debarred them from the higher scales such as those paid to shepherds. By the eighteenth century the gap had widened still further so that women habitually received half men's pay, a state of affairs deplored by the sympathetic Sir Frederick Eden in *The State of the Poor*: 'it is not easy to account for so striking an inequality; and still less easy to justify it' (quoted Hill, 1984, p. 187).

There is little evidence to suggest that, before the end of the eighteenth century, people disapproved of women carrying out farm tasks; the comment of Arthur Pringle, quoted above, strikes a new note in the contrast it makes between soft femininity and the 'rough' work of handling ordure. This theme was to be elaborated throughout the coming century. William Marshall sounded a different note of male prejudice when he explained in 1788 that he would only employ women if men were scarce, because of their propensity to waste time in gossip (Fussell and Fussell, 1985). But books on farm management written up to this period approve female employment in a wide range of tasks; before the nineteenth century, farm work for women was seen as natural and normal.

Interesting debates surround one traditional 'male' tasks, ploughing. It has often been argued that the invention of the plough, a heavy piece of equipment requiring considerable skill to operate, led to a diminution of women's responsibility in agriculture. This line is taken by Murdock and Provost, and echoed in Shorter's comment that women could not manage ploughing, 'great strength being necessary to manoeuvre a Norfolk plow behind a team of percherons' (Shorter, 1976, p. 517). This is also implied by Power (1975).

Whether inadequate physique really stops women ploughing is debatable. As we have already seen, women do substantial amounts of ploughing in Africa, and in Britain there are scattered references to women ploughing. The Fussells suggest that in the sixteenth and seventeenth centuries women ploughed on small farms, citing, for example, the case of Sarah Fell, who paid several women to plough for her in 1676 (Fussell and Fussell, 1985). Such reports often emanated from the South West; it was reported that a woman had been seen ploughing in the Mendips as late as 1800. Devonshire witnesses to the 1843 Poor Law Commission confirmed their own past experience of plough work. Mary

Puddicombe of Exeter spoke of leading bullocks and horses at plough; 'maidens would not like that work now', she said. Mary Rendalls recalled her days as a parish apprentice on a farm, when, she proclaimed, 'I did everything that boys did', and James Huxtable confirmed 'I remember formerly when girls turned out regularly with the boys to plough ... and were up to their knees in dirt' (PP 1843 xii, pp. 106, 109, 112).

Yet it is not entirely clear whether these women were taking responsibility for ploughing or merely acting as assistants to men, holding the teams of horses while the men performed the skilled task of steering the furrow. Such a division of labour, reported by Segalen in France, is movingly described by a fourteenth-century poet in *Pierce the Ploughman's Creed*.

> I saw a simple man me by upon the plow bending ...
> Four heifers went before him that had become feeble,
> Men could count all their ribs so rueful they were,
> His wife walked him with with a long goad
> In a short-cut coat cut very high,
> Wrapped in a winnowing-sheet to ward her from the weather
> Barefoot on the bare ice so that the blood flowed,
> And at the land's end lay a little wooden bowl
> And therein lay a little child lapped in clouts
> And twins of two years old upon another side.
>   (quoted Tickner, 1923, p. 19)

This stark picture of rural misery also indicates how the responsibility for children had limiting effects on married women: tasks they could break off to attend to babies' needs were, as Brown (1970) has argued, easier for them to undertake.

Nevertheless, even if women acted mainly as assistants to ploughmen, this does not prove that there is anything intrinsic in the task that debars women from it. Rather, as Middleton (1979) has argued, male assumption of this activity may relate to its importance as a feudal service to the lord of the manor, making it therefore symbolic of the family power wielded by the male head of house. Hanawalt (1986) goes further, seeing ploughing as a symbol of male social and household supremacy, constituted by men as a 'mystery'. Pictures of women ploughing during World War I prove that the task is within female capacity. Interestingly, one of Mary Chamberlain's 'fenwomen', Janet Hornigold, explained that her father had never taught her to plough because he liked to think he could do it better than anyone! Finally, he handed on this male mystery to her brother, but she professed no regrets at not having been taught, describing it as a 'boring' repetitive task; there is no suggestion that she would have been *unable* to do it (Chamberlain, 1983, p. 107).

We have considerable information on the role of women in agriculture in the nineteenth century, since it became a matter of public concern, and a series of commissions reported upon it. As the consolidation of large-scale capitalist agriculture brought an end to the subsistence farming activities of cottagers, the mass of agricultural workers, male and female, were reduced to the status of landless labourers. This did not immediately bring a diminution of women's employment, as, in arable areas at least, farming methods remained labour-intensive, and mechanisation developed only slowly. The cheapness of the labour of women and children made it attractive to farmers, who employed them in large numbers for wretched wages. However, capitalist development hastened the trend towards women being restricted to a limited range of tasks, at the same time encouraging the regional disparities already in existence. Finally, as Clark has shown, it severely diminished the economic contribution of the wives of rich farmers, who began to lead a life more resembling that of the leisured wives of the bourgeoisie, although on small farms women still might carry a heavy burden of domestic and household work.

Women's employment was most restricted in pastoral areas and in the South and Midlands. In East Anglia, they were employed in greater numbers, often in gangs, while in the South West, North East, Scotland and Wales their work continued to be more varied. In Northumberland, the bondager system prevailed, whereby the hired labourer or 'hind' was contractually obliged to provide a female 'bondager' to assist him. If he had no wife or daughter, he must find a non-family member to work with him. Though this custom died out over the decades, labourers' daughters continued to do field work right till the end of the century. This example illustrates the range of local variations. Indeed the 1843 Poor Law Commission, commenting on the influence of the 'habits of narrow localities', noted: 'The women of one village have always been accustomed to reap whilst to those of another in the immediate neighbourhood, the practice is unknown. Turnip hoeing is by no means an uncommon occupation for women, yet in many villages they never undertake it' (PP 1843 xii, p. 3).

Certain tasks, however, were identified as 'woman's work' all round the country. These included planting, singling and hoeing of root vegetables (especially potatoes, turnips and beet), weeding (especially pulling couch and spudding thistles), tidying fields, stone picking and spreading manure, picking beans, peas, soft fruit and hops, orchard work, haymaking and harvest work (including reaping with sickles, raking and winnowing) and attending threshing machines. According to the 1843 commissioners, these jobs were 'not the kind of work which it would answer to employ men upon' (PP 1843 xii, p. 27). In hop work, for example, men commonly set up the tall poles, while women tied the hops to them. It was considered that 'a man cannot get on' with what was described as an 'endless' fiddly job, while boys were not thought careful enough. As for picking, it was claimed a woman could pick more in a day than a man, presumably because of greater readiness to concentrate on a dull task (PP 1843 xii, pp. 166, 186–8). Male tasks, on the other hand, were said to require strength. Boys would start working at the age of nine or ten at simple tasks like bird scaring, minding poultry and livestock: sometimes they led teams at plough. At thirteen they progressed to the adult male tasks, such as ploughing, reaping, hedging and ditching, sheepshearing, harrowing and driving carts.

In the 1860s women were still carrying out these same 'women's' jobs, and it was noted that market gardening was employing large numbers of women and children. By the 1890s fewer women were employed, but they were still doing the same jobs: weeding, hoeing, hay and harvest work, as well as dairying and rearing calves (PP 1867–8 xvii; PP 1893–4 xxxv). Such work was marked by its drudgery and monotony, memorably portrayed by Thomas Hardy in his descriptions of Tess Durbeyfield working in the frozen turnip fields. These women, many of whom also bore responsibility for running a home, worked an average of nine hours, and longer at peak times like harvest. Dairymaids had perhaps the hardest life of all, having to start work at 4 a.m. and not being free of their duties until bedtime. Sir Richard Phillips, observing young country girls carrying baskets of raspberries and strawberries to market in London (a journey of 24 to 30 miles, carrying 40 to 50 lbs of fruit), simply described their work as 'unparalleled slavery' (quoted Hill, 1984, p. 194).

In the less central regions women continued to perform tasks now seen in the South East as male work. Cornish women loaded horses with furze, manure and sheaves of corn collected by their husbands, led the horses home and rode them back to the fields (Cook, 1984). In Devonshire women drove bullocks to the field, cleaned stalls, fed pigs, mixed lime and loaded packhorses. Mary Rendalls showed her determination not to be rated below men: 'I took a pride to it, when I used to reap, to keep up with the men' (PP 1843 xii, pp. 109, 113). In Northumberland in the 1860s women were reported doing 'every description of work', including the hardest, such as barn work, forking hay and filling dung carts. Here, too, the women exhibited a spirit of female independence: 'we fight to drive the carts, it is easier work than loading' said one (PP 1867–8 xvii p. 54). The remark tells us much about the vaunted male attributes of strength and skill!

In the 1890s in Wales women were said to be still doing the 'disagreeable work' of milking sheep, as well as leading horses, spreading dung and helping with threshing. Northumberland women were also still engaged in heavy farm work, as were their Scottish counterparts. The latter worked as dairymaids and byrewomen, as well as being 'workers', as female fieldworkers were called. Some had the status of 'cottars', holding tied cottages in their own right. They were better paid than their English sisters, the skill of the female specialists being acknowledged. Dairy- and byrewomen might earn £20 to £25 a year. Their work was no less heavy, though, as this milkmaid's testimony shows: 'We can't complain of our work; we start at 5 am, and then we milk till 7. We have breakfast, porridge, at 7 and a further breakfast at 8. In the house we start at once to work after meal ... Dinner is at 12; start as soon as finished to go and feed the cows; we work away with straw, turnips and other jobs till 4 ... Then feed cows again; rest from 5.30 to 7, then milk to 8; then fodder cows, which takes half an hour' (PP 1893–4 xxxvi, Vol. III, p. 68). Clearly the girl considered this to be a good job!

In East Anglia women's work took a special form. Here the gang system was prevalent, reportedly having originated in the Norfolk village of Castle Acre in the 1820s. This large 'open' village had a surplus of labour, which was exploited by subcontractors who organised gangs to carry out work in areas where labour was short. Some of the gangs were mixed in sex, but more characteristically they consisted of women and girls only. They travelled around for considerable distances, often being forced to sleep away from home in fields or barns. Children of six and seven were employed, carrying out the characteristically 'female' tasks of weeding, hoeing, stone picking and harvesting potatoes. This form of employment aroused considerable anxiety among middle-class observers, especially because of the use of young unmarried girls in the gangs. It was considered that gang work made girls 'bold and impudent', exposed them to risks of immorality and rendered them unfit for domestic employment and motherhood. Although gangmasters claimed to maintain strict discipline (one levied fines of 2d for swearing and tried to enforce silence, 'particularly among the females – an Herculean labour'), local clergymen, in particular, campaigned against the gangs. They even claimed that 49 out of 50 of the girls had illegitimate babies (PP 1843 xii, pp. 244–5, 252, 277–9; PP 1867–8 xvii).

As a result of the agitation, the Gang Acts were passed in 1867 and 1876, forbidding the employment of mixed groups and of children under ten. However, gangs still operated in Cambridgeshire, Suffolk, Norfolk and Lincolnshire in the 1980s, and indeed can be still found in East Anglia today, weeding, dealing with beet and potatoes and harvesting celery, still performing the same back-breaking, low-paid 'woman's work'.

The development of capitalist agriculture, then, pushed women into monotonous, low-status jobs, and deprived them of access to the range of skills possessed by the farmer's or cottager's wife in the pre-industrial period. Where new machines were introduced, such as steam-powered threshing machinery or reaper-binders, men took on the tasks of operating and maintaining them. Harvest work provides an interesting example of the effect of technological change on women's work.

Harvest was notable in the agricultural calendar, in that it required a great deal of extra labour; the wives and children of male labourers had traditionally been called upon to supplement the regular farmworkers. The division of labour varied with locality, but in the seventeenth, eighteenth and early nineteenth centuries women often had a central role as reapers, using sickles. The roots of this practice go right back to the medieval period, and Hilton (1975) provides evidence that in the fourteenth and fifteenth centuries men and women received the same rates of payment for sickle work. Old prints designed to teach English to foreigners show women with reaping hooks and rakes and the legends 'the woman reaps; the man sleeps' and 'the woman works; the shepherd snores' (Fussell and Fussell, 1985). Men also used sickles, but in many cases took the assistant role. In Northumberland in the eighteenth century, for example, women reaped while men gathered up the corn and made stooks. A similar arrangement was recalled by the Ashby family of Oxfordshire in the 1870s: 'A dozen, or maybe twenty, reapers, largely women, would work in one field, with men following to tie up the sheaves and another group to set them in shucks' (Ashby, 1961, p. 25). Reaping was skilled work, at which women could excel; in the late eighteenth century Philadelphia Baker and Sarah Cook were awarded prizes for reaping at the Bath and West of England Agricultural Society (Fussell and Fussell, 1985). Henry Stephens' *The Book of the Farm*, a well-known farming text of the mid-nineteenth century, recorded that 'with a sickle, a woman is as efficient a worker as a man; indeed, what is called a maiden-ridge, of three young women, will beat a bull-ridge, of three men, at reaping any sort of corn, on any given day' (quoted Hostettler, 1977, p. 96).

Technical advance threatened this female skill. From the 1750s on, heavier tools such as the bagging-hook and, notably, the scythe began to replace the sickle. The techniques employed were different. The mower (with scythe) cut the corn with wide swings in a wide swathe, letting it fall to the ground where assistants must collect it into armfuls, while the reaper (with sickle) collected an armful and cut it, gathering it in under the arm into a bundle. Where scythes and bagging-hooks were employed, it was women who took the subsidiary role, gathering sheaves and making bands for them, and following behind the mowers with a 'sweath-rake'. Roberts (1979) argues that wherever scythes were used males monopolised them, because of the greater strength required. One Berkshire villager described the resultant division of labour: 'Father with his broad-bladed fagging hook in his right hand and crooked stick in his left, slashed through the yellow stalks and left them gathered by his foot. Mother followed, swept a sheaf together, placed it on 'the bond', drew this tightly and fastened it by a twist. The children pulled the bonds' (quoted Morgan, 1975, p. 31).

The capture of harvest skills by men was made more complete by the introduction of the mechanical reaper. Men operated and guided these machines, and although at first women were still required to gather and tie up corn the advent of the reaper-binder (and later of the combine harvester) took that work from them too (Hostettler, 1977). By 1914 women's contribution to harvest was confined to the light work of raking, while men controlled machines and pitched corn and straw onto carts and ricks (PP 1919 xxxi).

Roberts, as noted above, believes that the exclusive use of scythes by men relates to physical differences between the sexes, specifically to men's superior height and muscular strength. Whether or not this is true (I have seen peasant women in Northern Spain using scythes), it affords a striking example of the tendency of men to claim as theirs any new skill created by technological advance. Judging from other similar cases, it may well be that arguments based on biological differences are employed *after* the masculinisation of a task, to provide rationalisation for the barring of women.

Perhaps the most notable change over the century, however, was the general withdrawal of women from all farmwork. The 1843 Commission estimated that women and girls constituted between a quarter and a third of the agricultural work force; but from this date the proportions decreased sharply. The 1867 Commission noted the absence of women from farmwork in a number of Midland counties, except as temporary help to husbands, and claimed that young girls were no longer going on to the land. Between 1881 and 1891 there was a 19 per cent decrease in women's employment in agriculture. According to census figures, women constituted a mere 3 per cent of farm labourers and servants in 1891 and this dropped still further to just under 2 per cent in 1901. Thus, the 1893 Commission on Labour could justly claim that women had virtually disappeared from fieldwork, especially in the South and Midlands, although they were still used for seasonal work such as hop picking and market gardening. Slightly more women were employed in the fringe areas. In South Wales, for example, the proportion of women was reported to have fallen from 32 per cent to 15 per cent between 1851 and 1881, with a greater fall in North Wales from 24 per cent to 5 per cent. By 1919 it had become the official view that women's employment had declined from the 1870s and more or less vanished in the 1880s, a view shared by Pinchbeck (see PP 1893–4 xxxvi; PP 1894 lxxxi Pt. II; PP 1919 xxxi).

The male takeover of farmwork extended to women's traditional areas, such as dairywork. Although it was reported that in Wales men had a 'traditional aversion' to milking, by the 1890s they were performing much milking and churning work. A picture of the Royal Agricultural Show in 1899, reproduced by the Fussells, shows men churning butter while women attendants carry pails about. This process was completed as milking was mechanised; the operation of a modern milking parlour is seen as highly technological skilled work.

Nevertheless, a note of caution must be sounded. Researchers have noted the extraordinary *invisibility* of women's farm work, partly because much of it takes place around the home (Boserup, 1970; New Internationalist, 1985): 'man, the breadwinner, is assumed and expected to be working in the fields. Woman, the wife and mother, has a veil of invisibility drawn round her when she does the same' (New Internationalist, 1985, p. 18). This may have applied in nineteenth-century Britain. Alfred Austin, one of the 1843 commissioners, complained of the tendency of both workers and farmers to mislead him about women's employment: their work was often overlooked. Census figures are misleading in glossing over seasonal and casual employment, which so often fall to women. A careful study of Gloucestershire done by Miller points to a significant gap between census data and the figures on women's employment as noted in individual farmers' wage-books. These suggest that not only did women work as casual labourers, but that higher numbers were employed permanently than the official figures show. Miller argues that women were extensively employed when male labour became unobtainable (Miller, 1980).

However, as Eve Hostettler's interesting study of Stephens' *The Book of the Farm* shows, the prevailing *image* of farm work by the end of the century was masculine. This was symbolised by one plate in Stephens' book from which a figure of a woman operating a turnip-slicing machine was removed in the 1891 edition. Even if in reality women still worked on the land, farming was by now ideologically viewed as 'man's work'.

Various reasons for women's withdrawal have been advanced. As stated, the progress of mechanisation, especially in the 1880s, was beginning to make redundant the type of unskilled routine labour performed by women, and as new machines such as tractors and harvesters came into use, men monopolised their operation. In addition, social attitudes of both men and women were changing, and it was this explanation which was particularly favoured by the commissioners in 1893. Male labourers, they argued, took pride in making their wives 'independent' of field work, apparently adopting the middle-class ideology of domesticity; one told them 'we have advanced from that. We keep the women at home, which is their proper sphere' (PP 1893-4 xxxv Vol. I Part III p. 174). Similarly, a meeting of labourers at Cirencester in 1872 had resolved that women should keep out of fieldwork since their place was at home with the children (Miller, 1980, p. 164). Behind this acceptance of changing family ideology, we may suppose, lay fear of competition, as jobs dwindled.

Women, too, were said to have become more discerning. 'They knows better than to work now,' one Dorchester labourer said (PP 1893-4 xxxv Vol. I Part IV, p. 27). This was not simply the result of material improvements to the farmworkers' position, for their lives remained desperately insecure and it was reported that even widows living off poor relief had spurned fieldwork. Possibly it had to do with the diminished status of the work, as Green argues in his history of agricultural labourers. He believed the rejection of the work by labourers' wives 'lies deep in the rank soil of social degradation when poverty drove their mothers to work as field labourers in gangs hovelled promiscuously like swine' (Green, 1927, p. 330). This is clearly a male reading of the situation and more crucial, perhaps, may have been the level of wages the women could earn, a point also emphasised by the commissioners, who commented that in Scotland a woman often worked as much as a man for half a man's wage. Women usually received only between seven pence and a shilling a day for a stretch of from eight to twelve hours. Jane Hyde told them 'I have worked 10 hours for 10d and then been grumbled at into the bargain. They pay so little we can do without it ... we can do as well without it as with it' (PP 1893–4 xxxv Vol. I Part IV, p. 102).

In Scotland the independent-minded women also objected to being given the worst work and being paid less for it; dressing turnips, handling dung and looking after the 'cauf hole' (the place where chaff was stored), a dusty job invariably assigned to women, were particularly disliked. Younger women, seen as more adventurous than their elders, were reportedly leaving the land for the towns, seeking work in the expanding areas of retailing and clerking (PP 1893–4 xxxvi pp. 98, 117–18). Such a woman, it was claimed, would 'thank the stars that she is at last leaving the unwomanly job for domestic service.' It is interesting that these women did *not* regard their lower pay as just, a sentiment echoed in the statement of Daisy Reed, one of the few female farmworkers Charles Kightly records among his *Country Voices*: ''cause I could do everything a man could do, jest about: but they never gave me no man's money' (Kightly, 1984, p. 39).

Another influencing factor was the changing definition of femininity. This theme was prominent in the reports of 1843 and 1867, in which numerous comments from farmers and local dignitaries (especially clergymen) concerned the impropriety of fieldwork. They were obsessed with the moral effects of working outdoors, especially where the sexes were mixed. Farm girls were described as 'disagreeably rough and rude in their manners', employing 'coarse and filthy' language, and there was much muttering about drunkenness, sexual horseplay and extramarital pregnancies.

Few people argued that fieldwork was detrimental to health and in fact several witnesses commented favourably on the women's fitness, their 'size and ruddy looks' (PP 1843 xii, pp. 9, 23, 89). Northumberland women were described as 'physically a splendid race' who could 'vie with the men in carrying sacks of corn' (PP 1867–8 xvii, p. 53). However, middle-class observers continued to emphasise the moral dangers they perceived. Commissioner Reverend J. Fraser was one who did consider women's physique too 'delicate' for farmwork, but was more worried still over the threat to femininity; 'not only does it unsex a woman in dress, gait, manners, character, making her rough, coarse, clumsy, masculine; but it generates a further very pregnant social mischief, by unfitting her or indisposing her for a woman's proper duties at home' (PP 1867–8 xvii, p. 16).

The wearing of masculine clothes was another aspect which shocked observers. Scottish women, who sensibly wrapped straw round their legs to keep damp out and hitched up their petticoats, were described by the 1893 commissioners as 'heavy-clad and rather bulky personages with elephantine legs' (PP 1893–4 xxxvi Vol. III, p. 14). This distaste may have been linked to concern that the girls were becoming too independent, an idea put forward by Kitteringham in her excellent study of Victorian farm girls. She quotes, for example, the verdict of Dr Julian Hunter:

> That which seems to most lower the moral or decent tone of the peasant girls is the sensation of independence of society which they acquire when they have remunerative labour in their hands ... All gregarious employment gives a slang character to the girls' appearance and habits, while dependence on man for support is the spring of modest and pleasing deportment. (Kitteringham, 1975, p. 129)

What the women themselves thought of their work is less clear; as so often the bulk of commentary comes from men. Some may have relished it, like Mary Hunt: 'I was always better when out at work in the fields; and as for hard work, I never was hurt by it. I have carried half a sack of peas to Chippenham, four miles, when I have been large in the family way' (PP 1843 xii p. 68). It was claimed that younger women aspired to higher-status jobs, such as domestic service or shopwork, while by contrast many married women were said to like the sociability of the fields. Despite middle-class fears, it was rare for women and men to work in the same group; they performed different tasks, or if engaged together worked on opposite sides of the field. Women seem to have enjoyed the chatter and humour of a large female group, and even single girls often contrasted fieldwork favourably with the tedium of being 'idle' or confined to housework (see Kitteringham, 1975).

Flora Thompson in *Lark Rise* relates that by the 1880s most women had given up fieldwork, but notes how some older women clung on to it having 'a liking for the open-air and a longing for a few shillings a week they could call their own'. Such women, whom she describes as 'strong, healthy, weather-beaten, hard as nails' declared that they would go 'stark staring mad' if they had to be shut up in a house all day (Thompson, 1946, p. 47). But such women were the last survivors of a generation who so fiercely prized independence. Younger girls were perhaps coming to accept the constrained and patriarchal Victorian definitions of what it means to be a woman and to be 'womanly'.

By the time of World War I few women, apart from members of farmers' families, were engaged in agriculture (officially at least), except in some traditional female tasks like fruit picking, and most of these were employed on a seasonal or casual basis. During the war, women were pulled back into the work force, and by 1918 at least 175,000 women were working in agriculture. The Report by the War Cabinet on Women in Industry suggested this might change the image of farmwork so that it was no longer seen as a 'somewhat degrading occupation' for women. The report referred to women's 'special skills' in certain types of work, such as dairying, stock-keeping and market gardening; these, of course, were the traditional 'women's skills' and reflected the association of women with domesticity and home management. More significant is the fact that during the war women ploughed, drove tractors, worked with horses and as shepherds and engaged in forestry and lumbering (PP 1919 xxxi, p. 99; Tickner, 1923; Brittain, 1928). Braybon and Summerfield relate the story of Annie Edwards who learned to plough: farmers would come to watch, marvelling at this 'unbelievable' sight. The incident reveals the strength of men's faith in their own superiority (Braybon and Summerfield, 1987, p. 74).

The 1946 Report on Equal Pay reveals that in the interwar years men regained their monopoly over specialist jobs; indeed, it was reported that women rarely worked as general farm labourers but had once again become confined to casual and seasonal work and to the usual 'female' jobs. This, the report claimed was due to women's lesser strength. It would require two women to do one man's job at, for example, bagging potatoes or forking hay. Agricultural economists claimed that women's output exceeded that of men in certain fiddly jobs like picking peas and cutting flowers, that in most jobs they achieved 70–90 per cent of male output, but in jobs requiring strength or staying power, such as loading potatoes or tractor driving, their output was only half men's. Evidence of women's achievements in the previous century must throw doubt on these findings, especially since women rarely performed these tasks and had not had the chance to build up speed and stamina through experience nor to develop muscles through constant exertion.

The resurgence of this argument about natural endowments shows how quickly and pervasively myths about strength and skill regenerate themselves, even in the face of quite recent evidence as to the competence and capability of women in farming. The Equal Pay Commission had acknowledged that in comparison with other occupations segregation was much less firmly entrenched; 'before the war there were no tasks in agriculture exclusively performed by women, nor were there any tasks except a few really heavy ones requiring a man's greater strength or staying power which were never performed by women.' Yet they then went on to endorse the myths when they claimed that World War II, as well as enabling women to engage in agricultural work 'formerly considered beyond their physical capacity', also allowed them to undertake 'for the first time to any appreciable extent general all-round farm work hitherto performed almost entirely by men'. So much for the women of Scotland and Northumbria and many centuries of history (PP 1945-6 xi pp. 87-9)!

In World War II the pattern repeated itself. 'Tasks considered beyond their physical capacity' included not just traditional heavy work such as digging and loading, caring for cattle and carting, but also the newer mechanised tasks, such as tractor driving, operating cultivators and threshing machines and spraying. Although women successfully took on all these tasks, the postwar period again saw them restricted to less specialised and skilled jobs, and a return to casual, temporary, seasonal and part-time work. The continued advance of mechanisation and centralisation, the spread of large-scale farming and the development of 'factory' farming methods have, in any case, further reduced the need for labour since the war. Howard Newby argues that this has affected men more than women. But men have managed to retain the specialist and skilled full-time jobs, as Newby's own figures indicate. In 1975 women made up only 8 per cent of full-time hired workers, but 45 per cent of seasonal and casual, 58 per cent of part-time workers: overall they formed 24 per cent of agricultural labourers, a higher proportion than in the prewar decades (Newby, 1980, p. 123). Yet women still perform the traditional, monotonous, low-paid tasks: fruit and flower picking, market gardening, hopwork and, to a lesser extent, fieldwork such as harvesting potatoes. In 1981, Census figures showed them as only 0.6 per cent of those employed in operating farm machinery; this, however, was an advance on 1971, when none were recorded as employed in this occupation.

The story of women in British agriculture, then, demonstrates clearly the interpenetrated effects of capitalism and patriarchy. Capitalist agriculture in its early stages made much use of female labour to cut costs; the jobs it generated for women were in part the continuance of tasks they had traditionally been responsible for within the pre-industrial family, when, characteristically, they had either been responsible for work located within the home area or worked as assistants to men in the fields. New jobs, such as those in root crop production, were also assigned to them, jobs marked by monotony, lack of training and thus labelled 'unskilled'. Further capitalist development reduced the need for manual labour, and as farming became mechanised many women lost their jobs or moved into other areas of employment. New machine-based jobs, whether skilled or not, were taken by men. In periods where male labour was suddenly withdrawn, as in the two world wars, women were pressed into service to perform all sorts of jobs, however 'skilled' or 'heavy' they might be; but, as soon as the men returned, myths of natural endowment and female incapacity were employed to justify the male takeover. Women themselves seem not have fought for specialist jobs, perhaps because in industrialised societies farming and the outdoor life do not fit readily with what are now perceived as the desirable female characteristics: prettiness, sexiness, delicacy, refinement, domestic skills. It is all too easy for the land girl in her corduroy trousers to be portrayed as a bit of a joke. Only farmers' daughters seem able to defy the stereotypes, riding tractors and carts and managing cattle.

Although the regional variations that characterise Britain are repeated on a much more dramatic scale worldwide, similar trends can be discerned in other countries. In pre-industrial conditions, women contribute extensively to agriculture. In colonial America, for example, although the association of woman with the home, man with the field, had been carried across from the European civilisations, women on pioneer frontier farms were often involved in all sorts of heavy work, such as clearing land and felling timber alongside their husbands; while in the slave economy on the Southern states gender was no obstacle to the use of black women in all sorts of gruelling agricultural work, such as hoeing, lumbering and ploughing (Wertheimer, 1977; Matthaei, 1982). On the frontier women continued to carry out all sorts of gruelling work right through the nineteenth century, a handful even acting as cowgirls and many taking up the offers of the Homestead Act and becoming landholders in their own right. More generally, after the Civil War the development of capitalist farming saw the increased employment of women as farm labourers around the country just as in Britain, but further development limited their numbers. In 1900 only 8 per cent of agricultural workers were women. However, in 1982 they made up 15 per cent of agricultural labourers, with thousands more acting as unpaid family help (United States Bureau of the Census, 1984). The pattern has been very similar to Britain.

In industrialised societies where farming has become highly mechanised woman's role has usually diminished, but where small-scale peasant-style farming lingers on, women are likely to be more involved in fieldwork, although in a subsidiary role to men, and often on a seasonal basis, for example, in France and Italy (see Thompson, 1982; Segalen, 1983). Even here, mechanisation reduces women's involvement as, for example, has been the case with Norwegian farms where mechanisation has driven women from the cowsheds (Slettan, 1982). In small-scale farming areas in France, such as Brittany, the same is true. Women have not had the necessary training to carry out the technical tasks so they are restricted to 'manual work of a repetitive nature' and to helping out in times of special need; one farmer's wife described herself as a 'stop-gap' (Segalen, 1983, pp. 180–1).

Meanwhile, in the Third World, women continue to disprove all the myths of female incapacity by shouldering the bulk of fieldwork and sustaining the major food subsistence needs of the society.

5

FISHING

If agricultural work presents us with a confused and complex picture of
shifting patterns of sexual differentiation, the fishing industry by contrast
is marked by a sharply defined division of labour, and one which is
replicated in many fishing communities in different countries, regions and
at different historical periods. Basically, it is men who go out in boats to
catch fish; women have rarely gone to sea. Consequently, fishing has a
strong image as a man's trade, although in fact, as Thompson, Wailey and
Lummis (1983) argue in their comprehensive study of British fishing
communities, it has always been 'peculiarly dependent' on the work of
women. Their work, historically, has been to deal with the catch once it
has been landed, and to assist their menfolk in a variety of subsidiary tasks.
Fishing in Britain, traditionally, was work for the whole family. As well as
displaying a clear sexual division of labour, the fishing case illustrates
another persistent feature of the process of sex-typing: its root in the
sharing of tasks within the family.

Like farming, the catching of fish and crustaceans has been an important
part of humankind's productive activity from the earliest times. In most
societies men have been responsible for sea fishing, particularly where
boats are used. Boatbuilding and 'hunting of large aquatic fauna' are listed
by Murdock and Provost (1973) in their survey of the sexual division of
labour as two of the most exclusive male tasks. Fishing itself is less
exclusively male, being categorised by them as a 'quasi-masculine activity'
(although it is notable more confined to men in European countries); while
the gathering of 'small aquatic fauna' is, world wide, a task more
commonly carried out by females. The majority of the societies sampled in
this study are tribal societies, and Murdock and Provost note that as
societies become more 'complex' and more industrially developed there is a

greater likelihood of male monopolies developing in masculine and 'quasi-masculine' tasks, as in the case of fishing.

In non-industrial societies, women may be involved in gathering shellfish and also sometimes with inland fishing, in streams and rivers. For example, Australian aborigine women fished in creeks, while Polynesian women took their canoes into small inlets off the sea (Lewenhak, 1980). Women of the Lele tribe in the Congo tend fishponds, just as farmers' wives did in medieval Britain (Oakley, 1976a; Fussell and Fussell, 1981). Women of the Agta tribe of Luzon in the Philippines join with their menfolk in river fishing, using spears to catch fish underwater; less active elderly people may specialise in collecting shellfish and shrimps (Estioko-Griffin and Griffin, 1981). In Papua New Guinea men and women together push 'skimming nets' along to scoop up fish close to the shore (Pownall, 1979). Japanese peasant women of the feudal epoch not only helped their husbands with nets and handling the catch, but dived for shellfish as some women still do in South-East Asia today. However, cases such as that of the women of Tierra del Fuego, who amazed European travellers in the nineteenth century with their deep-sea fishing prowess, remain the exception (Lewenhak, 1980). In an earlier sample of 565 societies, women were the main providers of food in only one of those societies dependent primarily on fishing and marine hunting and gathering, the Yahgan of South America (Brown, 1970). On the other hand, dealing with the catch on shore, including the marketing of it, is frequently women's responsibility in less industrialised societies. For example, in Grenada women receive and market fish, each boat having its attendant team of women 'usually the wives, mistresses or girlfriends of the eight-man crew' (Epple, 1977, p. 178). In Ghana, where women have traditionally controlled selling and processing of the catch, the advent of outboard motors for canoes has brought into being a new class of female entrepreneurs, who provide financing for the expensive motors to the fishermen (Christensen, 1977). Whereas in Britain we think of fishmongering as a male trade, in Portugal it is often done by women; in the fish house at Braga market in 1988 there was not a male marketer in sight.

Going to sea has been considered a quintessentially male task and has acquired strongly masculine connotations. The world of 'those in peril on the sea' is portrayed as rough, hard, physical and dangerous, especially in the case of deep-sea fishermen. Risks are certainly great. In the nineteenth century there were many deaths among fishermen, from drowning or accidents at sea, and the treatment of pauper apprentices, especially, assumed scandalous dimensions (Tunstall, 1962; Thompson et al., 1983). According to Tunstall, in the 1950s and 1960s death rates in the fishing industry outstripped those in mining. The trawlermen he studied in Hull had a fatalistic, gloomy attitude to their work, yet the life was apparently highly addictive: 'the boy who goes fishing and sticks at it seems to prefer to work and live in a world of men' (Tunstall, 1962, p. 116). Fishermen found it hard to give up the thrills of life at sea and settle to the perceived monotony of shore jobs. As one told Tunstall, 'When you get it all down and you go aft for a pot of tea with a nice sweat on, it's all right, I can tell you' (Tunstall, 1962, p. 117).

Other studies of fishermen reveal the same attachment to the work. Judith Cook, talking to oyster fishermen on the Fal river, noted their spirit of independence; 'when they go out in their smacks, no man's their master,' she was told (Cook, 1984, p. 117). Inshore fishing has remained an essentially family business, and family members often share a boat. Such men display the small businessman's spirit of self-sufficiency and involvement in the enterprise. Offshore work, too, promotes a strong sense of pride and pleasure in skill, in deck hands and skippers alike. A skipper can build up a tremendous reputation on the basis of his successful management of a boat and crew, and his ability to locate the shoals of fish, which can assume almost mythic dimensions. Lummis describes the East Anglian fishermen of the period 1880–1914 as a work force 'with an immense amount of industrial pride and a deep identification with their work'; such men gain satisfaction from developing identities as 'good workers', competent and hard-working (Lummis, 1985, pp. 50, 53). A skipper, in particular, is helped by a strong physique and a tough personality. It is not surprising that such men often develop a strongly male leisure culture of heavy drinking, brash spending and pursuit of 'good-time girls', such as that observed by Tunstall in Hull.

Family tradition remains strong in fishing, and men pass on these values to their sons. Scottish inshore fishermen used to teach the various tasks of the trade to their boys, and take them out for short trips to get them used to the sea; 'every father was hard on his sons – breaking them in for the sea' (Thompson et al., 1983, p. 240). Essays written by fishermen's sons in Hull show how they have internalised their father's culture: 'a fisherman's life is a rugged life,' wrote one; 'I think its exciting,' while a third perceptively commented: 'I like the sea because you get a way from the weman' (Tunstall, 1962, p. 110).

In many fishing communities the presence of a woman on board a boat before it set out was considered to bring bad luck and women were kept away from piers and nets (Porter, 1983; Cook, 1984; Thompson et al., 1983); indeed, women have been virtually excluded from sea fishing. Thompson et al. point to some of the exceptions; there are occasional records of women on boats in Scandinavia, Spain, Brittany and in other peasant communities. For example, along the Baltic coast women used to go out in small boats to catch bait. There is no real evidence of women in boats in Britain although nineteenth-century census data always recorded a handful of women as being fishermen: 1002 in 1851, and in 1871 364 in

England, 1029 in Scotland. However, there is no indication as to what these women were actually doing. Thompson reported that there were a few female boat owners in the Shetlands from the 1890s onwards. Even rarer are the occasions when women have penetrated the man's world of deep-sea fishing. Thompson reports that some nineteenth-century Labrador cod boats took on women as filleters and cooks (traditional women's roles, as we shall see). Similarly, women have been used for processing work on Russian 'fish factory' ships, which stay at sea so long that the preserving work must be done on board, rather than the fish simply being stored on ice (Thompson et al., 1983, pp. 173–4, 343). A notable example of women's involvement in deep-sea fishing is in Australia, where women work on trawlers as deck hands, and even as skippers; this appears to be one society where women have been notably successful in throwing off the nineteenth-century legacy, with its stereotypes of women as fragile, vulnerable and home-bound.

However, in most Western societies women's tasks traditionally have been the subsidiary ones: preparing and selling the catch, helping with lines, nets and bait, and providing any necessary help to the men in the fishing communities. In the British case this was related to the traditional organisation of the fishing industry, which was based on the work of families within a tightly integrated community. As capitalist entrepreneurs took over the organisation of the industry the assignment of tasks to men and women gradually altered, and women were slowly relegated to less and less responsible tasks. To understand the process fully, it is necessary to outline briefly the changes that took place in the industry between the eighteenth century and the early decades of the twentieth.

The development of the industry was a complex process, and there were considerable local variations in methods, technology and structure of ownership. Crudely, however, we can trace the pattern as follows. In the eighteenth and early nineteenth centuries the industry was family- and community-based. Groups of family members owned boats, and all necessary tasks were shared among the family. There were two common types of fishing activity: inshore fishing was for haddock, small fish and crustaceans, using small lines, nets or traps, while some fishing involved venturing further out, to catch ling, cod and other large fish with great-lines. Herring, mackerel and pilchards were also caught by inshoremen using drift nets.

From the 1830s, the expansion of the industry began to change this pattern. Organisation of the industry slowly devolved away from the fisher families to the curing houses or fish merchants, who took control of marketing and also of overall planning and co-ordination. Subsidiary tasks like processing (gutting, curing) and net-making, formerly performed in the family, were now centralised and done on a wage-labour basis, the curers and mechants hiring women. A variation was in the Shetlands, where deep-sea great-line fishing was organised by capitalist landlords. In this intermediary stage many fishermen still owned their boats; in Scotland, typically several families would club together to own a boat and a share system was employed in allocating earnings. However, a growing number of crew members were hired on a wage-labour basis with no ownership shares, and there was a slow penetration of landsmen owners, particularly the fish merchants. In England in the East Coast ports, the new trawling industry, which developed from the 1840s using bag-nets to catch cod and other deep-sea fish, was organised on a similar basis; but here the proportion of hired hands was higher, as was the number of non-fisher owners.

The advent of steam-powered boats in the 1880s and 1890s hastened the proletarianisation of the fishing labour force. These boats were too expensive an investment for fisher families. Some of the new owners were fish salesmen, who had taken over from the old curing firms; others were new entrants to the trade, who typically acquired over time other related interests, for example in ice or coal supply, boat building, insurance or fish processing. These were the new owners of the industry. Although some fishermen, notably skippers, continued to have shares in the boats, the majority of deck hands were now simple wage-earners. Nevertheless, even today traces of the old systems of share ownership or family ownership linger on, especially in the inshore industry in parts of Scotland and elsewhere (Gray, 1978; Thompson et al., 1983).

A classic example of the family-based pattern of work was the North Yorkshire inshore fishing industry, centred on Whitby and Staithes, which Peter Frank has researched. The industry seems to have remained virtually unchanged throughout the nineteenth century and up to the 1930s. The men fished in small 'cobles', often using long baited lines, in teams of three; each man had two lines, with 520 to 560 hooks, making a total of up to 4000 hooks to bait for each trip. The women's task was to collect the bait, mussels and 'flithers' (limpets), which they carried in 'swills' (baskets), sometimes walking as far as thirty miles on a trip, or, like the fishergirls seen by Arthur Munby, shinning down cliffs on ropes to reach the rocks. They then had to 'skane' (open) the shellfish, with spoons and knives, a job requiring strength, dexterity and speed. Next, the women had to 'cave' the old lines, cleaning them of old bait, seaweed and other debris, rebaiting them and coiling them in 'skeps' (oval baskets), another skilled job, as the lines must pay out smoothly and not snag or tangle (Frank, 1976; Horowitz Murray, 1984).

In Staithes the women also helped the men to push out the cobles. Other jobs, too were shared: men, if on shore, would help, as would children, with caving and baiting. Both sexes were involved with selling: the men would sell the fresh catch, but in the nineteenth century women also went around in winter selling fish which they had previously treated and cured, selling from baskets, or from stalls (Frank, 1976; PP 1843 xii p. 374).

The work done by women was both essential and hard, as an account of the life of Banffshire fisherwomen, quoted by Gray, demonstrates.

> The fisher wives lead a most laborious life. They assist in dragging the boats on the beach and in launching them. They sometimes, in frosty water and at unseasonable hours, carry their husbands on board, to keep them dry. They receive the fish from the boats, carry them, fresh or after salting, to their customers, at a distance, sometimes, of many miles ... it is the province of the women to bait the lines, collect furze, heath or the gleanings of the mosses which ... they carry home in their creels for fuel. (Gray, 1978, p. 13)

Women's work was also to preserve the fish, by drying with salt, pickling or smoking.

The Cornish pilchard industry was also marked by a family division of labour. In the 1850s wives and daughters, sometimes aided by hired girls, made nets (Razzell and Wainwright, 1973). A Mousehole fisherman recalled the tasks done by the wives and daughters: making and mending nets, making oilskin clothes and jerseys for the men, washing and packing the pilchards in layers of salt: the fish were arranged in rosette shapes, with their tails in the middle. Processing fish is a rushed job, if the fish are not to deteriorate, and in the 1870s it was reported that, if needed, the whole family, men, women and children, would pack the fish together (Phillips Bevan, 1877; Cook, 1984, pp. 86–7).

Women have frequently been assigned the fiddly task of dealing with shellfish. For instance, in Marshside, near Fleetwood, women were involved in the traditional shrimp industry in the 1840s, shelling the shrimps, dipping them in boiling water, and then selling them. With the railway came the potted shrimp industry, which took the retailing job away from the women, but they continued to shell the shrimps and make baskets for holding them (Thompson et al., 1983). Lummis (1985) reports that East Anglian fishermen's wives boiled shrimps and cooked and dressed crabs for the holiday trade. In Newlyn Judith Cook (1984) visited a crab wholesalers, where men were boiling the crabs while girls performed the time-consuming tasks of prising the meat out of the shells.

Although commercialisation and modernisation of fishing and the decline of family-based forms of work organisation, led to the loss of some of the women's tasks, as at Marshside, they also provided new forms of female employment. Women played a particularly important part in the herring industry. As Thompson et al. explain, from the mid-nineteenth century, there were three ways in which their work could be organised. In Scotland a part of the industry remained family-based, and women continued to do the subsidiary tasks; making and mending nets, gutting and filleting the herrings. Another group of women worked in the centralised fish houses or 'smokehouses' on the fish quays of the expanding ports in Scotland, the North East and East Anglia, preparing kippers; the herring were split, gutted, dipped in brine, hung up and smoked. Women performed all these tasks as one woman explained: 'You dinna go in right straight as a filleter. They say that the fish trade's nae a trade, but it is. You start wi' the bottom – headin', washin', picklin', tyin' smokies, goin' into the kelns, learnin' to pack – everythin' ' (Thompson et al., 1983, p. 169). Such work was hard and often involved working late at nights to meet the demands of the incoming fleets, which shocked observers, like Alexander Redgrave, the factory inspector, in the 1870s. But women have recalled the pleasure they took in the work, involving as it did membership of a highly companionable work group, with a considerable degree of self-determination; singing, joking and flirting with the fishermen added spice to the work. As one explained, 'it was a free and easy time, you weren't restricted like – you know, in a factory where there were bosses' (quoted Lummis, 1985, p. 125).

A third type of employment was that of the Scottish herring girls, who 'followed the herring' down each year to East Anglia, gutting, salting and packing the fish. The girls worked in groups of three, two gutting and one packing. As late as 1936, there were still 2600 girls who followed the fleet from Scotland. They often had to sleep in groups in roughly made accommodation such as wooden shacks, but once again the freedom, companionship and mobility of the job, along with the chance to meet a husband, seem to have compensated for the hardships.

The other major task for women was net-making and mending. In Buckie, Scotland, the family might join together in work on the nets: children preparing needles, women cleaning the nets and mending smaller holes, the men attending to corners, fitting weights and seeing to the overall shaping. Once again, this shows the family-based nature of the origins of the sexual division of labour in fishing. In communities like Buckie a wife was indispensable for a young man starting out to earn for himself: 'no one can be a fisher and want a wife.' This was even more the case in the remote crofting and fishing communities in the Highlands and Islands, where wives had to take their share in the hardest work on the croft (sheepshearing and dipping, carrying loads, hand-digging the fields) as well as their fishing tasks (Thompson et al., 1983, pp. 234, 340).

It is worth stressing that, despite the prevalence of the sexual division of labour outlined above, there was much sharing of tasks in this way as long as fishing retained its family base of organisation. This illustrates the flexibility of the division of labour in the household production era, as discussed in chapter 2. Another notable example is described by A. J. Munby, who visited the oyster-fishing village of Langwm, near Milford Haven, in 1871.

The boats were loosed at last and brought to shore; there was a general orderly bustle; men and women took down the long oars, put their paniers and mussel-jars aboard and settled to their seats, and pulled off; and so we started, soon after 8. What a sight it was, when our division of the fleet, some thirty boats strong, pulled out of the wide harbour in long procession upon the glittering waters of the haven! ... I watched them all dropping down below New Milford, to the oyster grounds, and saw the women heave the dredgenets over-board. (quoted Hudson, 1974, p. 292)

As fishing moved to a capitalist basis, net-making machinery, which had been developed from the 1820s, began to be used, but women continued to work on the nets, some of which were still made by hand. In East Anglia in the late nineteenth century women were employed as net-workers and 'beatsters' (menders), sometimes working in workshops, sometimes at home. In the 1950s Tunstall (1962) observed one such woman, who worked in and outside of her terraced house 'braiding' trawl nets. These were skilled tasks, and entrée to work was often achieved through family connections. Jessie Thacker, a skilled net-maker explained that though the trade was dying out, so far machines could only produce straight lengths of net, so that the subtly shaped trawls still had to be made by hand (Cook, 1984, p. 107). Descriptions given by the women of this work are similar to that given by Anita Desai of a net factory she visited on Froya Island in Norway: here women were making nylon nets by hand for trapping fish in fiords and inlets. The women were considered 'much better' at the work than men (New Internationalist, 1985, p. 106).

As mechanisation transformed the fishing industry, women's jobs were particularly affected, but women have continued to perform the modernised food-processing tasks, in canneries and frozen food plants. The expansion of employment choices for women since World War II has broken down, to some extent, the pattern of wives working within the fishing industry (see Porter, 1983). Nonetheless, Tunstall found that, though the Hull fishermen he studied preferred their wives not to work, some were employed in the fish-processing plants (Tunstall, 1962).

The extension of trips made by deep-sea fishermen has necessitated the crew performing various traditional female tasks (net mending, gutting, filleting) on board the boats. Perhaps for this reason, some of these tasks are now performed by men on shore. In Hull, for example, filleting, carried out on the dockside, is considered a semi-skilled male job (Tunstall, 1962). The job, along with 'bobbing' (unloading the trawlers) is performed by ex-fishermen among others. But, on the other hand, a whole new range of 'women's jobs' has been created inside the processing plants. Barbara Garson provides a detailed description of work at the Bumble Bee cannery in Oregon, where women workers, many employed on a low-paid casual or seasonal basis, process salmon and tuna for tins. Women clean, skin and bone the fish, removing parts of the flesh for catfood and splitting the fish into can-sized pieces. They also act as gutters, slimers and liver pickers. All this work is highly subdivided and women specialise in specific activities, in contrast to the herring girls, who had learned to perform the range of tasks. Male jobs at Bumble Bee were carrying crates, driving machines and timekeeping. Garson describes how one of the women, stultified by the monotony of fish-cleaning, applied for a job as 'gitney driver', a gitney being a small fork-lift truck used for transporting crates. She was told no woman could do the job, as if the crates fell from the truck they weighed 35 lbs, too heavy for a woman to lift; she had to stay in her line-bound 'woman's job' (Garson, 1977, pp. 23–41).

A similar set-up was seen by Desai in Norway, although the plant she visited was more highly mechanised. Again, women did all the handling of the fish, skinning, cleaning and boning it, operating machines for sorting, cutting and packing, while the 'heavier' work of driving, carrying and trolley-pushing was done by men (New Internationalist, 1985). In both factories it was notable that the men's 'heavy work' involved much greater mobility, freedom from tight supervision and the pressure of the line, while women stood monotonously at work all day, fish in one hand, tool in the other.

The nature of the work performed by the women in the canning factories – subdivided, routinised, repetitive, indoor, static, highly supervised – is in sharp contrast with the work of the Yorkshire inshore fishwives, or even with that of the smokehouse women and the Scottish herring girls, although the onset of capitalist organisation had involved some task degradation in the latter cases. Before the development of the factories, women's work with fish retained strong outdoor connections, and the masculine image that the trade had acquired over the centuries had rubbed off on these women. To nineteenth-century male observers, their lifestyle seemed notably unfeminine.

Early in the nineteenth century, Sir Richard Ayton had noted that women gathering cockles and mussels at Port Isaac had hitched up their petticoats in an unseemly fashion, though men trying to take advantage of this unaccustomed display of female flesh were rebuffed, he observed, with words and fists if necessary (Hill, 1984, p. 221). In 1875 Redgrave described the East Anglian fish-house women as 'robust and ruddy ... singing, laughing, full of slang and rude jests bandied about between men and women'. This rough behaviour he considered to be influenced by the nightly allowance of two pints of beer given to the workpeople. Even more scandalously, women were described as lying down on the quay to snatch a couple of hours' sleep in order to carry on working into the small hours (PP 1875 xvi, p. 21). These working conditions, like outdoor farm work, were deeply offensive to the Victorian patriarchal sensibility. In 1877 another observer commented that, although the scene on the fish quays was 'eminently picturesque and busy' this form of employment was hardly suitable for 'feminine associations'. The herring curers, he continued, 'are noted for their robust, animal health, and perhaps not unnaturally, for their somewhat free and unrestrained manners' (Phillips Bevan, 1877, p. 202). The Scottish herring girls, too, were described as 'real, hard, tough girls': 'they used to work in the open. They used to wear oilskins just above the elbow and their arms used to be red, absolutely red, with the salt and the wind' (Lummis, 1985, p. 123).

The development of capitalist fishing removed women from the fish quays to the secluded, protected, indoor environment of factory and cannery, in a way which the Victorian commentators would have approved. From the beginning, they outnumbered men in the food-canning industries, which, in 1871, employed 1425 women in Scotland and England, as opposed to 958 men (Phillips Bevan, 1877, p. 198). Such jobs struck observers as suitable for women, linked as they were with domestic food preparation and being safely isolated from the male outdoor world. The move indoors, however, deprived women not only of independence but of status. Porter in her study of Newfoundland women recounts that the old fishing work was remembered with pride, while work in the frozen fish factory was experienced as unpleasant and demeaning. The girl who worked in the factory no longer saw her work as in any way connected with the fishermen's work, while the older women had shared the traditional knowledge passed down by fishing generations (Porter, 1983).

In fishing, then, we see a classic case of a sharply marked sexual division of labour, rooted in family sharing of tasks. Men obtained from early on a virtual monopoly over sea-fishing. Such an arrangement seems almost inevitable in societies where the care of house and children was firmly assigned to women, for it was clearly necessary for one marriage partner to stay on shore and run the home. The married woman's association with child care would almost inevitably exclude her, in settled pre-industrial societies, from work involving frequent, long and irregular absences from home. This exclusion, however, became more assured as a culture of masculinity developed around fishing, along with a symbolic view of women as polluters, manifested in the widespread tabus surrounding women's connections with boats. These cultural elements have served to reinforce a view of fishing as an essentially male task, so much so that women would not even think of trying to force a way on to the male territory of the trawler and drifter. There is perhaps no other task in which women have, even now, made so little inroad. In Britain in 1971 no women were recorded in the Census in the occupation of fisherman. The 1981 figures show a small advance; there are now eighty, which may represent the start of a breakthrough in this area.

The principal tasks done by women, net-making and processing the catch, were, however, crucially important, skilled and responsible tasks, similar in economic significance to the farmwork done by women in pre-industrial societies. Up to the latter part of the nineteenth century, the significance of women's contributions was emphasised by the roles they often took in helping with the marketing of the catch. Scottish fishermen, who retained the family-based fishing system into the twentieth century repeatedly emphasised to Thompson and his associates the impossibility of operating as a fisherman without a wife. Few would marry with people from outside the fishing community, for it was vital to find a partner who had been brought up with a knowledge of these important skills (Thompson et al., 1983).

Once net-making, fish processing and packing had become defined as 'women's work' they continued to be seen as such even when the family system broke down in the face of capitalist reorganisation. Where formerly some tasks had been shared within the family by men and women (cleaning nets, collecting bait, baiting hooks, etc.) centralisation and capitalist development reinforced the division of labour, so that tasks became more narrowly specialised and sex-typed. No doubt this tendency was reinforced as well by Victorian prejudice, since these female jobs were so similar to the jobs performed by women in the home – food preparation and needlework – that it was easy to characterise them as 'fit' work for women.

Thus, as in many other cases, while capitalist reorganisation of the industry was grounded upon an already-existing sexual division of labour, its effects were to intensify and secure the sex-typing of jobs. This process is highlighted further by the development of the canned and frozen food sector. This has heralded the further debasement of the female role in the fishing industry. Although many fish cleaners, canners and packers are fishermen's wives, they are far removed from the masculine world of boats and nets, of the hustle, bustle and excitement of the fish quay. They perform degraded, low-paid tasks, often on a casualised basis, under the control of men, with none of the autonomy enjoyed by the fishwives and herring girls of the nineteenth century. As Porter's work shows, these women have lost all sense of connection with the mainstream of fishing activity, and all sense of involvement in the skills and traditions of one of humankind's oldest occupations. As so often, subsidiary tasks shaped within the family have been transmuted to inferior, degrading tasks within the factory environment. From the masculine world women are excluded, on grounds which can frankly only been seen as traditional and irrational. If a rationalisation is provided, it is likely to be on the grounds of women's inferior physique, or of the admittedly dangerous nature of life at sea. But such rationalisation is rarely called for, since, in Britain at least, there has been virtually no challenge by women to men's assumption of the fisherman's role.

6

MINING

Along with fishing, coalmining appears as perhaps the most exclusively and essentially masculine of occupations. In Great Britain this is now quite literally true. Women were excluded from working underground in mines by the 1842 Mines Act, and by the 1970s they had also disappeared from surface work at the pits. The 1981 Census recorded that 0 per cent of underground workers and 0.4 per cent of all workers in the mining and quarrying industry were female. Mining, thus, presents us with a paradigmatic case of total gender-based segregation. Apart from a few clerical workers and the odd visit below ground of female medical personnel, mining has become an all-male industry.

If we look back at the history of mining before women were banished from the pits, there are many parallels with the case of fishing. In coalmines in Scotland, Wales and England at the beginning of the nineteenth century there was a clear sexual division of labour which, as in fishing, was rooted in the family system of organisation which still prevailed in many areas. There was the same growing condemnation of women's work in mining as unfeminine and unsexing, and the same hardening out of a masculine work culture. Later in the century, the surface tasks, which women seem to have relished, were removed from them as mechanisation developed, but in this case, not even degraded tasks were left for the women to perform. The coming of automatic machines for cleaning and sorting coal at the pithead has, in Britain at least, completely removed one field of employment from women.

There is a certain amount of uncertainty surrounding the history of mining in pre-industrial Britain. Jane Humphries in her influential article on the Mines Act argues that the employment of women was a short-lived phenomenon: far from being a relic of 'feudal barbarism', it was a product of the onset on capitalism and exchange-based production, and of the proletarianisation of the peasantry. This assertion, for which little evidence is provided, seems in line with Humphries' desire to explain the patterns of employment in mining entirely within a Marxist framework of the analysis of capitalist relations of production and her scepticism over the primacy afforded to patriarchy as an explanatory category in the work of many feminist historians (Humphries, 1981). Yet her own account also emphasises the family-based nature of work organisation in the mines, a feature which alternative interpretations have picked out as central. Lewenhak (1980), Pinchbeck (1981) and John (1984) all claim that the work of women and children in mines goes right back into the feudal or pre-industrial epoch and that it is attributable to the subsistence activities of families seeking fuel; this they attained both by picking from the surface in the equivalent of open-cast mines (an activity similar to that of the 'sea-coalers' of the North East) and by scrabbling down under the surface in rudimentary pits.

Women's work in mines, then, started by their giving assistance to their menfolk within the family economy, and as mining became commercialised by large landowners and proprietors their employment continued. Pinchbeck and John cite odd references to female mineworkers from the fourteenth century onwards, although these are too few to provide firm evidence one way or another. However, by the seventeenth and eighteenth centuries women's employment seems to have become fairly well established, and, as John and Hill argue, by the eighteenth century it was regarded as quite natural and normal (John, 1984, p. 20; Hill, 1984, p. 200).

Some support for this interpretation is provided by an official source, the 1851 Mines Commission Report, which outlined the history of mining in parts of East Scotland. Here, until the last decades of the eighteenth century, landowners had engaged colliers in a lifetime contract: this system of 'slavery' was said to have lasted right through from the twelfth century, during which time 'the female sex of the collier population were serfs or slaves like their husbands fathers or brothers' (PP 1851 xxiii, p. 49). Those who tried to evade the yoke could be fined up to £100, or, as an old collier recalled be 'placed by the necks in iron collars called juggs' or alternatively yoked to the gin horse and made to run backwards all day (PP 1842 xvi, p. 450).

By the time this system of bondage came to an end, a clear division of labour had developed between the sexes, which was replicated in other districts where women worked underground, such as Lancashire and Yorkshire. While men performed the central task of 'hewing' or 'getting' the coal, women and children carried out subsidiary tasks: young boys habitually started work as 'trappers' (opening air doors for carts to pass through), a job sometimes also done by young girls; women and girls, sometimes helped by boys, transported coals from face to shaft and possibly from shaft to surface. These tasks were, of course, absolutely essential so that, as Robert Bald, a visitor to the Scottish mines in 1812, explained, 'let a collier be ever so expert at his occupation, if his wife or daughters be indisposed, all his exertion goes for nothing' (Hill, 1984, p. 213).

When the 1842 Commission investigated the work of women and children in the mines, it found that the employment of females was confined to four areas: Yorkshire, Lancashire, South Wales and East Scotland. Here girls, like their brothers, might start working at the age of six or seven. Figures for seven areas in Scotland indicate that about 24 per cent of the work force was female. In the Durham and Northumberland coalfield the employment of women had died out around 1780. In Staffordshire no women were employed underground, but many worked on the pitbank, as was the case in the tin and lead mines of Cornwall, where about 5000 were employed. The Commission reported that in some Yorkshire collieries 'there is no distinction of sex, but the labour is divided indifferently among both sexes, except that it is comparatively rare for women to hew or get the coals, although there are numerous instances in which they regularly perform even this work' (PP 1842 xv, p. 24).

In fact, the evidence of the report tends rather to confirm Humphries' contention that 'everywhere they were employed women did the same work' (Humphries, 1981, p. 8). Although women, girls and boys might indeed be used interchangeably at many tasks, there was a clear divide between their work and that of the adult male hewers. Young girls sometimes worked as trappers, but the main female tasks, as Humphries argues, surrounded the transport of coals. In England women and girls worked as 'hurriers', 'drawers' and 'putters', dragging and pushing trucks or 'corves' of coal. In Scotland they were 'bearers', carrying coals in baskets to the shaft and even on occasions up ladders to the face. In Wales they worked as 'windlass-women', winding coals to the surface. Other female jobs were filling the corves at the face and 'riddling' (sieving) coal. In Scotland they helped clean the roadways of the mines, and in Wales they operated pumps to clear water and did 'pouncing', a type of boring work using logs when new shafts were sunk. At the surface, the bankswomen were involved with loading and unloading coals, weighing them, riddling and sorting. In tin, lead, copper and zinc mines they worked at 'dressing' the ores. Their tasks included washing, sieving, sorting, grading, and 'spalling' and 'bucking' (breaking up lumps of ore or mashing it with heavy mallets). Women also might wheel barrowloads around the site.

As must be apparent from this list, much of the women's work was extremely hard and heavy, requiring considerable strength and stamina. Robert Bald had observed that it took two men to lift a basket of coals, weighing 170 lbs, on to the back of a woman (Burton, 1976, p. 33). The

Commission's estimates exceeded his: Scottish women were carrying weights of up to three hundredweight! A six-year-old was found carrying 56 lbs in a wooden basket, a work she not surprisingly described as 'very sair' (PP 1842 xv, p. 18). So much for the inability of women to handle 35 lb crates of fish!

In Wales, it was reported that while women refused to push trucks, men and boys turned their backs on windlass work. One sixteen-year-old windlass-woman explained that men disliked winding, it being 'too hard work for them', while Hannah Bowen, who handled 400 loads of between one and a half and four hundredweight daily, described her job as 'good hard work' (PP 1842 xv, p. 31; xvii, p. 573).

It was not, therefore, lack of strength which debarred women, in the main, from working as hewers. Indeed, fourteen-year-old Rebecca Hough, who was chiefly employed as a hurrier but helped out with other tasks including hewing, claimed that hurrying was the hardest work she had to do; Ann Hamilton also spoke of the toughness required for hurrying, in an interesting comment which turns on its head the masculine stereotype of female weakness: 'lads are no fit to stand the work like women' (PP 1842 xvi, pp. 257, 484). Possibly it could be argued that hewing required a different kind of exertion, more muscular and immediately draining, while women's tasks drew more on sustained energy and stamina; but a more convincing explanation for the male near-monopoly of hewing is the way authority devolved in the family. Hewing was the central mining tasks; it fell upon the hewer to co-ordinate the work of his assistants. In addition, in the regions in which women were employed underground the contractual system was one in which the hewer alone was hired directly by the proprietors. He then employed his own team of assistants, and paid them himself. The system clearly encouraged the use of family labour, since then the whole of the employer's handout was retained within the family unit; it also mirrored the family arrangement of pre-industrial families, where ultimate control of the household's pool of resources lay with the male head of house. Mark-Lawson and Witz (1988) see this as one type of patriarchal control strategy which they call 'inclusion'; this gave way, as family work systems collapsed, to alternative strategies of exclusion. If men had no direct authority over their womenfolk they preferred to bar them from industry.

Women, then, infrequently worked as hewers. One Lancashire witness actually declared that in his region 'girls and women never get coals, and always remain drawers, and are considered equal to half a man' (PP 1842 xv, p. 156). This claim was exaggerated, as evidence suggests that a few women were employed as hewers in Lancashire, and slightly more in Yorkshire. However, there are indications that such women were probably either providing occasional reinforcement to men, as in the case of Rebecca Hough, or were substituting for incapacitated male relatives, as was

Margaret Boxter whose husband had 'failed in his breath'. In such cases women apparently were more than adequate replacements; it was reported of one that she earned more than her husband (PP 1842 xvi, pp. 248, 475).

The kind of career of a woman might have in the industry is exemplified by the case of Hannah Hughes of Ebbw Vale. Daughter of a miner, and now the wife of another, she started work in the pit at fifteen filling and drawing trucks, boring and performing 'all the light work the same as the man did, excepting with the powder'. Whether the 'light work' excluded or included hewing is not clear, but it is significant that she was debarred from handling explosives, a task not only dangerous but involving technical knowledge, which, as we have seen, was so frequently withheld from women. Later she moved to the surface, where she worked unloading, cleaning and stacking coal, an improvement in her opinion: 'I liked working in the level very well after I got used to it, but I like the work outside best' (PP 1842 xvii, p. 625).

This preference was probably shared by many. The 1842 Report presents an ambiguous picture of women's responses to underground work. Many, especially the younger girls, lamented its hard and tiring nature. Margaret Jacques, a seventeen-year-old bearer, complained: 'it is horrible sore work; it was not my choice, but we do our parents' will' (PP 1842 xv, p. 29). Fourteen-year-old Agnes Reid also disliked it: 'few lassies like it,' she said, and it often made them cry (PP 1842 xvi, p. 436). Many young girls complained, in addition, of beating and brutal treatment by the hewers.

The Scottish women's work caused particular resentment. Jane Watson explained the vicious circle in which they were caught; 'it is only horse work and ruins the women; it crushes their haunches, bends their ankles and makes them old women at forty. Women so soon get weak that they are forced to take the little ones down to relieve them' (PP 1842 xv, p. 30). Many women, she added, experienced miscarriages or stillbirths as a result; another woman claimed to have miscarried five times (PP 1842 xv, p. 30). The sense of imposition and indignity in the term 'horse-work' re-appears in a comment of Isabel Hogg; 'You must just tell the Queen Victoria that we are guid loyal subjects; women-people here don't mind work, but they object to horse-work' (PP 1842 xv, p. 30).

However, not all women disliked the work, and many saw it as preferable to the limited alternatives that faced them. Mary Ann Watson told the Commission that underground work had not harmed her and would not harm her children. Ten-year-old Ann Winchcliffe asserted she would rather be in the pit than at school! A Mrs Day pointed out that employment chances were limited so that girls who did not go into the pit 'must take a poke and go begging'. It was claimed by one young witness that the fear of losing work was so great that most girls would pretend to the commissioners that they liked their jobs. These young women clearly had achieved a realistic, though fatalistic, appraisal of their future, exemplified in the wry, if confused, assessment of Ann Fern: 'I like being in the pit, but I would rather go to service, but I never tried ... I care nothing about where I am. It's hard work going in the pit ... I should be worked hard anywhere, I dare say' (PP 1842 xv, pp. 29, 74; xvi, pp. 276, 296).

Surface work was more positively viewed. In Wales, the commissioners were told that it was preferred to other types of employment, notably domestic service, because it was relatively well paid and freer. Girls said they wanted to work all the days they were permitted (PP 1842 xvii, pp. 381–2, 513). A similar verdict was returned, over a century later, by the pitbrow women interviewed by Angela John, looking back on their work. One enthused, 'Oh, I loved every minute of it. Oh I did ... And it was healthy job, it was hard, it was heavy, but it was healthy' (John, 1984, p. 179).

The attitudes of the men in 1842 were equally mixed. Some colliers deplored women's underground work, considering it unsuitable and emphasising its demoralising effects, but others preferred a system which kept the family together. James Waugh had sent his children early down the pit 'to keep them out of mischief'; another man believed the pit was better for daughters than the factory (PP 1842 xvi, pp. 282, 481). Employers, too, had mixed opinions, some opposing the employment of women and even debarring them from their own pits. Others clearly found the system to their advantage and defended it, declaring that women made better workers, a point on which many of the colliers were in agreement with them. Girls were said to work harder than boys, to play around less, to be fitter and suppler, more attentive to their work, more punctual and easier to control (PP 1842 xv, p. 27; xvi, p. 283; xvii, p. 202). Revealingly, they were also praised for their acceptance of a secondary role: 'they make far better drawers than lads. They are more steady ... A lass never expects to be a coal-getter, and that keeps her steady' (PP 1842 xv, p. 27).

However, the most prominent theme in the statements of male witnesses, and surely, as the work of both John and Humphries suggests, the most crucial in swinging public opinion against underground work for women, was sexual morality. Never, in all the numerous attacks on the various forms of women's employment which appeared over the course of the nineteenth century, was the theme of sexuality made so explicit or conveyed in such blunt language. The particularly shocking feature of pitwork was that heat and humidity led many men to work virtually naked, and girls too sometimes worked naked to the waist. 'No brothel can beat it' the commissioners commented (PP 1842, xv, p. 24).

The reader of the report was provided with a wealth of salacious details. 'I have seen many a one with her breasts hanging out,' witnessed a

Lancashire collier, while a boy explained how the girls' trousers were often frayed by the chain which passed between their legs as they pulled the carts, so that 'we can see them all between the legs naked.' Colliers spoke of having intercourse with girls in the mine, of horseplay between groups of adolescents and of all sorts of debauched behaviour: drunkenness, swearing, fights in which clothing was ripped off; 'the women are wickeder by th' half than the men,' said a Lancashire man. The result, it was claimed, was that many girls had illegitimate children or 'lived tally' (cohabited). One woman told how she had frequently been paid twopence by the canalboat loaders 'to show my breeches' and how the women used to pelt with coal one naked miner who commonly importuned them (PP 1842 xv, pp. 25, 32; xvii, pp. 202, 211, 214).

These bacchanalian descriptions may well have been as exaggerated as Sir Richard Ayton's earlier claim on his visit to Whitehaven pit that men and women 'excited by passion' were apt to indulge themselves with any passer-by, not caring 'if it be father or daughter, brother or sister' (Hill, 1984, p. 214). But such reports of unbridled sexuality were bound to raise Victorian moral fervour, especially when combined with the apparently contradictory charge of the loss of femininity and of 'unsexing'. One Lancashire observer commented that, as women wore trousers, 'the sex of the female is best discernible by the necklace of blue or red glass beads and by her earrings which are usually worn' (PP 1842 xvii, p. 161). This juxtaposing of unfeminine appearance with feminine frivolity represented the worst fears of the middle class about working-class decadence. No wonder such girls were inevitably described as unfit for 'performance of mothers' duties' (PP 1842 xv, p. 35).

In her account of the Mines Act, Humphries argues that the exclusion of women from underground work cannot be attributed to patriarchy; the male workers had no reason to fear female competition or downward pressure on wages as women formed non-competing groups and were anyway under their authority. Nor did they display any desire to force their wives into a purely housewife role. Our survey of the 1842 Commission's evidence certainly confirms the lack of wholehearted support for exclusion from both male mineworkers and employers. On the other hand the chief impetus for exclusion, which came from middle-class crusaders and politicians, acting with strong support from the press and public opinion, can only be described as having patriarchal elements. While it may be argued that the Commission was only responding to the women's own complaints about their work, it was not so much the hard and burdensome nature of the work as its 'immoral' and 'unfeminine' nature which was played on in the report and in subsequent debate (see John, 1984, for similar view). Humanitarian principles may indeed have been involved in the case of reformers like Lord Shaftesbury; but the passing of the Mines Act has surely to be seen as the triumph of the emergent Victorian view of femininity and the female role. As such, it paved the way for subsequent redefinitions of what was 'fit' work for women. At the same time, it enshrined the attitude of paternalist protection towards women which was exemplified in the subsequent pairing of women and children as 'minors' in the Factory Acts. Since the removal of a source of cheap labour was clearly to the disadvantage of the capitalist employer, it would be hard to interpret these actions of the state in anything but a patriarchal framework. Moreover, John provides evidence that the working-class press, such as the *Northern Star* and the *Miners' Advocate*, supported the call for exclusion of women not just from underground but also from surface work, as part of the evolving campaign for the 'family wage'. By the 1860s, the opinion of miners seems to have swung firmly against the use of women in *all* pitwork.

Nevertheless, many from the mining community campaigned against the Mines Act, notably some of the women it was designed to protect. In Wales and Scotland in particular, there was little alternative employment for women; John reports that by 1845 only 200 of the 4200 Scottish women displaced from the mines had found new jobs. It was not surprising that they furtively returned to the pits, where many women worked illegally. In 1845 the mines inspector Tremenheere knew of 200 such women in the Wigan area alone (John, 1984, p. 57). Women used back passages, stairs and tunnels to creep into the pits, sometimes disguising themselves as men. In 1851 women were still working underground in Nantyglo and Blainau; in Scotland 'the poor women, thinking themselves unfit for other employment, often eluded the overseers and stole into the mines dressed in men's clothes' (PP 1851 xxiii, p. 50). Even in the late 1860s women were still working in Welsh pits, and it is instructive that A. J. Munby, a fierce supporter of the pitwoman's right to choose her own destiny, saw the exclusionist campaign in terms of male competition. He wrote:

They've took the bread clean oot on oor mouths, aye, every mother and maid,
An all for to pleasure the menfolk, as wants to steal oor trade!
Well, if it's hard an mucky, who knows that better nor me?
But I liked it, an it was my living – an so it had to be.

(quoted John, 1984, p. 54)

Despite growing male resistance, women continued to work as bankswomen and also as ore dressers or 'bal maidens' in the Cornish mines. Phillips Bevan estimated that there were some 7000 or 8000 of these in the 1870s (Phillips Bevan, 1876, p. 10). The 'pitbrow lasses' worked at a variety of tasks, but especially on the screens (machines for sieving), cleaning and sorting coal. In 1874 6.25 per cent of surface work was done by women, whose employment was highly concentrated within certain areas, such as Lancashire. By 1900 it had declined to 3.13 per cent, as processes like screening became more automatic (John, 1984, p. 71). The bal maidens of Cornwall have been studied by Gill Burke, whose figures show an increase in their numbers in the 1840s and 1850s, but a decline from the 1870s, as a result both of technological development, such as a mill for mashing down ores, and of mine closures. By the twentieth century only a handful remained.

Although the system of family employment had been destroyed by the Mines Act, John's work indicates that most the pitbrow lasses came from mining families; many of the Wigan colliery girls had previously worked below ground, and the majority married miners (John, 1984, p. 115). Although the work was heavy and could be dangerous (women fell down mineshafts or were crushed by heavy trucks) both groups appear to have enjoyed their work. Burke portrays the bal maidens as strong, independent women. The *Ladies' Journal* summed up the life of such a girl in these words: 'out in the sunshine, a free woman, mistress of herself, enjoying her work and the cheerful society of her companions' (quoted Burke, 1986, p. 192).

Such a picture was not likely to appeal to men! Although the 1842 commissioners had generally exonerated surface work for women as a healthy and respectable occupation, a note which was to become the main theme of subsequent male thinking was sounded in the comment that 'By the constant exertion of their strength, the muscles acquire a development and their carriage a manner, which may be somewhat out of character with feminine appearance' (PP 1842 xvii, p. 366). From the 1850s on, steady pressure mounted against surface work as unsuitable for women, culminating in attempts in the 1880s and 1900s to make it illegal. Propaganda centred on the degrading and unfeminine nature of the work. The *Morning Chronicle* in the 1850s described the 'swart-faced' Staffordshire bankswomen as having lost 'every womanly feature and attribute': 'The women work at rude and unsexing labour ... partly assuming their habiliments and altogether adopting the coarseness of the men' (quoted Ginswick, 1983, pp. 84–5). Wearing men's coats – or, even more scandalously in the case of the Wigan lasses, trousers – was considered particularly degrading, as was the association with the blackness of the pit, 'their skins engrained with dirt, which is very often never washed off from Saturday to Saturday', as the *Chronicle* correspondent put it (quoted Ginswick, 1983, p. 90). The masculine associations of the work were comprehensively attacked by A. J. Mundella in 1872, who deplored the women's wearing of 'coal-heavers' hats', their smoking pipes, drinking in pubs with the men, and even brawling in the streets with them afterwards (John, 1984, p. 180). Phillips Bevan, a more dispassionate observer of the same period, saw nothing 'indecorous or degrading' in the work, but noted that 'public opinion' was swinging to the view that this work was 'not suitable' for women (Phillips Bevan, 1876, p. 10).

However, the various campaigns failed to eliminate women from pitbrow work, although the declining proportion of women to men, noted above, may reflect the opposition of miners to women's employment in areas where male unemployment was often rife. In 1911 a clause was passed on pitwork, forbidding the 'lifting, carrying or moving anything so heavy as to be likely to cause injury to the boy, girl, or woman' (shades of the 35 lb fish crate). Such legislation, however, was so vague as to be fairly unworkable. World War I predictably witnessed a large increase in numbers of pitwomen, from 6500 to 11,300, although this was resented by male miners who asserted their belief that women should be in the home (Braybon and Summerfield, 1987, p. 48). Clearly the men had switched from strategies of inclusion to exclusion, as Mark-Lawson and Witz put it. However, after that the number of women slowly declined: by 1953 only some thousand remained (John, 1984). In was machines rather than men, however, capitalist technology rather than patriarchal ideas, which gave the final push to exclude women from the industry.

In other countries women continued to work in mines, both below and above ground. Lewenhak reports that women worked underground in Belgium and Germany into the twentieth century. In India women continued to work underground until Independence, and are still employed as surface workers. In the 1960s they were 19 per cent of the Indian mining work force (and were similarly represented in Thailand, Hong Kong and Jamaica, among other countries). Here they worked in open-cast mines and at the pit brows; in India they were particularly found loading and unloading railway wagons, a job scorned by men as 'women's work' (Boserup, 1970, pp. 68–9, 80; Lewenhak, 1980, pp. 193, 254). Today women work in mines in China, and since the 1970s have taken up minework in parts of the USA such as Pennsylvania, Kentucky and Virginia. In 1982 women were 1.4 per cent of mine operatives, some 200,000 being employed (United States Bureau of the Census, 1984). Their campaign for access has been aided by the mechanisation of facework, making the work less strenuous and possibly less dangerous; the operation of automated cutters and shuttlecars calls for less exertion than swinging a pick or pushing a corve. Although the women faced initial hostility and harassment from both employers and male mineworkers, they have now apparently established a female bridgehead in the industry.

Although in many areas of employment increased automation has led to the substitution of women for men, this is unlikely to occur in British mines. Women have shown no interest in taking up this type of work, and both employers and miners have become used to the idea of the pit as a male preserve. Studies of mines or miners, like those of Burton (1976), Douglass and Krieger (1983) or Roberts (1984), emphasise the masculinity of the miner's world: toughness, danger, dirt and squalid conditions (no lavatories or washrooms underground), the cult of strength and endurance, male comradeliness and teamwork, a culture of rough joking and sexual bragging. Young miners must undergo initiation rites which emphasise physical endurance and male sexuality: grease being smeared on their genitals, submersion in pools, electric shocks and so forth (Roberts, 1984). As in the case of fishing, the exclusion of women was symbolised by the superstition, current in the North East pits from the 1850s, that to meet a woman on the way to the mine was dangerous. Once excluded, women became the other, threatening, polluting.

In most mining communities, it was the custom for married women to stay at home and commit themselves to domesticity and housework, the latter being particularly heavy in households where several male members would be returning daily filthy with pit dirt. Williamson's study of a Tyneside mining community emphasises the altruism demanded of miners' wives, and also the real sense in which they remained in the shadow of the pit, ears ever alert for the warning hooter (Williamson, 1982). Although exiled from pitwork, women remained identified with the mining community, witness the history of women's involvement in strike support activities throughout this century (Stearns, 1972). As Allen says, 'women and wives have been adapted to meet the needs of mining as effectively as miners themselves' (Allen, 1981, p. 74). Nevertheless, the role assigned to women was that of supporter, backup to the male, and domestic worker.

The mining industry, then, presents us with one polar case, that of total exclusion of women from an activity. It is of particular significance for two reasons. First, it provided an archetypal model for working-class family life, that of male breadwinner and female housewife, which, despite its limited applicability in reality, has taken deep-rooted hold in the popular imagination. Secondly, it has established parameters for the kind of work which is popularly defined as for men only: dirty, dangerous, physically strenuous, a battle with the elements, demanding a kind of close defensive team spirit which, it is assumed, could never be achieved in a mixed-sex group. In environments where these conditions are replicated (building sites, lighthouses, oil rigs) women will find it hard to gain access; and they themselves are likely to view with incredulity the idea of women wanting to undertake such work.

B

The Secondary Sector: Manufacturing and Factories

The three previous case studies reveal common features: in all cases the sexual division of labour emerged from the allocation of tasks within patriarchal pre-industrial families; in all cases, women's economic role in these families was of crucial importance; in all cases, the development of capitalist production pushed women into a narrower range of tasks, devaluing their contribution and often depriving them of traditional skills; in all cases, a growing definition of the occupation as a whole as a 'masculine' area of activity, backed up by moral crusades which presented work within it as 'unsuitable' for women, led to major decreases in women's employment. In the case of mining this process of redefinition drove women out altogether. However, in none of these cases did women ever to any appreciable extent come into competition with men for the *same* jobs. Male workers, as a result, played little direct part in pushing women out.

As we turn to manufacturing industry a new dimension appears. In these industries manufacturers have habitually tried to cheapen production costs by employing greater proportions of women. In many cases this has brought men and women into direct competition for the same jobs. This in turn often led male-controlled unions to campaign for the exclusion of women from certain jobs and their confinement to others, usually low-paid, low-status ancillary jobs. Thus, in these areas, male workers have been directly responsible for restricting women's opportunities and reconstructing the division of labour.

This was, by and large, true of most industries which had come into existence before the Industrial Revolution. Industries which were only developed in the latter part of the nineteenth century, such as food and drink preparation, confectionery, cigarettes or electrical goods, often described as the 'new industries', present a rather different picture. Here jobs were often designed in such a fashion as to make them 'suitable' for women from the outset of production. Even here, though, the influence of developments elsewhere was felt, as the allocation of jobs to men or to women mirrored the sterotypes of 'men's' and 'women's' work which had been constructed in the older industries.

As a result, the sector as a whole presents a particularly stark picture of sex-typed tasks. The 1946 Royal Commission on Equal Pay was only able to find, within the whole of manufacturing industry, sixteen tasks in which there was any real overlap between men's and women's employment! Factories had become strange segregated environments, in which men and women worked in separate spaces, at different tasks. The case studies which follow show how this came about.

7

POTTERY

In the course of the world's history, responsibility for the production of earthenware vessels and containers has more commonly rested with women than with men. Lewenhak (1980) argues that in non-industrial societies pottery has often been a female monopoly, for example among certain Amerindian and African tribes: among the Nandi it is tabu for any man to come near a woman while she is making a pot. Lewenhak's argument is confirmed by the Murdock and Provost (1973) analysis, which reveals that around the world pottery-making has been a largely female activity, with the male participation index at only 21 per cent. Pottery ranks as an exclusively female activity in many African tribes, such as the Tiv, the Azande, the Tallensi and the Masai, and has done so in many other societies such as those of the Kurds, the Armenians, the Fijians, the Pawnee and Creek Indians.

Murdock and Provost argue that the growth of occupational specialisation often ends this female domination. In particular, Lewenhak indicates that the invention of the potter's wheel changed the sex of the potter. As in the case of the plough or sickle, this technological development tended to push women into a subsidiary role.

The early history of pottery-making in Britain remains obscure, but tradition within the industry portrays it as having developed as a family trade. Within this, women's major role up to the seventeenth century was the marketing of the ware, although it is likely that wives, along with children, gave general help to the husband-father potter. Occasional women may have practised the potting task themselves, though these seem to have been few in number. A study of fourteenth-century Shrewsbury traces the existence of one female potter, who, as was frequently the case with widows, was practising the craft after the death of her husband (Hutton, 1985). Research by Weathergill (1971) into the Staffordshire industry between 1660 and 1760 also provides sparse evidence of female participation. In the developing factory system children, not women, acted as assistants to the potters, turning lathes and wheels and carrying clay and pots for them. Records of Whieldon's manufactory for 1750–3 record that only one of the forty-three employees was a woman, and at Baddeley's in 1761–2 there was only one out of 129. Early eighteenth-century wills show that there were a few female potters, such as Hannah Simpson and Dorothy Wedgwood, both of Burslem, but they were insignificant in number. However, Weathergill suggests that, in these early days of the reorganisation of the trade on a factory basis, traces of the family system remained, and that in fact wives, sisters and unspecified 'wenches' may have worked as unpaid assistants to the potters: as they did not receive wages from the entrepreneur or master potter, they do not appear in the records.

Factory organisation of the industry on a capitalist basis, as the above study indicates, started unusually early, but this did not involve mechanisation, and traditional hand techniques continued for some time. Indeed mechanisation of the industry proceeded extremely slowly, and was not completed until after World War II. The most notable early development, therefore, was the introduction into the factory of a highly specialised division of labour, with the processes formerly performed by one family being broken down into a large number of tasks performed by specialists in different departments. This innovation is credited to the firm of Wedgwood some time around the 1750s. Up to then, according to Simeon Shaw, the nineteenth-century historian of the industry, a good workman could throw, turn and 'stouk' (put handles on) pots. Thereafter these became separate departments alongside numerous other specialisms. Although evidence is sketchy, it seems to have been at this point that women began to enter the manufacturing process in considerable numbers. This may well have been due to the shortage of labour in the area for a rapidly expanding industry. Shaw comments: 'the Flowerers now scratched the jugs and tea-urns, with a sharp pointed nail, and filled the interstices with ground zaffre, in rude imitation of the unmeaning scenery on foreign porcelain; and in this art women were instructed, as a constant demand was made on men for the plastic branches' (Shaw, 1970, p. 177).

By the end of the century, women dominated in certain departments. Flower-making, painting, gilding, burnishing (rubbing up the gilt with agate or bloodstone), and scouring (rubbing off loose grit or lumps of clay from the ware with sandpaper and brushes) were the main female jobs. Wedgwood also used them in the 1750s to perform the new task of transferring engravings on to porcelain. An official investigation into the origins of sex segregation in industry commented that 'from this time decorative processes have become more and more reserved for women, partly on account of their special aptitude for the work, partly no doubt on account of the lower rate of wage' (PP 1929–30 xvii, p. 15). The latter reason was probably the more cogent, as contemporary accounts emphasise a view of decorating as fairly unskilled work. Jacqueline Sarsby, in her interesting discussion of the industry, quotes Josiah Wedgwood's comment about the burnishing he had seen performed by women at the Chelsea pottery: 'I believe it is neither a secret or very curious art for Women only are employed in it' (Sarsby, 1988, p. 15). Although the talents of individual craftswomen were recognised, types of decorating which were considered more skilled, or particularly artistic, such as designing engravings or patterns, or intricate free-hand painting, were commonly performed by men. The master decorators of the epoch were all men.

By 1800, then, pottery was clearly a mixed-sex trade. The first of a series of government reports that looked at the industry, the 1816 Commission on the Employment of Children, reported that about one third of the children working on the potbanks were girls. But this report, unlike subsequent ones, did not treat sex as an important issue. Later reports focused specifically on the employment of women, and provide an elaborated account of the sexual division of labour through the course of the century.

Almost all tasks in the industry were assigned to men or women only, so that sexual segregation was fairly complete from an early date. In the clay rooms components were ground, mixed, sieved and squeezed through presses. This was considered heavy, mucky work, and was exclusively performed by men. In the 'making' departments men took the main tasks. The thrower, who shaped pots initially on a wheel, had two female assistants beside him. One turned the wheel for him with a treadle, the other, the 'baller', handed him lumps of clay. In the 1850s the thrower, whose work is of course highly skilled, earned 30 to 40 shillings a week while the baller earned eight. Likewise the turner, who milled, ridged and shaped the pot after an initial drying, had a female assistant, the 'treader' who turned his lathe. By the 1850s some lathes and wheels had been mechanised, making the female assistants superfluous, but the hand method continued to be in use as late as the 1870s (Phillips Bevan, 1876). Women continued to do subsidiary work in these two departments carrying clay and ware about.

Men were also responsible for 'pressing', or making hollow-ware (bowls and dishes) and flatware (plates and saucers). This was done on a machine called a jigger. It was normal for boys to start work as assistants in these departments, either as 'mould-runners', who carried moulds full of ware to the ovens and empty moulds back, or 'wedgers', who performed perhaps the most onerous job on the potbank. This involved banging huge lumps of raw clay into a malleable form, by hurling it to the ground from a height.

These jobs were hard and back-breaking and the gruelling life of the young apprentices, who were often brutally treated by their masters, is chillingly described by Arnold Bennett in *Clayhanger*.

> The business of Darius was to run as hard as he could with the mould, and a newly created plate adhering thereto, into the drying stove ... The atmosphere outside the stove was chill, but owing to the heat of the stove, Darius was obliged to work half naked. His sweat ran down his chest and down his back, making white channels, and lastly it soaked his hair ... When there were no moulds to be sprinted into the drying-stove ... Darius was engaged in clay-wedging. That is to say, he took a piece of raw clay weighing more than himself, cut it in two with a wire, raised one half above his head and crashed it down with all his force upon the other half, and he repeated the process until the clay was thoroughly soft and even in texture ... At eight o'clock in the evening Darius was told that he had done enough for that day, and that he must arrive at five sharp the next morning to light the fire ... When he inquired how he was to light the fire his master kicked him jovially on the thigh and suggested that he should ask another mould-runner. (38–9)

Bennett drew his material in part from the autobiography of Charles Shaw whose *When I Was a Child*, reprinted in 1977, describes his early life in the Potteries. He started as mould-runner and wedger, and was then promoted to making handles for a cup-maker.

Another male preserve was the dipping room, where pots were immersed in a glaze containing borax, soda, potash, lead carbonate and sometimes arsenic. This was the most dangerous work on the potbank, leading to terrible illness caused by chemical poisoning, including stomach complaints, bronchitis, consumption, convulsions and complete paralysis of the wrist and arm. The most dangerous task performed by women was scouring, which exposed them to inhaling dust, and led to 'potter's lung'. Anny Williams told the 1843 Children's Employment Commission, 'it stuffs a person up very much in the stomach. Not many scourers live long ... We all feel overloaded upon the chest; sometimes we cough very much, especially in the morning' (PP 1843 xiv, p. c6).

Men were dominant in warehousing and packing, and monopolised furnace and oven work, which was laborious, hot and involved heavy lifting, and required people to work at night. Other male jobs in the clay departments were modelling and relief work (both by hand and with moulds); men sculpted Parian ware and the moulds for what we now call 'Staffordshire' figures. Both sexes were involved in making 'saddles' and 'stilts', little pieces of pot which were placed between the unbaked pieces of ware to keep them separate in the 'saggars' in which they were placed in the kilns. Women were also sometimes employed as spongers and 'scallopers', smoothing or decorating the rims of pots.

In the finishing departments, women had a more prominent role. The majority of painters, decorators, gilders and burnishers were women, although men continued to perform work judged to be more skilled and 'artistic'. In 1851 male painters earned 20 to 50 shillings, female 9 to 12 shillings, and this differential was maintained in 1871, when men earned 42 to 63 shillings, women 14 to 20 shillings (Ginswick, 1983; Phillips Bevan, 1876). Nevertheless, for both girls and boys painting was considered skilled work, requiring a seven-year apprenticeship, which was entered into at the age of eleven or twelve. The *Morning Chronicle* in the 1850s described the occupation as follows:

> Artistic skill, in the higher sense of the term, is, of course, rarely required. The operative requires knack rather than art. To make a good china painter, however, a man (sic) must be endowed with an eye susceptible of the grace of form and the harmony of colour, and he must possess a hand skilled in the necessary manipulation and perfectly steady. The circles formed outside and round the rims of vessels are traced with beautiful steadiness of finger and brush. (quoted Ginswick, 1983, p. 119)

Most firms had separate rooms for men and women painters. In the 1840s, for example, Hannah Barker was in charge of six rooms containing seventy women and children, with only three men working in them, as gilders. At Adams, the management explained 'the males and females, while on the premises, do not associate with each other; each have their separate departments' (PP 1843 xiv, pp. c3, c15). Elizabeth Bates, a twenty-nine-year-old paintress, explained that these departments contained a better class of girl than those in departments who 'mix with the lads' (PP 1843 xiv, p. c87).

Women were also employed in the printing section. Here it was characteristic to work in teams of three or four. The male printer would hire a female transferrer, who in turn hired one or two assistants. The printer heated an engraved plate and printed with it on very thin paper. The cutter, a young girl aged between nine and fifteen, would cut it out, using scissors or a long nail. Then the transferrer would apply the paper to the ware, which was rubbed to make it adhere, and finally the paper was soaked off. Transferring was considered skilled work, and it was traditional for girls to start as cutters, working up through rubbing to transferring. The cutter's job was very much that of a girl apprentice, and these children were required to do a range of other jobs, including cleaning the shop, fetching coals and lighting the fire, fetching water and disposing of damaged ware. The work was onerous, and might start as early as six in the morning. Like their brothers, these girls endured a baptism of fire.

Women, then, performed two types of work. In what was known as the 'clay end' they worked as assistants to men or performed subsidiary tasks like sponging or scouring. These were, one suspects, very much the tasks they would have undertaken when the work remained in a family setting. In the decorating shops, however, they had important roles in their own right, not as assistants to men (except in the print shop). This work was considered skilled and involved an apprenticeship of the traditional kind. Paintresses and decorators, in particular, who worked in segregation from men, were considered to be drawn from a superior type of girl.

From about the 1870s, the combined effect of technological development and factory legislation began to alter the existing division of labour. Clement Wedgwood told the Factory Commission in 1876 that the Factory Acts were forcing his firm, albeit most reluctantly, to employ women and girls instead of boys, so that women were now more commonly found in the clay end, especially in hollow-ware and flatware (PP 1876 xxx, p. 344). Phillips Bevan, writing at about the same time, noted that the traditional male jobs of wedging, mould-running and pressing were being mechanised. This made them easier for women to perform. Mechanised jollies and jiggers for hollow-ware and flatware had in fact been invented in the 1840s, but the men had resisted their introduction, and it was not until boy labour became scarce in the 1870s that they were widely adopted. Their use facilitated the introduction of women. Similarly, although it was reported that some physically tough women took over the old job of wedging by hand, the jug-mill, easily operated by women, was coming to replace that process (Phillips Bevan, 1976; Burchill and Ross, 1977).

Clara Collett's report on women's employment in the industry in the 1890s reveals that change was in progress, but also how slow that progress was. For many decades the old hand processes could be found co-existing with the mechanised ones, sometimes even on the same potbank. In the factories Collett visited women were performing a mixture of new and old tasks. The thrower still had a female assistant, though in the turning department the lathes were steam-powered. Women were working here as spongers, and they were also found assisting the flatware pressers. Children, both boys and girls, were acting as mould-runners, released from school under the 'half-time' system. Women were working as handlers and at 'towing', smoothing plates with tow on a machine called a whiffler. Girls were making cups using the jolly, and others were sorting ware in the warehouses. Women were even to be found in the dipping room, rubbing off glaze. In sum, while women continued to occupy their traditional jobs, especially in the finishing departments, many more were now working in the clay end, in new jobs or jobs formerly reserved for boys. The old pattern of sex-typing appeared to be in decay (PP 1893–4 xxxvii, Pt. I, pp. 61–3).

The process of innovation continued to create new jobs for women in the 1890s. New decorating techniques, such as aerography and lithography involved women; in the production of fireclay sanitary ware, women were used to paint glaze on baths and lavatories. The technique of casting was replacing some of the old forms of 'making', and many women were employed in this new area, increasingly so as the new century got under way (PP 1929–30 xvii).

Table 7.1 Estimated proportion of men and women workers in china and earthenware, 1851–1929

Year	Men	Women
1851	69.5	30.5
1861	68.4	31.6
1871	64.7	35.3
1890	63.3	37.7
1895	61.2	38.8
1907	53.8	46.2
1921	48.6	51.4
1929	49.9	50.1

Source: *PP 1829–30 xvii*

The development of the industry through the nineteenth century, then, involved a slow but steady trend towards feminisation, as the figures in table 7.1 indicate. The figures reflect the fact that, as the 1930 Report on Women in Industry explained, 'whenever a new process has been introduced women have if possible been employed in it' (PP 1929–30 xvii, p. 17).

The process of feminisation was consistently opposed by the men who argued that much pottery work was unsuitable for women, being too heavy and dirty. This opposition started as early as the 1840s, when Charles Shaw's father, a painter and gilder at Davenports, was involved in a strike over feminisation: 'a new manager there introduced new methods of conducting the business. For one thing, he introduced female labour in a department which had hitherto belonged almost exclusively to the men' (Shaw, 1977, p. 89). The motives of the strikers, according to Shaw, were a general distaste for change coupled with the fear of a 'serious reduction in wages'. However, this particular strike failed and Shaw's father was sacked.

In 1867 the hollow-ware pressers declared their opposition to feminisation; 'women are better occupied at home' (Burchill and Ross, 1977, p. 148). Their campaigns had apparently retarded the introduction of the automatic jolly, but ultimately the men's resistance was ineffective. This may well relate to the weakness of union organisation in the industry. Many unions were formed in the course of the century, but few survived long or had extensive membership. The unions persistently failed to win their campaigns against what they saw as the abuses of the industry, particularly the practice of annual hiring and of 'good from oven' (non-payment for pieces of ware which got damaged in or before firing). In view of their weakness, the men may have concentrated their policies on defending what they saw as the key jobs, such as throwing and turning. Burchill and Ross in their history of the men's organisation comment that the skilled and heavy jobs were retained by men, and until World War I 'male and female jobs ... were regarded as discrete, and no doubt family income was regarded as the decisive factor' (Burchill and Ross, 1977, p. 148).

Grieco and Whipp, in their interesting study of women's role in industry, argue that in many pottery families the woman might in fact be the central breadwinner or fill an almost equally important economic role as 'broker', placing family members in different departments of pottery work (Grieco and Whipp, 1986). To drive women from the industry, therefore, would have meant at the least a lowered standard of living for the pottery families, at the most a complete disruption of the existing system of gaining and controlling employment. When male workers are faced with such a dilemma, a common strategy is to try to reinfoirce sex-typing more strongly, even if it means yielding some newly created jobs to women. In this way, men can reduce the threat of female competition and resulting downwards pressure on wages, whilst keeping open employment chances for their wives and daughters and maintaining family income (see Grieco and Whipp, 1986; Bradley, 1987).

In other occupations we have observed that middle-class campaigns over moral issues have helped to secure the removal of women from paid employment. The pottery industry was not untouched by moral scaremongering. The commissioners in 1843 described the throwing and turning rooms as 'emporiums of profligacy', asserting that 'sexual intercourse in these departments is of very common occurrence.' Women in mixed departments were called to witness to the coarse and 'indecent' language used by male workers, and its detrimental effect on women working with them (PP 1843 xiv, pp. 218, c80). Working people were not averse to spreading these reports. Charles Shaw described how while the throwers and turners kept up the old practice of 'honouring St Monday and St Tuesday', young women and male apprentices were left at work alone; 'merriment and frolic were the order of the day.' He claimed that drinking, feasting and horseplay were common in the clay end, and sometimes the girls, excited by alcohol, were induced to stay on at night: 'whoever came early next morning saw a veritable pandemonium ... Men were seen still stupefied with drink, and young women, blear-eyed, dazed, with a stupid shyness dawning upon them, with woebegone faces, and with tumbled and torn garments' (Shaw, 1977, p. 50).

Interestingly enough, similar rumours and gossip marked the potbanks when Jones went to observe them over a hundred years later. Jones believed these tales to be essentially mythic, and considered that pottery workers as a whole were highly respectable, with old-fashioned views on sexual morality. There was a strong tendency to impute immorality to people in *other* departments, labelling them as being of a 'low sort' or a 'rough lot' (Jones, 1961). This was a common theme throughout the nineteenth century (for example, in the 1890s towing girls were described as a 'very rough independent set' (PP 1893–4 xxxvii, p. 62)). Sarsby found the same attitudes prevailed among the women and men she talked to in the 1980s, recalling their work at the beginning of the century: clay end girls were seen as rough, even as 'ladies of easy virtue', while decorators were considered 'posh' and pretentious. One woman, described the clay end as 'horrible'; 'the people are different, shouting and gawping at each other – where we have got to be nice and quiet, it's the posher part ... I used to hate going through, and they're gawping and swearing at the men, and they think they sound big ... (Sarsby, 1985, pp. 72–3).

These sexual scandals, however, did not have the same effect as in mining and agriculture, perhaps because the sheltered and segregated decorating departments offered women the option of respectable and 'womanly' employment within the industry. Nor were the reports of immorality coupled with propaganda about the de-sexing effects of pottery work. The image presented, then, was not strong enough to deter women from pottery, especially as it offered tolerably well-paid and secure work. The male potters were not among the working-class aristocrats in terms of pay, and apparently did not object to their wives working, although in fact many married women did give up their jobs.

There is considerable debate as to whether the patterns of sex-typing I described above can be linked into family relationships, as I have suggested. In a recent paper Bellaby (1986) has argued that the nineteenth-century pottery industry cannot be considered a family trade, since neither were whole families hired to work in it (as in textiles, or, as we have seen, in mining), nor was there any strong tradition of family recruitment, as least until the last decades of the century. Sarsby (1985) takes a similar position, arguing that women's roles in pottery cannot be seen in family terms, since, in the main, women were not employed as assistants to men, but as single, independent wage-earners. Drawing upon the detailed study of family relations within the industry carried out by Dupree (1981), which establishes, for example, that only 20 per cent of potters' wives worked outside the home in the 1860s, she argues that the notion of family connections was an ideological construct, used to reinforce a characteristically paternalist management style and to obscure the importance of women's work in the industry.

Although it is clear that contracts with employers were indeed on an individual not a family base, I believe that, nevertheless, family relationships were of great significance in the industry. Evidence suggests that a family recruitment system was in existence and that family connections were strong within factories. The 1843 Commission spoke of the 'employment of whole families' in the industry, a contention supported by details provided of individual workers. Margaret Powlson, a twelve-year-old thrower's assistant, said her mother was a burnisher, her father a wedger. Ellen Turner's mother was a transferrer and she herself worked as a paper-cutter for her printer father. Her brothers worked as a mould-runner and a turner. James Hulme acted as mould-runner for two days for his father, a bowl-maker, and then for somebody else for the remainder of the week (PP 1843 xiv, pp. 215, c57).

This may not have been the case for all employees, but some sort of family-based recruitment system was certainly reported to be operating throughout the century. In the 1890s Clara Collett reported that throwers' and turners' assistants were mainly married women, 'men in several cases bringing their own wives to work with them', and that in many instances, especially in the printing sector, 'husband or wife or child worked together' (PP 1893–4 xxxvii, pp. 61–3). The work of Grieco and Whipp also reinforces these findings. The family tradition was still strong when Jones studied the Potteries; he reported many families in which successive generations had followed one another into the industry, often in the same department.

Evidence from Dupree's study can bear alternative interpretations to those offered by herself and Sarsby. Although her figures indicate that miners' children were as likely as potters' to work in the industry, they also show that there was a high incidence of family links; of 155 children working in pottery, 87 per cent had an immediate family member in the industry. Intermarriage was quite common, 48 per cent of potters' sons marrying potters' daughters, 41 per cent of potters' daughters marrying potters' sons. Although by mid-century most potters' wives did not work, if they did there was a high probability that it would be in the industry, and the majority of married women potters were potters' wives. Dupree's figures for 1861 show 74 per cent of wives not working, 21 per cent working in pottery, and only 5 per cent employed elsewhere (Dupree, 1981, pp. 141, 156, 174, 181).

Sarsby (1988) also argues that the portrayal of women in the industry as assistants to men, in the way I have outlined above, may be misleading. She believes that these gender stereotypes, as she call them, may be used to mask the reality of the central contributions made to the trade by women as independent craftswomen. This is an interesting view and deserves consideration, especially as we have noted similar processes at work concealing women's activities in agriculture. In industry, too, it may well be that women do a lot more 'men's work' than we are aware of. However, Sarsby does not to my mind produce entirely convincing evidence that this was the case in pottery, in the nineteenth century at least. Here it seems that many women did take assistant roles. However, the survival of elements of family tradition, as outlined above, made it possible for *all* women to be seen, and indeed to see themselves, as subsidiary workers to men even when they were *actually* working on an individual basis as skilled workers. To this extent Sarsby is right. A manufacturer's comment from 1876 neatly encapsulates the local view of workplace relations: 'the work of the men cannot be carried on without the *assistance* of the women and children' (PP 1876 xxx, p. 542, my italics).

Developments in the twentieth century followed the path already set. The 1919 Report on Women in Industry noted that a number of tasks were now apparently performed by both sexes; these included pressing, casting, cup-making, handling, decorating and warehouse work. In all departments, however, it was noted that women were given 'lighter descriptions of work' (PP 1919 xxxi, p. 16). In casting for example (the operation which was replacing pressing), women were said either to help men or to work alone on smaller pieces. Wedgwoods stated that 'in casting, the smaller articles and, therefore, the lighter moulds are given to the women ... Heavy and more responsible work is performed by men' (PP 1919 xxxi, p. 123). Decorating was largely by now an all-female occupation, but men were still used for the more skilled hand work.

During the war, it was noted that some 5000 women had taken over male jobs, in such areas as dipping, turning and plate- and saucer-making. However, it was argued that men and women were still not performing exactly the same work. Women were making the lighter and smaller articles; men carried out traditional hand techniques, while women were given the mechanised versions of those tasks. Although the traditional sexual division of labour was decaying, this emphatically did *not* mean an end to segregation. This confirms the arguments of Braybon and Summerfield, discussed in chapter 2, that processes of dilution were more apparent than real. Jobs were taken apart and reconstructed in such ways that women continued to be assigned the 'inferior' tasks.

Between the wars women continued to make advances: by 1935 there were 30,902 men and 37,635 women employed in pottery. An investigation into the industry noted that women were working on many newly automated tasks, like throwing and turning, while continuing to work as pressers, casters and handlers and in the warehouses. Sarsby (1988) argues that during this period the old confinement of women to 'lighter' tasks was abandoned. Women she interviewed remembered that few men had been involved in casting, while women were producing all sorts of items, including the heaviest. Indeed, at this time, many women managed to become 'missuses' getting access to skilled work and employing their own teams of unskilled women assistants. This seems to have been the high period for women in pottery. The TUC, reporting to the Commission on Equal Pay in 1945, also claimed that women and men were now doing 'identical or similar work', though apparently piece rates for women were a third lower than men's. By contrast the investigating committee reported that in the manufacturer's view the work was still segregated: 'generally it can be said that the articles made by women are the less difficult shapes and the smaller sizes' (PP 1945–6 xi, pp. 69, 70). This distinction could, of course, be used by the manufacturers to justify lower wages paid to women, and it is possible that by World War II segregation was at a minimum level. Certainly male employment had diminished, and only older men, kept on by the paternalist employers, continued to perform traditional 'male' hand tasks.

However, by the time Jones went to the Potteries in the late 1950s, a structure of sex-typing had apparently re-emerged. This post war reversal of a trend was, as we shall see, common to other industries, possibly resulting from the growth of union strength and reputability after the war, which allowed the male unionists to bargain with the employers and ensure themselves of the best jobs.

Jones presents us with a picture of an industry still in the throes of mechanisation and technological change. He found that men were in control of all major 'making' tasks, including operating the semi-automatic systems of potting, using moulds, jollies and jiggers. These jobs he considered to require expertise rather than real skill, but a five-and-a-half to seven-year apprenticeship was still obligatory. In factories other than the one he observed, more fully automatic processes were being introduced, but he does not report on whether this involved the use of women. Girls continued to do some ancillary work, including sponging, which Jones described as 'simple and monotonous to the last degree'. The more skilful task of scalloping was now done by machine.

Engraving was still carried out in the old way, in one-man, three-woman teams. In the painting rooms thirty men were responsible for underglaze painting, while the women did the less testing overglaze work. Nevertheless, this calls for skill: it took Jones an hour and a half to do what a girl could do in five minutes! Women were also employed on a newer process, silk-screening, sticking on tiny, thin prints. Women's wages, ranging between £5 and £8, were still half the male levels of £9 to £14. Jones' verdict on the sexual division of labour could have been applied to 1843: 'either the men were the centre of things, with women doing ancillary jobs, as with the makers and the printers; or else they were a class apart, secure in the mastery of highly skilled trades' (Jones, 1961, pp. 31, 128, 154). Only in the warehouses did women exercise authority over men; here they were responsible for polishing, burnishing, wrapping and examining, while men did grinding (the old female task of scouring) but were mainly employed to carry ware about.

The attitudes of workers apparently played an important part in maintaining gender roles, which were threatened by continued technological development and the degrading of tasks. One older woman had retained her wartime employment as a cup-maker, but, while acknowledging her individual competence, the potters were firm that making was 'a man's job', and resisted the idea of introducing women. On the other hand, a screenprinter told Jones when he tried his hand at it that he was doing quite well 'considering you're a man'! She explained: 'in the nature of things, men could not work as fast as women. On the other hand women could never work as carefully as men. Decorating the china ware, with rich and expensive colours was a man's job. They did it slowly, and they did it perfectly' (Jones, 1961, pp. 35, 110).

Such stereotypical ideas, as we have seen before, are quick to establish themselves. Thirty years previously women painters and designers, such as Clarice Cliff and Susie Cooper, had been pre-eminent in the trade. Susie Cooper was a middle-class girl, imported on the design and management side, but Clarice Cliff was a local paintress made good. She organised a team of girls, nicknamed the 'Bizarre Babes' after the colourful range of ware they produced, who worked freehand on the pots to produce their own original designs. Their creativity and skills earned great profits for their employers, yet, apart from Clarice herself, they received minimal credit or financial reward. As so often the skills of women are obscured and ignored by themselves as much as by others.

The current state of the division of labour is outlined by Sarsby. In 1981 the proportion of women employed had fallen slightly, to 48 per cent. Men perform many of the longstanding male tasks: firing, slipwork (mixing the clay), dipping, mould-making, turning and much of the casting work. In the decorating departments they continue to be given the work defined as creative and artistic, such as enamel painting, while women are assigned more routinised decorating work, mainly lithographing (which has replaced the old form of transferring), but also burnishing and gilding. But they are again more numerous in the clay end: they carry out automated making tasks, sponge and tow, make flowers, cast and dip smaller items and work in the warehouses; these are the jobs into which they have spasmodically penetrated since the 1880s. These are general patterns, but Sarsby stresses that definitions of 'men's' and 'women's work' is extraordinarily variable between factories. A comment from a manager is highly revealing of the arbitrary yet persistent nature of sex-typing: 'I don't think that's the type of job on this particular factory is a woman's job ... In our particular company, I don't think it would work out with a woman as placer' (quoted Sarsby, 1988, p. 139).

Despite this continued fluidity around the border of the division of labour, the physical segregation of men and women is perhaps greater than ever. Only in rare cases do women in the clay end work as assistants to men. By and large, even when engaged in similar types of work, men and women work apart in single-sex groups, often in different rooms. As often in manufacturing, divisions between the sexes are marked by territorial distinctions. The inferior status of women is reflected in pay differentials. As we have seen, women's pay has habitually been a third to a half that of men, and even in 1983 they only averaged 70 per cent of men's hourly earnings (Sarsby, 1985, 1988).

Capitalist development of the pottery industry, then, has been marked in an unusual way by the continual erosion and reconstitution of the sexual division of labour. As Sarsby says, at different times women have carried out virtually every potting task. This has occurred because of the extreme fragmentation, from an early stage, of the labour process, and because the pace of mechanisation has been slow and its application uneven. Hand and machine tasks have coexisted for an unusually long period. However, over time, jobs have characteristically become sex-typed, with men retaining for themselves those generally considered to be heavy or skilled. Although unions have not been very strong or militant in the industry, the extraordinary strength of tradition in the Potteries area has helped the men in this endeavour. While the sexual division of labour remains fluid around the newer jobs and processes, the physical segregation of men and women, apparently voluntarily espoused by both sexes, ensures that 'men's work' and 'women's work' remain differentiated and are not allowed to merge.

8

HOSIERY

In the 1980s the word 'knitting' conjures up a quintessentially female image. Knitting is a skill taught by mothers to little girls and withheld from little boys, who tend to identify it as 'sissy'. For adult women it is one of the most cited activities in surveys of leisure pursuits. According to the General Household Survey's 1983 report on leisure, 48 per cent of female respondents had been engaged in needlework or knitting in their spare time in the preceding four weeks, and Deem in her study of women's leisure in Milton Keynes found knitting to be among the four or five most popular home-based leisure pastimes (Deem, 1986).

It has not always, however, been so exclusively feminine an activity. Fred Boughton, describing his childhood in the forest of Dean, recalled how he and his brothers had been taught to knit as part of a whole package of domestic and work skills which their parents passed on to them as equipment for survival in adult life (Burnett, 1984). Such an experience was not unusual in the nineteenth century; and in preceding centuries, it has been common for old men as well as old women in rural areas to utilise spare time in knitting socks, an activity which could be pleasantly combined with sitting outside the home gossiping, or even strolling about! 'In populous Pennine valleys like Garsdale and Dentdale, and in parts of Wales, both men and women knitted stockings as they walked from home to home and from village to village' (Everitt, 1967, p. 426). Moreover, although handknitting has developed such strong identification with female cultures, the history of mechanised knitting, first on 'stocking-frames' and then on powered machinery, has, in England at least, been dominated by men.

The case of the machine-knitting or 'hosiery' industry bears some interesting similarities to that of pottery. This industry, too, was subject to early capitalisation, with accompanying fragmentation of the division of labour. But, in contrast to pottery, the early capitalist entrepreneurs developed production by means of technical improvements without imposing a factory system until much later, when machines were harnessed to steam power. In fact part of the hosiery industry continued to be run on an outwork basis until the end of the nineteenth century. These processes of change affected the sexual division of labour which had developed in knitting families, as employers tried to cheapen costs by employing women; once again, the defensive tactics of male workers were important in redefining a new sexual hierarchy. As in pottery, the ultimate result was the confinement of women to tasks seen as 'secondary' and the almost total physical segregation of men and women in the factory environment.

Murdock and Provost (1973) have noted the association of women with 'soft' raw materials, predominant among which have been the various threads and fabrics used for making clothes. The provision of clothing is one of the six tasks which Novarra (1980) identifies as almost universally 'women's work'. Among the various techniques associated with garment-making, we should therefore expect to find knitting as historically a woman's task. In fact, the early history of handknitting remains obscure. Knitted caps were available in Britain in the fifteenth century, and it is recorded that the first knitted stockings were brought to England from Mantua in the sixteenth century and copied. Once the technique was known, it became part of the accepted armoury of skills by which women of all classes could provide for the needs of their families, and was a useful 'bye-occupation' for struggling peasant families in the 'proto-industrial' stage of the eighteenth century (Felkin, 1967; Malcolmson, 1981).

The invention of the knitting frame provided the impetus for a new, more commercialised industry. It was invented in 1589 by the Reverend William Lee, popularly said to be his response to a frustrating courtship of a woman who preferred knitting to his attentions! Its commercial potential was soon realised, and a manufacturing system on guild lines evolved, based on London. The guild tried to control entry to the trade, by establishing apprenticeship rules; these expressly forbade women to operate frames, except, as was usually the case, the widows of guild members. This no doubt, also signified a similar customary exemption for wives and daughters. However, entrepreneurs, attracted by the relative cheapness and efficiency of the knitting frame, found the guild restrictions frustrating and started to infringe the apprenticeship rules. When the guild responded with litigation, and the operatives by smashing frames of offending masters, the latter took evasive action by moving into the East Midlands. From around 1710 the industry developed in the 'three counties' of Leicestershire, Nottinghamshire and Derbyshire. The apprenticeship system gradually decaded, as operatives began to employ their wives and children as helpers and a family production system was established.

Production of hose and other knitted goods was now run on a 'putting out' basis. The masters or 'hosiers' owned frames and yarn, which were rented out to the 'stockingers', as the knitters were locally called; finished goods were taken by the knitters, or collected by middlemen and taken, to city warehouses for marketing by the hosiers. The industry generated a large stratum of such middlemen (also known as 'undertakers' or 'bagmen'), many of whom became employers in their own right. Some knitters were found in the towns, but many worked in the villages, where displaced agricultural labourers turned to knitting or supplemented seasonal agricultural work with part-time manufacture. Villages like Wigston and Shepshed became the classic locus for what has been described as 'proto-industry' (see Hoskins, 1957; Levine, 1977).

The sexual division of labour which evolved in the eighteenth century was a classic one, later idealised by both manufacturers and male operatives, although it was quickly to be eroded. In the hosiery household, the husband worked the frame, the wife seamed and stitched the stockings, girl children learned to seam from the early age of five or six (or even three or four) 'as soon as ever a female has judgement enough to know how to take a stitch to seam' (PP 1845 xv, Minutes I, p. 277). Little girls were also set to look after babies, some being sent out to 'nuss and seam'. Boys were responsible for winding yarn on to bobbins, before beginning to learn to knit, which they did sitting beside their father and learning simple processes first, then working up 'by steps' (PP 1845 xv, Minutes II, p. 123). But some boys also learned to seam, or looked after younger children, according to family resources and needs. Where there were no family members, the stockinger would have to pay outsiders for assistance with seaming and winding; according to Levine, this encouraged young stockingers to early marriage and childbearing; a family team was necessary for a viable business.

Hosiery, then is an interesting case of an industry early established on capitalist lines, based on a fragmentation of the production process which utilised the sexual hierarchies of a patriarchal society: inferior or subsidiary tasks were allotted to women, and children were trained within the family for their adult roles.

But capitalist development, though the pressure of competition, also threatened this sexual division of labour. Evidence for the period from the late eighteenth century until 1840s is complex and often contradictory (see Bradley, 1987), but signs indicate that hosiers were employing women as knitters from at least the 1780s. Chapman's study (1967) of hosiery masters suggests that some girls were being taken on as apprentices in the 1770s. Witnesses to a series of government commissions in the early nineteenth century confirmed that some women were operating frames, although disagreeing over the extent and dating of such a change. In 1833

William Felkin, hosier, local historian and amateur statistician, estimated that there were 13,000 men, 10,000 women and 10,000 children operating frames, with another 27,000 women and children engaged in finishing tasks (PP 1845 xv, p. 17). Although this may have been an overestimation of the extent to which the knitting task had been feminised, harder information given to the 1845 Commission on the Condition of the Framework Knitters confirms the trend, as employers enumerated their work force. For example, in one Leicestershire village, Enderby, 26 frames were worked by men, 14 by women and at Alfreton, in Nottinghamshire, 104 were worked by men, 40 by women. By 1855 another report showed that things had gone even further, with two employers reporting that two-thirds of their frames were worked by women (PP 1845 xv, p. 102; PP 1854-5 xiv, p. 290).

In the towns production was by now located in workshops, where an overseer was able to keep an eye on the quality and quantity of work and to prevent embezzlement of yarn, said to be rife in the cottage industry. In her study of hosiery, Osterud (1986) argues that the association of women with the home kept them out of workshops; but some of the evidence gives a different impression. While one glove branch knitter said there were no women in his shop, another spoke of many female employees, predominantly single, all of whom he claimed worked in shops (PP 1845 xv, Minutes I, pp. 24, 87). A *Morning Chronicle* reporter of the 1840s visited workshops where women and children worked on the ground floor, men on the top floor (Ginswick, 1983). There seems little doubt that women had, in fact, made some penetration into every sector of the industry.

The reason why is clear: the employment of women and young people helped maximise profits. Although the industry was based on a piece-rate pay system, women's output was less and they were given the cheaper types of work, so that their wages tended to average about half to two-thirds those of men. This situation was useful to the employers because of a curious and perhaps unique feature of the industry; an acknowledged part of the hosiers' profits came from the 'frame rent' which workers paid weekly on the frames they operated, whether or not they were fully, or even partially, employed. In an industry characterised by demand slumps and overstocked with labour, it paid the hosiers to share the work out thinly over a number of frames. The employment of untrained young people ('colts') and women was favoured as they paid the same rent for their lower output; thus, the employment of women was one of a variety of tactics by which, quite literally, hosiers made capital out of frame rents (PP 1845 xv, pp. 103-4).

This might appear to be a clear-cut case of the substitution of women for men, as part of the logic of proletarianisation, in line with Humphries' arguments discussed in chapter 3. However, the process was more complex. As in other cases, women did not do exactly the same work as men. Within the knitting process, there was a further subdivision into finer and coarser processes: men tended to predominate in the better-paid sectors, requiring greater skill and experience, such as fancy work, while women made basic stockings in coarser gauges on the old-fashioned or 'narrow' frames. Where man and wife worked their frames side by side in cottages, men tended to knit legs, women the tops and feet. Women, in fact, were viewed by the men as inferior in skill or strength. A Leicestershire knitter, Walter Upton, explained the logic of the division of labour:

> I should apply of course for the best work for my own hands, because I am most expert in the business, and if my wife worked, she could not work above half her time . . . They are not so much consequence as we, therefore it is in that way that we look out for the best jobs for ourselves. (PP 1845 xv, Minutes I, p. 194)

One employer explained that when he rented a fine-gauge frame to a man, it was usual for the worker to apply for a coarse-gauge frame for his wife (PP 1854–5 xiv, p. 447). Ideally, these different aspects of knitting could be seen as complementary.

> 'I'm promised a three legger soon, a nice house I've found and shop,
> But without you'r willing Mary, all this happy plan must stop,
> For I want you, that is Mary' – Thomas here began to stutter –
> 'If I get the legger working, will you come to be my footer?'
> (*Hinckley Journal* 1859, quoted Bradley, 1986a, p. 8)

There was considerable debate as to whether women were really less skilled, or whether it was simply that their responsibility for household duties prevented them from spending a full day's work on the frame. Some manufacturers maintained that the best women could equal men in output and quality. However, there was one clear sense in which Upton was right in describing women as 'less expert': women were not given training in the mechanics of the frame. Male knitters, by contrast, were much more than just operators: they knew how to set up a frame, how to get it in trim when it was new, how to adjust it for different fabrics or stitches, how to service and repair it. It was claimed that frames worked by boys, women and old men suffered much more from wear, tear and deterioration, and a woman knitter would need a man in attendance to maintain and adapt the frame (Bradley, 1987). This exclusion of women from technical knowhow was to persist into the factory era and marked a major boundary between men's and women's work. The case lends support to Cockburn's arguments (see chapter 3) that monopoly of technical knowledge is a major device by which male supremacy is secured.

The impact of capitalist industrial development, then, was slowly to break down the established pattern of family-based segregation, by opening up the male job to women and bringing the sexes fairly directly into competition with each other, to a greater extent even than in pottery. This posed a dual challenge to men: it pulled down wages and threatened their economic livelihood in an occupation characterised by under-employment and unemployment, and it jeopardised their patriarchal authority in the home, where men traditionally had directed and co-ordinated their families' labour; in the words of village knitter Storah Wise: 'We consider every head of a family in our village to be the head of his work. We have always been very independent in that respect' (PP 1845 xv, Minutes I, p. 180). Wise's remark illustrates the point made by Sonia Rose in an illuminating article drawing on the hosiery case, that traditional notions of masculinity centred on 'a man's capacity to direct and organise his family's economic contributions because of his possession of skill' (Rose, 1986, p. 125). It is feasible that the allotting of coarse work to women, as described above, was one way in which men attempted to maintain their sense of masculine superiority, rather than being a reflection of lower female capacity. A similar dilemma for men and a similar outcome is described in Gullickson's case study of spinning and weaving in Auffay, a French proto-industrial community; as women moved from spinning into weaving they, too, were given tasks seen as less skilled, making different fabrics from those woven by men (Gullickson, 1986).

The economic aspect was, however, of great concern to the men and their representatives, a few of whom were beginning to move towards a 'family wage' policy (Bradley, 1987). One male knitter considered that 'this female system was one of the greatest evils we had to labour under' (PP 1845, xv, Minutes I, p. 139). But since feminisation was only one of a range of 'evils' against which the male operatives were fighting, their campaign against it was less concentrated (and therefore even less successful) than that of the potters. They were campaigning on a range of other abuses, such as frame rents, middlemen's charges and the use of potentially deskilling technology, the 'wide' frames, which knitted not a fully-fashioned 'wrought' stocking as did the 'narrows' but a flat piece of material from which stockings were cut out and stitched together. This threat to their traditional skill and control was seen, rightly, as more alarming than the erosion of sex differentials.

The move to factory production, which did not occur until the late 1850s, seemed set to continue both these trends of feminisation and task degradation. Male operatives over the past few decades had resisted attempts at reorganisation on a factory basis, resenting the loss of freedom and control and the imposition of regular working times. It was easier to employ women, who were less recalcitrant to authority. Besides, newly invented types of machinery could easily be operated by young and untrained women, as in one of the first successful factories, owned by Thomas Collins. Girls aged thirteen to seventeen were employed on his rotary machines: 'these frames require nothing of mechanical skill. You have nothing to do but to turn the handle by the hand, and any boy or girl can turn these frames, if there is anyone to look after them to see that they work rightly' (PP 1845 xv, Minutes I, p. 138). This enabled him to dispose of his adult male outworkers whom he regarded as 'insolent' and 'saucy' (PP 1845 xv, Minutes I, p. 77). The belated adaptation of hosiery machinery to steam power confirmed this trend; another early factory was run by Thomas Corah who made similar comments: 'in one case a man works one frame and his wife works another; all they have to do is merely to notice that the thing is going on rightly' (PP 1854–5 xiv, p. 202).

The evidence of this and other early factories suggests that young men and women were the first hosiery factory workers, as was the case in cotton textiles (see Gullickson, 1986). However, by the 1870s the sexual division of labour had resegmented, with a return to a pattern quite close to the old family-based eighteenth-century ideal. Indeed one observer reported that it was common for a whole family to work in one factory, distributed through the varying departments 'with one girl left at home to make the beds and cook the dinner' (Cassells, 1873, p. 63). Osterud, in her study sees this, rightly, as the perpetuation of traditional family relationships in a new work environment, although she ignores the extent to which the demand for cheap labour had disturbed those relationships in the intervening period.

In the factories of the 1870s men had returned to dominate knitting, operating the larger and less automated frames. Several types of machines were employed: 'circulars' produced tubes of fabric which were then ironed into shape, and 'rotaries' produced flat pieces of fabric for cutting up and stitching. These machines, which as Corah had explained required little skill in operating, were replacements for the 'wide' frames which had already degraded traditional skills. The most important machine was the Cotton's Patent, the first to produce satisfactory fully-fashioned goods, thus replacing the old 'narrow' frames. This was considered the 'heaviest' and most skilled work. Rotaries and Cotton's Patent were worked by men only, but in Nottingham some women worked with men on circulars. However, the majority of women worked at finishing and warehousing tasks. These 'secondary' tasks, like seaming, stitching, embroidering, buttonholing, folding, pressing, packing, etc., had been greatly increased in number as the move to factories and mechanisation boosted the productivity of each knitter. The proliferation of such tasks may have absorbed the pool of female labour, enabling men to regain the monopoly over the more complex machinery: here they had the added advantage of their mechanical expertise, more important where the actual operator's skills had been diminished.

The growing power of Victorian ideology of separate spheres and 'fit work for women', which we have seen was so important in other areas, also had some influence here. There was considerable concern about the morality of factories, which employers countered by emphasising the respectability of the girls they employed. Muggeridge, head of the 1845 Commission, pronounced knitting 'unhealthy' for women (on dubious medical grounds), while considering seaming 'quite a woman's work' (PP 1854–5 xiv, p. 171). A. J. Mundella, ex-knitter, leading Nottingham hosier and Liberal politician, who was another of the factory pioneers, shared this view, and colluded with union leaders in establishing gender norms for the industry. He believed 'it would be an awful thing to have only women and boys employed in a trade' (PP 1867–8 xxxix, p. 82).

As leading light of the Nottingham Arbitration Board (which he established in 1860 to promote consultation between hosiers and operatives), Mundella had an important influence on the organisation of the trade and had won the trust of the hosiery unions. Drawing on Lazonick's study of the cotton trades, Rose has argued that capitalist employers sometimes disregard opportunities for deskilling, when they wish to use a section of the male work force as part of the structure of labour management, and also to promote a climate of co-operation rather than confrontation (Rose, 1986). This was apparently the case here, at least until the 1880s.

The resulting arrangement of the sexes was a good one for the male operatives. Like the potters, they had found a solution to the dilemma between the desire to have female family members working and the fear of female competition. The men now constituted a core work force of reasonably well-paid knitters (also monopolising the heavy, wet work of dyeing, bleaching and scouring); and their wives and daughters could go on contributing to the family budget by performing subsidiary tasks, some in factories, others in the domestic sector which survived into the 1890s, yet others doing outwork sewing for the factory sector. Women had been returned to their assistant role; an employer in the 1890s characterised them as 'auxiliary' workers, or perhaps 'assisting a man with a machine to run on for him when he transfers to the frame' (PP 1892 xxxvi, Pt. 2, p. 91). The proper gender order had been restored.

As a result of these developments, the proportion of women in the industry rose steadily from 42 per cent in 1851 to 51 per cent in 1881 and 68 per cent by the turn of the century. It was estimated that in 1907 nearly three-quarters of the factory work force were women, while another 25,000 were outworkers.

These figures also reflect renewed attempts by some employers to substitute women for male knitters. This became a major trend in the 1880s and 1890s, when the truce between hosiery manufacturers and unions appeared to break down (significantly the Arbitration Board had collapsed in 1884). There were now available to the manufacturer two versions of the production process. The one established in the 1860s, which I have elsewhere referred to as the 'integrated task' (Bradley, 1987), involved men acting as operators and also doing some of the mechnical work, setting up and servicing the machines. Expert mechanics would also be employed for repair work and more specialised maintenance tasks. As Parr has argued in an interesting paper, such an arrangement rested on the firm conviction of both male employers and male workers that men possessed mechanical aptitude by virtue of their sex (Parr, 1986). The other possibility was to degrade the knitter's task by splitting off the mechanic's functions from the operator's and using women operators with male overseers and mechanics in attendance. Some anti-union firms took this option, often combining it with a move into the villages away from the towns, where it was easy to get non-union labour. One such firm explained, 'they would not allow us to put a woman on, although a woman can work the machines by power just as well as a man; but of course when we moved them to Foleshill we put women on to the machines and employed men to look over them' (PP 1892 xxxvi, Pt. 2, p. 95). The employers preferred women because they could pay them less and also, it was claimed by the union, because they were more obedient, easily terrorised by overseers and managers, who prevented them joining the union (PP 1892 xxxvi, Pt. 2, p. 60).

This struggle between male unionists and the employers over the use of female labour continued right through both wars. In World War I labour shortages meant that the unions were forced to accept dilution procedures and allow women to work on all sorts of machines. During the war the proportion of women rose from 75 per cent to 80 per cent, with 3000 being redeployed on to men's jobs (PP 1919 xxxi). But as in other wartime industries the unions were able to impose their own conditions on the employers: dilution was to be for the wartime only, and on Cotton's Patents one man was to supervise five frames operated by women. Predictably, male witnesses, while conceding that 'on many machines, owing to their intricacy and delicacy, the women are superior to the men', claimed the redeployed women had not been successful: 'in quality and quantity of work the women are not as good as the men. The women do more damage to the machines, they cause more waste, and require more supervision' (PP 1919 xxxi, p. 90). Perhaps this is hardly surprising, as the work normally required a lengthy apprenticeship!

In the interwar years, however, union power and support waned and employers returned to feminisation policies. In 1922 it was reported that about a third of Cotton's Patents in Leicester were still being worked by women. Union campaigns against feminisation reflected both economic and traditional patriarchal motives. A major concern was the erosion of wage levels, but arguments about differential physical capacities and the propriety of using women on work described as 'more suitable for men' were also aired: the countermen (packers and folders) told their employers 'it isn't a proper thing to have a woman at such work' (quoted Bradley, 1987, p. 364).

The economic worries were real enough, for essentially the knitters were fighting to retain their trade in face of the spectre of redundancy raised by reports of factories such as Klingers (a Tottenham firm, outside the traditional hosiery areas and thus remote from union sanctions). Here girls worked a 49½ hour week for less than £2: 'all the machines are worked by women, mechanics do all the altering and repairs etc. Girls straight from school are put with another female for two or three weeks, then put on a set of heads. Klinger is often in the factory, any person not suitable is dismissed at once. No week's notice' (union records, quoted Bradley, 1987, p. 141). It was fortunate for the male workers that technical innovations were favouring twenty-four-hour operation of new types of machinery; the spread of night shift systems, which necessitated the use of male labour, would help keep women from knitting.

The only exception to the men's hostility to women working on men's machines was where daughters (as well as sons) were brought to work as 'helpers' on the larger machines. Where patriarchal family authority was firmly reflected, women's labour was not seen as a threat. Since this was clearly a practice that permitted the seepage of women into the trade (just as in the domestic period) it might be viewed as economically irrational, but demonstrates how firmly rooted was attachment to the idea of the family work-unit under the male head, as we have also seen in the pottery case.

In the meantime the majority of women continued to work on tasks traditionally seen as 'woman's work', jobs requiring 'sharp eyes and deft fingers' and 'close attention' (Bradley, 1987, p. 149). Some of these jobs, as in the pottery industry (and in cotton textiles), took on the character of female 'trades' or 'skills', although they never achieved comparable status or rewards to male skills. Among these were the jobs of 'overlocking' (the mechanised version of seaming) and 'linking' (known in America as 'looping'). The latter involves closing the toes of stockings. While a machine does the actual closing, the linker has to 'run on' the minuscule loops to points on the machine. With the use of fine man-made fibres in the 1930s this became a most demanding job, and, like other female skills, was acknowledged to demand great expertise and experience, if it was to be done effectively and at sufficient speed. These skills assigned to women, however, as Westwood argues, are of the kind which women are considered to possess 'naturally'; thus they are ranked inferior to skills assigned to men which have the character of being culturally acquired (see chapter 3). So much is this the case, that many commentators argued that the skills were in fact hereditary, passed from mother to daughter.

Skilled hosiery workers cannot be trained in a week or two, nor is there any other area of the country where girls and women have that intangible something which makes them not just operatives but good operatives. Employers have argued the pros and cons of heredity for years, but they are faced with the indisputable fact that in the Leicester area hosiery workers, particularly women, have nimble fingers, sure hands and adaptability. (Leicester Corporation handbook of the 1930s, quoted Bradley, 1987, p. 149)

Linking, in particular, was considered to be 'in the blood': 'either you are a born linker or you aren't' (King, 1948, p. 149).

The hosiery case provides particularly clear and interesting evidence of the ways in which notions of skill are socially construed and manipulated to benefit powerful groups. Another good example was countering, which became a male monopoly from the 1870s. This job consisted of processing stockings after their return from the dyeing departments: pairing, folding and packing them. The work was originally performed by women, but in the East Midlands became entrusted 'only to men who have had long training and have acquired a more accurate eye' (PP 1863 xviii, p. 269). The skill was considered to lie in the ability to match pairs exactly. Yet, since 'good eyesight' is considered a female physical attribute, it is hard to see how the counterers could support their case that the job was unsuitable for women, and indeed in other locations (for example in Scotland and America) the job was performed by women without any opposition.

Not surprisingly, employers tried to use women as counterers, despite union resistance. The agreements made in Hinckley during World War I are another interesting indicator of the persistence of the family labour tradition and of how notions of skill and the sexual division of labour were involved with patriarchal family authority: 'a female relative of a counterman, if not already employed in the hosiery trade, may be introduced by him and taught by him; he will draw the wages of both and make his own arrangements with the female for her portion of the remuneration' (PP 1919 xxxi, p. 133). The struggle over countering persisted right up till the 1960s, when automatic machinery for pairing was developed, thus eliminating the core skill. The task was then further degraded into pairing, folding and packaging, each performed by different workers, often women. In hosiery factories today counterwork is one of the few mixed jobs, though within each factory custom often dictates that the team of packers is single sex.

World War II brought a return to dilution policies, under similar conditions, but in 1945 the various small local hosiery unions joined together to form the National Union of Hosiery Workers, which entered immediately into national negotiation with the employers. Agreements over apprenticeship rules and the operation of three-shift systems acted to exclude women from 'male' knitting tasks. There was a return to the climate of co-operation and compromise of the 1870s, whereby employers accepted the claims of the core group of male knitters. In addition, acute shortages of female labour in the postwar era of economic reconstruction meant that the available women would be channelled into the traditional female tasks. Linkers, in particular, were in desperately short supply. The job required two to three years' training, and one study found that nine out of ten recruits failed to master the skill (King, 1948). Curiously employers never tried to solve the problem of the undersupply of skilled female labour (which has persisted through to the 1980s) by raising wages to a par with men's! Apparently the convention that women shall only earn about two-thirds of men's wages is sacrosanct.

A report by the Board of Trade in 1946 gives a full picture of the sexual division of labour at this crucial strategic juncture. Seamless and fully-fashioned stockings were knitted 'principally' by men. Both sexes knitted socks, but although women's output was as high as men's per machine they were allowed to operate only three-quarters the number of machines. Women and girls did finishing work and operated glove machines, said to need 'close attention, good eyesight and nimble fingers'; attempts to train men for this work had failed. Indeed, the report specifically mentioned the difficulty of getting men to do tasks traditionally designated as 'women's work' (and thereby considered inferior). Overall, women were operating smaller and less advanced machines, although these might require considerable skill (Board of Trade, 1946, pp. 33, 36, 53).

In the years following the war, some women who had substituted for men retained their knitting role, and others continued to be employed on smaller machines. However, by the time Sallie Westwood conducted her observation at 'Stitchco' there were no female knitters in this large hosiery company. The traditional divisions in the industry, between males as knitters and women as sewers, males as core workers and women as assistants, have been largely re-established. My own interview with employers in sixteen firms revealed that only a quarter employed female knitters, and in all cases only one or two. In three of these factories a two-shift rather than three-shift system was operating: protective state legislation has now a key role in hosiery in maintaining sex-typing. However, custom is also crucial. This dictates that all work on sewing machines is done by women; managers reacted strongly against the idea that men might become machinists, seeing it as a 'sissy' job': 'you can imagine what boys would feel about being a machinist' (Bradley, 1986b, p. 109).

At 'Stitchco', as in many hosiery factories, an almost complete physical segregation of the sexes is maintained through sex-typing (Westwood, 1984). The practice of men and women working in different departments, often on different floors, prevailed in the 1870s, in line with Victorian ideas on propriety, and has persisted into the 1980s. Only in very small factories do constraints of space ensure that men and women work side by side. Westwood has vividly described the gendered work cultures which evolve; their sex-specific rituals, customs, forms of talk, also act as a barrier to the breakdown of segregation and sex-typing. Managers asserted, no doubt correctly, that people prefer to work with their own sex: 'if I were a woman, I'd want to be in a garment factory with lots of other women' (Bradley, 1986a, p. 22). They also believe that black and white workers work better apart, and it is not uncommon to find departments, even whole factories, segregated by race.

In the late 1980s hosiery, in common with most industries, is beginning to feel the effects of computer technology; computer-controlled knitting machines can be programmed to run different patterns and weaves, removing much of the need for skilled workers to set them up and adapt them, just as in engineering; computer-aided cutting machinery can do away with the skilled and dangerous work of cutting with a band knife. The machines are costly and are being introduced very slowly, but clearly their application could lead to another attempt to introduce women as knitters; one manager admitted to me that it would be in his interest to use semi-skilled married women on the new machines. If the male unionists fail to maintain their position, this could lead ultimately to a virtually all-female industry, unless there is a compensatory movement of men into 'women's jobs', which, as we have seen, appears unlikely. Masculine self-images and stereotypes are set firmly against such a desegregation.

The possibility of a feminised industry appears more probable as this development has already occurred in other countries. In Scotland a small and long-established knitting industry, centred on Hawick, was from its initial stages based on women's labour. In the domestic period women operated knitting frames, and with the move to power continued to work as knitters, even on large machines. According to the president of the Hawick manufacturers, before World War I 80 per cent of labour on Cotton's Patents was female, with all other work done by women, except for scouring, pressing and packing. Girls started work at fourteen, and gradually learned to operate machines, although, even here, they were not totally in command of techniques: 'generally a woman does not look after her machine as well as a man, and on the power frame requires more overlooking. In some cases an extra mechanic is necessary' (PP 1919 xxxi, p. 90). Although this was seen, rather curiously, as increasing the cost of production, shortage of male labour in the area made it likely that women would go on being knitters.

As this case indicates, it was open to manufacturers to choose either the 'integrated' or the 'degraded' version of the knitting task. The latter option tended to dominate in Canada and America. Joy Parr's research into the Canadian industry portrays knitting as an ambiguously gendered task (unlike seaming which was unquestionably seen as 'woman's work') (Parr, 1986). The Ontario firms she studied were in the early twentieth century using both men and women as knitters, but, despite a shortage of female labour which meant recruiting English hosiery workers to the mills, they seem to have preferred to use women; presumably this enabled them to keep wages down. Employers used both knitting options. Parr describes how in the daytime women and boys operated machines, with male 'fixers' (setters up) and mechanics in attendance; on the night shift (from which, as in England, women were barred) men performed the integrated task operating and 'fixing', aided by male mechanics. The use of the more automated machinery from America favoured this flexible approach.

Male workers and the employers colluded in the notion that while men 'controlled' machines women only 'cared for' them. But despite the stress on their mechanical superiority, men received no more pay than women and they were unable to influence the pattern of work organisation. The major cause of this difference from England seems to have been the lack of unions in the industry up to 1946, when men began to flex their industrial muscles; however, in this postwar period there were better-paid options available outside what essentially had become a feminised industry. The fact that any male knitters at all were retained may be ascribed to the presence and influence of foremen and technicians from England, who favoured English custom and wanted to retain the image of knitter as craftsman. Indeed, Parr makes the interesting point that engineeers and technical innovators had a crucial role in furthering the collusion between male workers and employers; their literature and their descriptions of machinery propagated the image of the knitter as male.

In America the industry had a long history and the sexual division of labour was subject to great fluctuation, with a strong tendency to feminisation. According to Baker (1964) production of knit goods was a woman's task up till the end of the eighteenth century, when men began to operate frames. With the move to power frames (called looms in America) both sexes operated machines, with women quickly penetrating into a range of knitting tasks, especially on the more automatic and smaller machines; in 1850 women and girls were 64 per cent of the industry's employees, while they were still only 42 per cent in Britain. Fully-fashioned knitting machines, however, were not introduced until the 1870s and these, Baker tells us, were invariably operated by experienced men. But they were never as important in the industry as the more automated circular machines of various types. Meanwhile, as in Britain, numerous female tasks had been created, 'light handwork such as mending, stamping, sorting, folding and boxing, which called only for dexterity, exactness and willingness to repeat a series of simple movements all day long' (Baker, 1964, p. 21). 'Topping' and 'looping' were higher-ranked female specialisms, although they had originally been performed by men, with bleaching and dyeing the major male monopolies.

As elsewhere, where women worked knitting machines mechanics were needed to set up, repair and service the machines, though women were able to replace needles and bobbins and keep the machine producing correctly. This was the case when women moved into fully-fashioned work during World War II; by 1943 95 per cent of knitters were female (the fully-fashioned sector being smaller than in Britain). Although it was considered that men's 'technical knowledge and aptitude for mechanics' (Baker, p. 141) would continue to recommend them as preferred labour after the war, this did not prove to be the case. American employers have chosen to use more highly automated techniques and to break down the task into maintenance and operation, in the Canadian fashion. The strength of the British trade unions and their ability to build an agreement with their employers seems a major factor in accounting for the greater persistence of the integrated pattern in Britain, along, perhaps, with the fact that the New World economies provided a wider range of highly paid opportunities for male workers.

The hosiery case reveals very clearly, then, the socially constructed nature of gender-assigned tasks and skills, which can be differently allotted and developed in different cultures, using broadly similar technologies; but it also reveals that while 'male tasks' can be permeated by women (where employers are motivated to cheapen labour costs and tighten control, and where men are not able to organise successfully against these developments), 'women's work' is relatively impermeable by men, stereotypes of masculinity being firmer than those of femininity, or, at least, more desperately clung to – by men!

More than any case we have previously looked at, hosiery shows the possibility of an occupation being feminised, with women taking over work close to that performed by men. However, we should emphasise again that the work was not identical; for when women are brought in they almost always perform tasks which have been reorganised, degraded or technically transformed; there is no simple substitution. In this industry, then, as in the others we have so far viewed, we see the sexual division of labour shifting and collapsing, but this does not mean in any sense an end to sex-typing, as transformed jobs simply switch from being 'male' to being 'female'; while, once jobs have had the stigma of being characterised as 'woman's work', in manufacturing at least, it proves remarkably hard to get men to do them.

9

SHOEMAKING

There are many resemblances between the boot and shoe industry and the hosiery industry. In both cases the traditions set in the family were important in shaping the sexual division of labour and a family-based system of outwork lasted into the 1890s; in both cases male unionists fought to retain the jobs they saw as theirs and the employers tried at times to use female labour on new machines as they were introduced. The major difference is that the men of the boot and shoe industry had built up over the years a much stronger and more determined union organisation, along with a tradition of resistance to innovation, which enabled them to hang on to their traditional 'male' jobs much more successfully than the knitters had done. As a result, shoemaking presents us, in the case of Britain at least, with one of the firmest and most enduring examples of sex-typing within manufacturing industry, in marked contrast, say, to pottery, where the boundaries between men's and women's work were so constantly being redrawn.

By tradition, shoemaking in Britain was one of the more firmly male trades. According to Lewenhak (1980), cutting of leather has been a task monopolised by men in most societies, contrasting sharply with the processing of textiles. The toughness of the raw material may have something to do with this, for it requires more strength to cut out pieces of a shoe than pieces of a garment. Murdock and Provost (1973) have noted the frequent cultural identification of hard materials with men, soft with women. The association of skin and leather with the hunting and slaughtering of animals may also have helped to make their primary processing a male responsibility. However that may be, in medieval England most shoemakers (or sutors and cobblers, as they were also called) were men, though there is evidence that women were also in the trade. For example, there were three 'sutrices' in Oxford in 1380, and one in the West Riding in the same period (Clark, 1982). Fourteenth-century Shrewsbury, where no female shoemakers were recorded, may perhaps have been more typical (Hutton, 1985). Snell's research on apprenticeship suggests that numbers increased over the centuries; in seventeenth-century Southampton eleven girls were apprenticed to cobblers, four to cordwainers (Snell, 1985, p. 280). But as in most craft occupations, women were the exception rather than the rule (see chapter 2): for example, Snell's sample of parish apprenticeships in the eighteenth century showed five girls apprenticed to cordwainers to thirty-three boys.

Women appear to have entered the industry in larger numbers chiefly through the progress of subdivision. Under the traditional apprenticeship system, the young shoemaker would learn to carry out all the operations involved in making a shoe, boot, slipper or sandal: cutting out parts, assembling them and preparing the footwear for sale. One man would 'make through' each pair of footwear. However, within the family it made sense to hive off some of the simpler tasks to women and children, since assembling a pair of shoes was a lengthy process. Certainly by the nineteenth century, and probably long before that time, the wives and children were assigned certain less skilled tasks; children were set to 'stabbing' (making holes for sewing) and women to sewing together the pieces of the upper ('closing' or 'binding'). Some finishing jobs, such as ornamentation, fitting of laces, eyelet-making, were also done by the women. As capitalist interests gained hold of the industry and factories and workshops were set up, women and children continued to perform these tasks, both as outworkers and in the factories.

The first shoe factory was opened in Stafford in 1787, but progress in this direction was very slow. A more immediate effect of capitalist development was, as in the case of pottery, to effect a subdivision of the shoemaking process so that the workpeople became specialists in certain operations only. It may be useful here to describe the various processes involved in making a boot or shoe. As reorganised by the capitalist entrepreneurs, the industry was broken up into four separate departments. First was the cutting or 'clicking' department, traditionally the most skilled part of the job; considerable experience and expertise were required to cut pieces economically out of the hide and to fit pieces to the grain of the leather. Allied to this work was 'rough stuff' cutting, the cutting of soles and heels, which was a low-status job. The second department was 'closing', the area where women entered the industry, though men also performed this task, especially in the case of heavier footwear such as men's boots or Wellingtons. Thirdly, there was the task of 'making' or assembling the whole shoe. This involved several steps; the upper was shaped on a last and fitted to the insole; linings were inserted; finally the sole proper and the heel were attached. This last process had traditionally been performed with an awl and thread, but in the 1850s a process of riveting was introduced which opened up the possibility of using less skilled labour. In general, however, these tasks retained the label of 'skilled' work and were said to be beyond the capacities of women. Finally, in the finishing department, a wide variety of tasks to complete the shoes were carried out: burnishing, waxing and polishing, 'knifing' (trimming round the edge of sole and heel), 'scouring' (smoothing the sole), inking and glazing the heels and fitting various trims. For many of these jobs it was claimed that considerable strength was needed. The workman had to press the shoes hard against his chest, which was said to be very detrimental to health, and thus unsuitable for women.

These four departments formed the basis of organisation of the industry throughout the nineteenth century, and the same system largely prevails today. The major change is that many of the finishing operations, now mostly performed by machines, have been incorporated into the 'making' stage: the finishing department is now usually known as the 'shoe room' or stock room, and work there is mainly of a light nature, such as cleaning, labelling and boxing.

Most women and children were drawn into the industry through the family. The *Morning Chronicle* correspondent who visited Northampton, a key area of production, in the 1850s wrote of the shoemakers' families: 'If there are any children at home, they will be certain to be found – whether male or female – occupied in some department of the shoe trade' (quoted Razzell and Wainwright, 1973, p. 8). As the industry slowly moved into factories and workshops, closing continued at first to be largely done 'outdoors', in the workpeople's homes. But mechanisation hastened the move to 'indoor' production. The sewing machine was adapted to stitching leather in 1852, and this promoted a major upheaval in the industry. Its introduction disturbed the male workers. The 1860 Select Committee on Master and Operatives learned that in Leicester and Kettering, two rapidly expanding newer areas of shoe production, which concentrated particularly on women's shoes, 'people who knew nothing about the shoe trade whatever, and, if I am rightly informed, girls and boys and women who never saw a shoe made, scarcely, now work these machines in making shoes' (PP 1860 xxii, p. 246). The introduction of the sewing machine eventually pushed men right out of the closing sector, where they had formerly performed the heavier work. Women were employed in the closing department at first in teams of three, two 'fitters' to each machinist: the fitters' job was to hold the upper pieces in shape for the machinist to sew. In later years these pieces were pasted together. By 1864, for example, Walkers factory in Leicester was employing 300 females who worked twelve hours a day, earning from 10 to 14 shillings a week. Another factory safeguarded the respectability of its female recruits by providing separate entrances for the two sexes, who also had different dinner times. Conditions in these newly built factories were generally agreed to be much better than in the small workshops where much of the making and finishing was still carried out, and where the worst of 'sweated' conditions prevailed (PP 1864 xxii, pp. 165–6). In these squalid and unhealthy workshops young boys were apprenticed as clickers, riveters and so forth; in some cases hand closing was still carried on here, but in 1865 it was reported that few parents were prepared to let their sons train as closers, since it was clear that sewing machines were rapidly making this technique redundant (PP 1865 xx).

Writing in 1877, Phillips Bevan confirmed the growing dominance of women in closing: 'although mainly the occupation of a man, women have of late years largely found employment, owing to the universal use of the sewing machine' (Phillips Bevan, 1877, p. 142). His figures show that, whereas in the older age groups men outnumbered women in the trade by ten to one, among the under-twenties a third of the work force was female. By the time of the Sweating Commission of 1888 it was reported that closing was 'invariably done by females', while in some factories women were also doing trimming jobs in the finishing departments (PP 1888 xx, p. 102; xxi, p. 106).

The story of the industry's development is complicated by the fact that the old family-based 'outdoor' system survived alongside the more mechanised factory sector until the end of the century. The spread of the many labour-saving machines, which now were being used in American factories, was slow in Britain, and strongly resisted by the workmen. In his survey of the industry at the end of the century, Head (1968) reports that until the 1890s closing, making and finishing were all frequently performed outside the factories, either in the homes or in workshops (especially in the London area). During this period the male workers managed to retain their virtual monopoly on the other three departments. Despite constant attempts by manufacturers to break the apprenticeship system and use cheaper labour, clicking, knifing and lasting retained some of their skilled status.

This male monopoly did not go entirely unchallenged. Phillips Bevan reported in 1877 that in one factory at Newcastle-under-Lyme shoes were being made almost entirely by machine; women were employed, on lasting and making as well as closing. Similar thinking was evinced at Clarks factory in Street, Somerset, as outlined in a company history: 'some savings in labour could be obtained by a more radical allocation of work between men and women. The division of the sexes between "binding" and "making" involved a somewhat arbitrary assessment of their relative capabilities. In the case of light footwear ... there were no physical reasons why women should not be able to assist in the "making" (Sutton and Sutton, 1979, p. 23). The authors describe how women were used in the making of children's shoes, although it is interesting that they were apparently as reluctant as men to see changes in the traditional practice introduced: 'some women were with great difficulty persuaded to learn the art,' they report.

Clarks was a highly paternalist factory in a remote rural area, which had succeeded in keeping unions out, but in many shoemaking areas the industry had a strong tradition of union activity and worker militancy. Hobsbawm (1984) has documented the history of the 'radical shoemaker' which goes right back to the pre-industrial period, but reached its zenith in the struggles against capitalist reorganisation of production. Cobblers and shoemakers were at the forefront of many of the protest movements of the early nineteenth century. Their unions fought persistently against the introduction of new machines and techniques, the use of cheap boy labour and the destruction of traditional skills. In the earlier decades of the century the men fought fiercely to retain the outwork system which gave them control of the work environment. 'Once within the infernal walls, once the damnable system is established, and your social degradation is secured for another generation, and you will leave your poor offspring a legacy for which they will curse your memory' a handbill of the Boot and Shoe Workers' Mutual Protection Society of the 1850s proclaimed (quoted Bythell, 1978, p. 215). But by the 1890s union leaders had switched their policy, fighting now to consolidate the factory system; they believed this would increase the power of the union and put an end to the wage-cutting tactics of sweatshop owners. Their struggles culminated in the great lockout of 1895, when the National Union of Boot and Shoe Operatives (formed in 1874) clashed head-on with the employers. Although that particular confrontation ended in compromise and weakened the union, it also resulted in the adoption of arbitration procedures and centralised bargaining; these paved the way for national agreements safeguarding the jobs of the men against feminisation.

Men kept women out of the male departments on the grounds that most of the work was too skilled for them to manage. Clicking was considered too dangerous, and other jobs required too much strength. It was, ironically enough, the men themselves who had allowed the women into the industry, through enrolling their aid as workers in the family. But they seem to have conceded the closing work without much effort, perhaps because of the nature of the work, the use of a needle being seen as a female skill. In the words of the Clarks' historians, 'a needle, some thread, a steady hand and strong eyes were the essential requirements in this tedious work, for which girls and housewives were ideally suited' (Sutton and Sutton, 1979, p. 16). Alan Fox, in his history of NUBSO, argues that the men's resistance to this idea of operating sewing machines was the root of women's takeover in this area (Fox, 1958); the sewing machine had quickly become associated with female labour, a factor which may have heightened the men's distaste for it.

Since the 1860s, the degree of feminisation in the industry has tended to reflect the relative proportions of traditionally 'male' and 'female' jobs created in any period, rather than being an indication that women were taking over male jobs, as in the pottery industry. The 1871 Census recorded 253,739 men in the industry and only 27,716 women (although it should be noted that part-time working and housework of women tend to be under-represented by the Census). Mechanisation of some of the male processes, which took place in the 1880s but gathered pace in the 1890s, following the lockout, led to a relative decrease in numbers of male jobs; while the spread of mass-produced fashion shoes for women increased the number of stitching and trimming jobs for women.

This pattern of change continued into the twentieth century, although there was also some absolute expansion of women's jobs in finishing. The 1919 Report on Women in Industry noted that 99 per cent of closers were women, but so also were 65 per cent of stock-room workers, engaged on treeing, cleaning and boxing. Average wages in 1906, according to the report, were 28 shilling and 8 pence for men, 13 shillings and a penny for women, a very typical differential; women and men rarely performed comparable tasks, but in the odd case where this occurred in stock rooms and closing departments, men earned 32 shillings on average, women 17 shillings.

Prior to World War I, it was estimated that there were about 110,000 men and 56,000 women in the industry, which demonstrates the effect of mechanisation since 1871. Over the wartime period the proportion of women increased to 43 per cent, 12,500 extra women being employed, and it was estimated that 11,000 to 15,000 women had moved into the men's departments, including the 'dangerous' clicking department. However, this did not necessarily imply a complete breakdown of sex-typing. As in the pottery industry, it was reported that in each department men carried out the harder and heavier tasks, women the lighter, with extra supervisors employed to look after the women. The Bristol branch of NUBSO, from an area where, we are told, the outwork system still lingered on and women 'generally worked as partners to the men', a couple receiving £3 a week joint pay, nevertheless found the changes unacceptable; 'some of the men's jobs which women are doing are not suitable for them,' they complained (PP 1919 xxxi, pp. 58, 92, 103, 105). The example reveals the workers' attachment to the family work system, which died hard; Cadbury et al. (1906) reported similar arrangements in Birmingham.

After the war women returned to their departments as had been agreed, although in 1930 it was reported that in Northampton, where male labour was short, women were operating some machines, such as sole-makers and heel-compressors, elsewhere operated by men. Census figures for 1921 reveal the combined effect of mechanisation and wartime dilution; 37,103 men and 33,776 women were recorded in the industry (PP 1929–30 xvii, p. 32). In 1946 the Equal Pay Commission estimated that the proportion of men to women had subsequently restabilised at three to two, and that departments remained highly segregated, although a new balance had been struck. Men retained clicking and press (soles and heels) work, lasting and many finishing operations where machines were involved. Women, however, now dominated in the stock rooms, with responsibility for glossing and packing shoes (PP 1945–6, xi, p. 73).

World War II again brought a labour shortage. Solutions of employing extra women, or alternatively of lengthening hours, were rejected at first by NUBSO. They feared that an increased burden of work would lead to absenteeism among the women (Summerfield, 1984). Inevitably, some dilution did eventually take place. The proportion of women rose from 35 per cent in 1924 to 42 per cent in 1935, thence to 44 per cent in 1947 and 46 per cent by 1951 (Fox, 1958, p. 586).

Betty Ferry, born in Hackney in 1922, described for a local history project her career in the shoe industry. She started work in 1936, at first in all-female departments, closing and sewing linings. Then she moved into finishing, inking soles, which boys would then wax, painting soles while boys operating buffing machines to smooth them. However, as the wartime labour shortage began to bite, she moved to a factory producing children's shoes: 'One could do several jobs here as they were short of staff owing to the fact that most of their workers had been called up for the forces. I started off by inking round the sole of the shoe. I was taught Buffing and Kegging, Buffing soles, Back Tacking and Pulling Over. I also did machining' (Hackney WEA, undated, p. 113).

We have clear evidence of the men's resistance to the expansion of female areas during these years. In 1913 the claims made by NUBSO for the coming year's National Agreement, included a call for the 'elimination of the tendency (which had given the Council some minor worry for some years) to introduce female labour into the clicking and press, lasting and finishing departments' (Fox, 1958, p. 345). The employers refused to accept this clause, but the agreements made in World War I probably helped to secure the men's position. NUBSO at first opposed female dilution, but was obliged to concede it, though under strictly regulated conditions similar to those made in the hosiery trade. It must be done only with union consent, only when men were unobtainable, and only for the duration of the war; women must be given the male rates for jobs they took over.

The attitude of NUBSO to women is exemplified in the comments of Leicester clickers' leader, Hill, who urged that the union should 'stand first for the men', although he claimed that as a married man he had 'a certain amount of respect for the ladies' (Fox, 1958, p. 370). The Bristol branch also demonstrated an obstinate separatism: 'there is a sentimental objection on the part of the men to women being in the same room as the men and men supervisors prefer to supervise men as they can discipline them more easily.' They made explicit their beliefs about male superior skill: 'women are not experienced enough to cut leather, which is done by the men. Pressing is not women's work at all. It is too heavy and the machines are complicated and dangerous. Finishing is absolutely unfit for women' (PP 1919 xxxi, p. 105).

In 1930 the NUBSO Annual Conference demonstrated its continued resistance to feminisation with a motion expressing 'determined opposition to female labour being engaged on operations hitherto performed by male labour' (quoted Fox, 1958, p. 485). This was reaffirmed in the National Agreement of 1938, showing that the men had increased their influence with the employers: 'it is undesirable that females should be employed amongst male operatives in the clicking, press, lasting and finishing departments, in which male labour is now almost exclusively employed' (PP 1945-6 xi, p. 73).

After the war, an interesting reversal occurred in Leicester, where it was reported that 'men are taking women's jobs'. A *Daily Mail* article told of men entering 'the closing department and stockrooms which at one time were jealously-guarded domains of the women'. This situation arose because of the labour shortage which also had affected the hosiery industry; the reporter speculated that girls had been seduced away from Leicester's two traditional industries by their more agreeable work experience in engineering and munitions factories; now they were loath to return to their traditional female jobs where tight piece rates and the pace of the sewing machines forced them to frenetic activity. This may be true, but the tenor of the piece is interesting in suggesting (as did the earlier case of Clarks' closers) that women could be as conservative in their attitudes as men; previously they may well have relished their 'jealously-guarded' pre-domination in the 'female' departments as much as men did theirs in the 'male' ones (*Leicester Industrial Handbook*, 1946, p. 36).

Sex-typing was eventually re-established, although it may be that to attract women back into the industry manufacturers were forced to raise the level of female wages. Fox reports that in 1955 women were getting 74 per cent of male rates, a higher figure than in any of the industries we have studied so far. By the time Goodman, Armstrong, Davis and Wagner studied the industry in the 1970s, a solid division of labour was again in evidence. Clicking, now done by electronically controlled presses, is still an exclusively male task, as is making. Women do closing and predominate in the stock room, carrying out cleaning, spraying, repair work, inspection and packing. Making now includes injection moulding, and technological change is concentrated in the male departments, so that the proportion of women continues to rise. In the postwar period women constituted 50 per cent of the work force; by 1975 they had increased to 56 per cent. Lack of strength is still given as the reason for women's exclusion from clicking and lasting (Goodman et al., 1977).

Turning to the American industry, we can perceive some interesting similarities with the British case, and some illuminating differences. In the colonial period, as in pre-industrial England, shoemaking was a male craft; the European migrants brought over the craft tradition, along with some of its militancy. As in England, women were drawn into the industry as closers, 'binders' in the American usage, although there is disagreement as to when this happened. According to Baker (1964), before 1800 all the work was done by men, either singly, or, during the War of Independence, working in a team. She claims that women did not start to work in the family at binding and trimming until about 1800. Matthaei (1982) states that women were only drawn into production as the work moved on to a putting-out entrepreneurial basis, which promoted subdivision of the production process, as in Britain. If this is true, there is clearly a strong argument to be made that in both countries it was the advent of capitalism which opened up this work for women. However, Wertheimer (1977) has a different version, by which women are claimed to have been binding shoes in the home from 1750 onward, and from what we know of the colonial household, with its tough, hard-working ethic of self-sufficiency, this is at least plausible. Wertheimer also provides evidence that, as in England, some women worked as shoemakers in their own right. In this version, women had penetrated the trade before capitalism took firm hold.

According to Wertheimer, the invention of the wooden 'shoe peg' in 1811 enabled women and children to carry out the 'making' of light shoes and slippers. This development is indicative of the tendency for American shoemakers to be less resistant to technological change than the British, or at any rate less successful in resisting it. All the major inventions which transformed the industry were American, and mechanisation proceeded at a far more rapid pace. As a result there was during the nineteenth century, as Lewenhak (1980) argues, a continual switching of some jobs between the sexes, as employers experimented with the new machines. Men operated some of the sewing machines (those for stitching heavier leather) when they were introduced in the 1850s, claiming that they were too heavy for women to operate (a sharp contrast with the British case). However, machines for lighter-weight shoes were easier to handle, and women operated these. The effect of the spread of machines, however, was to reduce the proportion of women in the industry as the productivity of each binder was sharply increased; in contrast, the male 'cordwaining' jobs remained unmechanised. In the following decade the proportion of women fell from 31 per cent to 23 per cent; there were 32,949 women, 72,305 men in the industry in 1850, while in 1860 there were 28,515 women with the number of men increasing to 94,515 (Baker, 1964, p. 29; Wertheimer, 1977, p. 86).

Machines for the various making tasks were introduced in the 1860s. Women were used at first on one of these, the Mackay sole-sewing machine, particularly during the Civil War period. However, according to Baker, 'it proved too heavy for them to manage', as was the case with the Goodyear welt machine, invented in 1872. Men took over these machines, and thus the traditional division of labour reasserted itself, similar to that in England. Women in the main stuck to binding and sewing linings, although they did assist in some of the preparations for lasting (Baker, 1964, p. 29). At this stage, shoemaking still retained some traces of its origin as a family trade, according to Wertheimer: 'entire families worked making the shoes, men and women performing different work' (Wertheimer, 1977, p. 169).

By the mid-1870s only lasting and clicking were not mechanised, and in the next decades machines for these processes too, were devised. In 1882 a lasting machine was invented, while from the 1890s clicking was performed using metal dies (Head, 1968). These changes mean a swing back towards feminisation, so that by 1911 a third of the work force was female. The 1900 Census pointed to the expansion of women's employment: 'women are largely taking the places of men ... in the operation of the lighter kinds of machinery' (quoted Baker, 1964, p. 29). By now, the industry was highly subdivided, there being some 150 separate operations. The trade had basically lost its skilled status, which may have facilitated the influx of women. However, the changes did *not* imply the breakdown of sex-typing. According to Baker, the dividing line between men's and women's work was still 'only slightly dimmed': 'by long custom men invariably did the heavy, clumsy but exacting work of cutting the leather, linings, and trimmings, and women performed the intricate stitching operations on the dozens of cut pieces – each process on its own group of machines, each operator doing one sort of stitching and no other' (Baker, 1964, pp. 30, 157). Men and women were rarely in direct competition for jobs.

Baker throughout her account seems to accept as truth the idea that women were incompetent or physically unfit to perform certain jobs. This was the argument of observers from the United States Bureau of Labor who reported in 1915. Lasting, for example, was seen as heavy, unpleasant work: 'there is no question of its unfitness for women. Most of the operations must be done standing – muscles of arms and backs are subjected to constant strain' (quoted Baker, 1964, pp. 157–8). Yet in the course of the war women 'managed' to perform many of these male jobs, including some of the clicking work.

As in England, the idea of the unsuitability of girls working in the 'men's department' was a deterrent to using them in some of the subsidiary tasks, and this may have helped to maintain the boundaries of sex-typing. Matthaei refers to an interesting study conducted by Helen Sumner in 1910. A survey of thirty-one factories revealed that 99 per cent of employees were in jobs working with their own sex only; of 3964 workers, there were only 10 women in 'male' jobs, 7 men in 'female' jobs and only 39 in jobs which were not clearly sex-typed (1 per cent) (Matthaei, 1982, p. 212).

In America as in Britain, the long-term force of technological change has been to increase the proportion of women. In 1960 57 per cent of the industry's work force were women; only clicking, lasting and machine maintenance remained male monopolies. These areas are far less labour-intensive than the female stitching departments. The major difference between the two countries was that in America the faster pace of mechanisation more frequently raised the possibility of the use of women on new processes and machines, with a less solidly effective union organisation to oppose such changes. Nevertheless, over the decades the traditional pattern of sex-typing continued to re-emerge, just as in Britain.

An interesting diversion from that pattern was found in Australia, which challenges the assumption made by Baker that the traditional male tasks really *were* beyond the capacity of women. The hand system of production persisted in Australia up to the 1890s, but here, although the male head of household was responsible for providing materials, measuring the client, co-ordinating the work and marketing and transporting the shoes, all the actual processes of making the footwear were performed by women and children. An extraordinary reverse occurred with the switch to factory production: women were relegated to the role of assistants to the men as a result of agreements between the male workers and the employers. Although some of the men actually conceded that the women were more skilled, they were pushed into the subsidiary work of stitching: thus many of the skills they had used when working in the home were abruptly snatched from them (Game and Pringle, 1983, p. 9).

The behaviour of male unionists, then, has been particularly instrumental in this industry in confining women to certain jobs and maintaining a strict gender segregation. Economic motives were paramount here; it is notable that, by comparison with other occupations we have looked at, there was minimal fuss or 'moral panic' about women's employment in the trade. The strict segregation of male and female departments, which, in the early days, often had separate entrances, probably prevented scandal arising. The fact that the main female task was sewing also helped define this work as one that was 'fit' for women.

Perhaps as a result of the male intransigence, this industry, uniquely among those we have so far studied, was marked by a militant, if sporadic, reaction from women workers; both in Britain and America groups of women attempted to fight back by demanding equality with the men, although, being less powerfully organised, they failed to make much impact on the behaviour or attitudes of the men. In America women shoebinders organised their own separate union, the Daughters of St

Crispin, in 1869. The union called for equality of pay: 'we demand for our labor the same rate of compensation for equal skill displayed, or the same hours of toil' (quoted Wertheimer, 1977, p. 170). This was a progressive enough demand for that era, but even more radical was the union's challenge to the idea that the type of work performed by women was inferior. The Daughters declared it to be 'equally valuable and efficient'. Unfortunately, the union collapsed in the depression years of 1873–7, and later the women united with the men in organisation, many of the radical activists joining the successful but short-lived Knights of Labor organisation (Wertheimer, 1977).

In England women were slower to realise the benefits of union organisation. Fox disparagingly describes the female closers of the 1860s and 1870s as 'weak in bargaining power and indifferent towards attempts to improve it' (Fox, 1958, p. 21). But by the beginning of the twentieth century NUBSO had made considerable headway in organising women: by 1917 about 20,000 of its 69,000 members were women. As we have seen, the policy of NUBSO was firmly oriented towards defence of male interests, and the organisation of women was a defensive move, to ensure solidarity in time of industrial action, rather than a recognition of women's special plight. There were, however, two attempts by women in the early twentieth century to improve their position vis-à-vis the men. In Leicester, the women's case found a champion in the fiery shape of Lizzie Willson, who, influenced by the feminist and suffragette activities of the time, fought to get the union to acknowledge the claims and interests of women. In Fox's disapproving words, 'Lizzie Willson was conducting, in fact, not only a class war but a sex war' (Fox, 1958, p. 309).

While conceding that women were right to see the male unionists as not taking their claims seriously and caring only for women's organisation in so far as it affected their own interests, Fox describes their reaction as hysterical and over-belligerent, following the 'largely psychopathic' example of the suffragettes. Male leaders were enraged by Lizzie Willson's activities; 'a man is not fit to arbitrate on a woman's cause', she declared in 1911, a statement which, no doubt, would have been seen as merely conventional if the nouns had been reversed! The separatist strand in her thinking culminated in her leading a breakaway female union, the Independent National Union of Women Boot and Shoe workers, which survived World War I and lasted through to the 1930s; in 1920 it had 1300 members, an indication of the support for Lizzie Willson's stance among women (Fox, 1958, pp. 309–12).

After the war the women's cause found another spokeswoman in Mary Bell-Richards, the wife of a prominent Leicester unionist. Although formerly supporting the men's line, she became convinced of the need for special organisation for women, founding a Women's Social Club in Leicester. At the 1922 Annual Conference she declared 'the sex-war in our

Union is forcing women to look well after themselves first' (quoted Fox, 1958, p. 484). She campaigned throughout the 1920s for an equal minimum wage with men, and, even more radically, for all departments to be opened up to women. The greater numerical strength of the men ensured that her motions were rejected.

Although these attempts failed to uproot the male sense of superiority, they indicate that in a context of general industrial militancy women had developed a strong awareness of their own situation, recognising that the low pay and limited opportunities which they encountered did not arise merely from the exploitative behaviour of the employers, but also were the product of the policies and attitudes of male unionists and workers; there was indeed a 'sex-war' to be fought. No other group of industrial workers we have studied so far seems to have reached a comparable state of feminist consciousness; for this we must look at the white-collar occupations where middle-class feminist influence was felt.

The shoemaking industry, then, presents us with a strong example of a persistent pattern of sex-typing. It is not altogether clear what originally brought women into the trade, whether it was a direct result of capitalist re-organisation, an indirect response to family poverty caused by proletarianisation, or whether its origin was in pre-industrial family work patterns. But once in, women were confined to certain jobs, and, despite mechanisation, the pattern has largely persisted unchanged since 1800. This stable pattern of sexual segregation has been maintained by male trade union action. In America, where the pace of mechanisation was faster and organisation less co-ordinated, there was greater fluidity in the sexual division of labour, but here, too, a similar pattern of sex-typing has in the long term prevailed. This, along with the Australian case, not only illuminates the important part played by unions in sex-typing (see Hartmann (1976) and Rubery (1980)), but also indicates the power of international precedents in shaping developments within a nation.

10

THE NEW INDUSTRIES

In all the industries so far considered, practices and traditions existed which long predated the advent of capitalist industrialisation. In this chapter we turn to industries producing new types of products, or producing them in a form only made possible by industrial advance. These have jointly been referred to by commentators as 'the new industries' and, perhaps inevitably in light of their lack of traditions, they have received less attention from researchers than the older industries. Some pioneering work is, however, now being carried out by Miriam Glucksmann (1986).

As we have seen, the sexual division of labour in the areas we have studied was highly dependent upon relationships and work practices in the pre-industrial stage. In the new industries, where no such traditional practices had been established, it might be supposed that relationships of a more equal nature could be established between female and male workers. This, however, was not the case. With remarkably rapidity, the new industries produced a structure of sex-typed jobs, which in many cases showed a more rigid sexual segregation than did older industries. Employers, given a free hand where no existing labour customs impeded them, organised labour processes in ways which used male and female labour differently.

These ways were noticeably consistent between the new industries, which pioneered, in Glucksmann's phrase, the 'prototypes' of new forms and relations of production, involving low-skilled assembly-line work (Glucksmann, 1986, p. 34). I have chosen to illustrate these developments by examining three industries, for which there is some reasonable degree of documentation in the Parliamentary Papers: tobacco, confectionery and electrical goods.

Tobacco

The tobacco industry straddles the line between 'old' and 'new' industries. Tobacco, although a fairly recent import to European societies, had been produced and processed before industrialisation. However, industrial technology enabled it to be used for new products, notably cigarettes.

In colonial America, cigar-making was a household industry performed by farm women as an additional source of income. It was, of course, done by hand. Women did it, according to Baker 'because the work was not heavy and skill depended on manual dexterity and a sensitive touch' (Baker, 1964, p. 32). Taxes imposed on cigars in 1861 provoked a general move into factories. Although the first cigar factory (opened in Connecticut in 1810) used only female labour, more commonly men were employed, especially for the skilled jobs. Superior quality cigars were made by male 'craftsmen', who performed all operations: shaping the 'bunch' of tobacco, binding and wrapping. With lower-quality goods women might be involved, but notably on less skilled operations, such as stripping the leaves, rather than rolling. Slave women and children were often employed at this work (Baker, 1964; Wertheimer, 1977).

From the late 1860s the division of labour altered, partly because of the use of immigrant tobacco workers from Bohemia (where tobacco production was done by women) fleeing from the Austro-Prussian War. Young Bohemian girls worked in teams, each performing a separate operation. Another European import was the wooden mould from Germany, which deskilled the work of shaping. The percentage of female workers rose from 10 per cent in 1870 to 28 per cent by 1890; by 1900 they constituted over a third of the work force (Wertheimer, 1977, p. 160).

The use of women, then, was linked to the process of subdivision, although originally women had been 'skilled' enough to perform the whole task. In the 1880s female employment was promoted by the introduction of tools and machinery for stripping tobacco and cutting wrappers. Women operated these machines, and soon only the best cigars were handmade by men. The Cigar Makers' International Union tried at first to keep women out, but had to admit defeat. As for the manufacturers, they maintained that women could equal men in attaining the 'highest possible skill' (Baker, 1964, p. 34).

The introduction of automatic machines in the 1910s confirmed the shift to female labour. Four unskilled women (often young girls) operated each large machine. Men took on a new role as mechanics and maintenance workers: also they worked as packers and selectors where it was claimed that considerable experience and judgement were needed in estimating the quality of handmade cigars (a claim reminiscent of that made by hosiery 'countermen'). However, as the standardised, machine-made product became dominant, male jobs were lost; by 1961 75 per cent of cigar workers were women (Baker, 1964, p. 168).

Other areas of the industry experienced similar developments. The manufacturer of tobacco (for chewing and pipesmoking) was earlier mechanised. Women and girls worked the semi-automatic machines, especially in the South, where slave women were preferred. In 1880, half of these workers were women. The making of snuff, however, was a male monopoly; according to Baker, this was the 'most complicated and oppressively odorous' tobacco-processing occupation. As so often, work defined as physically demanding and unpleasant was assigned to men (Baker, 1964, p. 30).

Cigarette-making, a classic 'new' industry, being a later development, was highly mechanised from the start. Men were used for heavier work, and for jobs requiring mechanical knowledge, while women operated lighter machines, also working as strippers, packers and labellers: these latter two have standardly become women's work in all 'new' industries. By 1940 women were 63 per cent of operatives, rising to 70 per cent by 1950. However, since that time the use of machines to replace the tedious job of stripping (taking leaves from stems) has led to a proportional decline in women's jobs. By the 1960s Baker found that women had ceased to operate the giant cigarette-making machines, though they worked in large numbers as 'catchers' (scooping cigarettes off the belt of the machines) and in packing. It may be that the association of men with technological mastery, as in other occupations, enabled them to regain jobs they had previously been in danger of losing (Baker, 1964, pp. 169–70).

Developments in Britain showed some similarities to the American case, and some differences. Since there was no pre-industrial tradition of women's tobacco processing, the first tobacco workers were men. In 1843 it was reported that there were no girls or women in the tobacco factories (PP 1843 xiii, p. 18). Parliamentary reports provided a detailed account of how things had changed by the 1860s. Roll tobacco and cigars were being produced. In the 'spinning' of roll tobacco, three children were employed per spinner. They were also working as packers and making 'bunches' of leaves for cigar-making. In Newcastle, Leeds and London girls as well as boys were employed. The work was described as 'very light and simple' and thus suitable for girls (PP 1865 xx, p. 80). Girls were employed turning wheels for spinners ('no skill or strength is required for this work'), stripping and 'pointing' (handing bunches to spinners). The male workers were responsible for training the children. This system, essentially a form of sub-contract, enabled women to penetrate the industry. Some were already working as strippers.

Employers readily explained the reasons for using girls. A London manufacturer explained, 'It is only lately that I have taken girls instead of boys to pack tobacco, I prefer the girls ... All our girls stop with us until they get too big for the wages we give' (PP 1865 xx, p. 82). Girls were only paid between 2 shillings and 6 pence and 4 shillings per week. In Liverpool Copes were employing 285 women among their 385 workpeople. They explained, 'the reason of our having so many girls is simply that our men had a dispute with us about the number of apprentices, and we did not choose to be dictated to. Now the only men we employ are the few who did not turn out when the rest did. So far as the work goes, girls, after some years' training, do it as well as men'. The girls were taken on at fourteen to serve a seven-year apprenticeship, just like boys. The firm did, however, find some disadvantages: 'they are more difficult to manage; it is entirely a matter of coaxing with them; if they are blamed, or put under strict orders, they prefer to go away; they do not fear the loss of work, for all look forward to marrying' (PP 1865 xx, p. 90).

This uncharacteristic departure from the stereotype of female docility is perhaps related to the Liverpool culture, where other types of factory work were available to young women. Another manufacturer, Mr Steel, who had first employed girls in 1850, was solving the problem by taking a firm line: girls were fined for singing or even talking at work, since, when he first employed them, 'they would curse and swear and dance around the room refusing to work' (PP 1865 xx, p. 92). Even now he considered them prone to 'hysterical fits', especially during menstruation, and he was faced by systematic pilfering practised by the girls as a group: even bodysearching was to no avail, as no girl would inform as to which of her fellows had let fall a plug of tobacco from her dress!

Subdivision, then, was one of the factors leading to feminisation, along with a version of subcontract which in many ways reintroduced into a later technology the practices of family employment systems; male union tactics also hastened the feminisation of the industry. By 1876 this trend was confirmed. In Glasgow it was reported that the employment of women was rapidly increasing and that boys were 'nearly the exception now'; at thirteen they preferred to leave the factory to learn a trade, while girls, without aspirations to skilled work, would remain (PP 1876 xxx, p. 706). At the Bristol factory of Wills and Co. girls predominated two to one. The factory manager gave interesting evidence of the Victorian taste for gender segregation: 'we find that they do not work well together in the same factories and we must either go in for all boys or all girls' (PP 1876 xxx, p. 649). Phillips Bevan, writing at the same time, noted that over 30 per cent of tobacco workers were now women; stripping he described as 'a work generally done by girls and women and involving a certain amount of skilled labour and dexterity' (Phillips Bevan, 1877, p. 186). Cigar-making was now largely a female job, requiring 'much experience', while tobacco spinning was essentially a male preserve.

By the 1890s this division of labour had stabilised. In Liverpool men sometimes made cigars by hand, but the bulk of less skilled, subdivided 'mould work' was done by girls (as in America). The elderly male workers were described as 'survivals of a time many years ago when men were employed'. In Scotland, it was noted that women and men never came into competition for jobs: men were spinners, women strippers and packers (PP 1893–4 xxxvii, Pt 1, pp. 68, 285). Details of elementary school leavers in the tobacco towns show how the industry had developed. In Bristol, 62 girls were entering the industry as opposed to 12 boys, in Liverpool 92 girls to 28 boys. In the newer centre of Nottingham no boys were going into tobacco work, compared to 48 girls (PP 1899 lxxv, pp. 40, 59, 66).

The War Cabinet's 1919 Report on Women in Industry gives a detailed picture of the first two decades of the century. Before the war cigarette-making by hand and packing, tobacco stripping and spinning and packing by hand and machine were 100 per cent female jobs; cigarette machinery operating and overlooking, tobacco cutting and drying were 100 per cent male. As in America, men had taken over the new cigarette-making machinery. Only in the making of 'plug' and 'bar' tobacco was there any overlap between the sexes. During the war, women took over about half of cutting and drying work, and three-quarters of cigarette machinery work; but in the latter teams of women were led by male supervisors. It was argued that in some jobs women's output was lower and they needed constant supervision; but it was conceded that on machinery their output equalled that of men. Nonetheless, after the war, by 'unwritten obligation', it was intended to return to prewar customs (PP 1919 xxxi, p. 114).

The industry was now seen, however, as 'primarily a women's trade' (PP 1919 xxxi, pp. 15). In 1928 72 per cent of the industry's workers were women. However, as in America there was a tendency for men to take over the larger types of machine when they were introduced, displacing numbers of handworking women; thus, by this stage is was claimed that the cigarette trade would never return to being an exclusively women's task as it had been in the handmaking era (PP 1929–30 xvii).

Information as to the current division of labour in the industry is provided by Anna Pollert's study of Churchman's tobacco factory in the 1970s. The company manufactured hand-rolling and pipe tobacco, plus the old specialities of plug, roll and chewing tobacco. Almost all work in the factory was performed in segregated departments. 'Wetting down', blending and cutting (the preparatory stages) were highly mechanised; men worked these machines. Women performed labour-intensive tasks: weighing, stripping, spinning and packing. Weighing was done by hand and by machine; either way, this was fiddly work requiring 'finger-tip precision and flying speed' (Pollert, 1981, p. 30). The male job of spinning had passed to women, as we have seen, at the beginning of the century, but was still classed as skilled work. These craftswomen were each assisted by a 'bundler', just as in the nineteenth century. Pollert comments:

The actual work was concentrated and incessant, doing the seemingly impossible task of spinning tobacco into a long unbroken cord – A slight hesitation and the bobbin would break the thread. Too little pressure and the roll would go bumpy. The spinner was a specialist craftswoman, with considerable control over her machine, but not on par with a 'skilled craftsman'. (Pollert, 1981, p. 32)

The job, in fact, is a classic example of the way skills are downgraded in status as women acquire them.

In the tobacco industry, then, a fairly continuous process of technological change has produced a rather flexible structure of jobs and corresponding shifts in the sexual division of labour. Overall, though, it can be seen that subdivision of jobs has resulted in increased proportions of women being employed: these have persistently been assigned to jobs seen as light or unskilled, men being made responsible for heavier work and for new machinery where technological knowledge is seen as relevant.

Confectionery

I have chosen confectionery as illustrative of the various food and drink-processing industries which have become in the twentieth century a major employer of women. In Britain in 1981 food, drink and tobacco employed some 270,000 women. Although not much information is available for these industries, what I have been able to find is interesting in illustrating the way in which men have persistently acquired control over jobs defined as skilled, even where this conflicts with prevailing wisdom and imagery about gender roles.

When Phillips Bevan conducted his survey in the 1870s the food and drink industry was in its infancy. In the canning and preserving factories which were just being developed in England and Scotland, three-fifths of the workers were female. A striking characteristic of these industries, as they developed, was that, despite women's vaunted superiority in the domestic sphere and the almost worldwide identification of women with the preparation of food in the home, most of the actual cooking tasks were done by men. According to Shorter (1976), the one task peasant men never performed in pre-industrial France was cooking; yet when food production moved out of the home into the public sphere men became the chefs and cooks, with women assisting as servers and cleaners; in food-processing industries, in the same way, men performed the core tasks with women confined to packing and doing the 'fiddly' bits.

The manager of a jam factory gave an interesting account of his rationale for employing men as jam-makers:

Men were more reliable in cooking the jam at an exact temperature with the aid of a thermometer. Women would trust to the look or smell and cook it as they would do in their own homes. The men who make the jam are paid high wages as skilled workers. (PP 1893–4 xxxvii, Pt I, p. 241)

Here women's expertise in the home is seen as a handicap in the factory, and a reason for denying them access to a more technological kind of expertise, which is then taught to men. In jam-making women were confined to washing containers and filling them, labelling and packing.

Similarly, in the early chocolate factories in Bristol and Birmingham it was reported that the numerous young girls employed there had nothing to do with mixing the chocolate and cocoa, which were considered skilled male jobs. The girls were confined to wrapping and packing; ornamental box-making was the best-paid female job at the Bournville factory. Like other factories employing young women, this was a highly paternalist institution. It provided the girls with a playground, a sick club, good cloakrooms and dining facilities, with a district nurse available. The girls were made to wear white Holland dresses for the sake of cleanliness in handling the confectionery. Thus a protective female environment was created for the young workers: 'the women work entirely apart from the men and are supervised by forewomen' (PP 1893–4 xxxvii, Pt I, p. 54).

By the 1900s these industries had become more mechanised, which increased the proportion of women. In 1890 women were 16 per cent of food and drink workers; this had risen to 36 per cent in 1928 (PP 1929–30 xvii, p. 6). In 1919 it was reported that men did the 'heavier work' such as jam-boiling and 'practical confectionery' (PP 1919 xxxi, p. 15). Women did everything else. They were attractive to managers because of their cheapness, and, it was reported in 1930 because of their dexterity, neatness and cleanliness: it was claimed they were suited by 'temperament' to sweet-making (PP 1929–30 xvii, p. 30). Thus they were employed in every possible process, except those which were seen as requiring 'physical strength and skill', notably mixing and transport.

The 1929–30 Report on Women in Industry referred specifically to the paradox of women's role in the food industries: 'though woman is the baker in the home, the baking trade has always been in the hands of men' (PP 1929–30 xvii, p. 21). In biscuit work men were assigned the task of mixing doughs, said to be highly skilled; this was justified on the grounds that it involved training, experience, and exposure to dangerous machinery. Women, however, were considered competent to take over operation of the new machines, first worked by men, which were entering the food industry, such as packing machinery. This nicely illustrates how men regularly succeed in manipulating the way in which women are allowed access to technology.

Comparable processes were observable in the USA. Wertheimer (1977) records that women contributed 50 per cent of the labour in the canning industry, but the actual cooking was done by men, while women washed and prepared the raw fruit and vegetables, put them into cans when cooked and labelled them. Baker, too, notes that in the transfer to the factory women had lost their traditional central role in food-making. Within the food industries, confectionery has become the second biggest employer after canning. By 1960, 50 per cent of confectionery workers were women. There is, predictably, a highly sex-segregated division of labour: men make the sweets and chocolate centres, women dip them in chocolate, using machinery or by hand, also performing decorating, packing, wrapping and inspecting tasks. Once again this division of labour is justified by Baker in terms of natural attributes.

> Women are especially adept at hand-dipping expensive chocolates. They work with candy centers and a small vat of melted chocolate or other icing machinery which must be kept at exactly the right degree of fluidity. They drop the candy center into the vat, then with great finger deftness lift it swiftly out of the chocolate, twist or twirl it to give a smooth uniform coating, stroke on a decorative, identifying mark ... and perhaps put a nut, a cherry, or other garnish on the top. (Baker, 1964, pp. 189–90)

Less expensive confectionary is coated automatically, and here women provide merely an identifying twist, using fingers or a forcing-bag with nozzle.

Such jobs as these are typical of women's work in food-processing. Thus, in the industrial sphere, women's contribution to food preparation has become marginalised: men or machines (increasingly the latter) do the mixing and cooking, and women are left to put the cherry or the icing on the cake.

Electrical Goods

Electrical goods production is perhaps the prime example of the 'new industries'; it is the one which Glucksmann particularly concentrates on in her study and which she claims to exemplify the development of a new pattern in the sexual division of labour which was to become paradigmatic of twentieth-century production methods. Today it is still a major employer of women, at least within certain areas and processes.

The earliest experiments in electrical production were carried out in Germany and America. Among the first products were cables and other equipment for the telegraph industry. In the 1850s Siemens in Germany was making electrical equipment such as insulators, batteries and instruments. In America in the 1890s Swan Edison started production of electric light bulbs and by the 1900s domestic appliances were being made.

Not much information is readily available about the earliest factories, but it seems that these enterprises, which were making goods for industrial consumption, originally employed only men. Siemen's London factory had twenty-five employees in 1861, all men (Scott, 1958). In 1881 the Electric Light and Power Generator company in London employed only men (Byatt, 1979). Edison's first lamp factory started with men only, making lamps by hand (Baker, 1964). However, as the industry expanded it rapidly became highly mechanised, and at the same time smaller products, characterised by fiddly assembly tasks, were developed. Women seem to have immediately taken up these jobs.

Techniques of production were developed in Germany and American and then introduced into Britain. It is not surprising, then, that in all these countries we find a similar division of labour. Women have been used for assembly tasks involving the manipulation of tiny parts and fine wiring, and also on assembly-line production where jobs are unskilled and repetitive.

Baker tells us that in America by 1910 women had become 36 per cent of the work force in the new electrical consumer industries. In certain jobs there had become predominant; in her words: 'technological advance combined with skill and patience enabled women practically to take over electric lamp manufacture' (Baker, 1964, p. 194). As stated, the first lamps were made by men. These workers had to be able to work with glass and wire, and to have some grasp of the scientific principles involved. Their products were costly and Edison soon redesigned his process to allow it to be done by machines. Soon 80 per cent of lamp-makers were women.

Mechanisation and subdivision in these areas proceeded with immense rapidity. In lamp manufacture by 1927 there were 237 operations required for making the socket alone. All these were done by women, who also wound and mounted filaments, tested lamps, made fuses and switches and so forth. World War I expanded the employment of women even further, where they took over from men and retained many of the jobs after the war. In the interwar period the consumer side of the industry expanded enormously. Women were involved in wireless assembly, putting together speakers, transmitters, receivers and condensers, while men's role was to assemble consoles and make cabinets. Television in its turn provided more female jobs after World War II such as wiring, soldering and other assembly tasks. By 1960 women constituted 40 per cent of the industry's workers (Baker, 1964, pp. 195–203).

As these processes and products were introduced into Britain a similar division of labour evolved. Before World War I it was noted that women were working in branches of electrical engineering where work was 'comparatively light' (PP 1919 xxxi, p. 8). This tendency was confirmed during the war as women were pulled into the manufacture of dynamos, switches, meters and so forth. As in American, women retained these jobs after the war and were also employed in gramophone and wireless production. The Report on Women's Employment summarised the division of labour.

Where work is hot, heavy, dirty or wet, or where skill only to be acquired
through long training is needed, the processes are for the most part carried
out by men ... Light repetition work requires little training, is undeniably
remunerative, and is preferred by women to work which requires a long
course of training. On the other hand it is a blind alley unsuitable for men. (PP
1929–30 xvii, p. 24)

Presumably women were considered quite happy to enter a blind alley!

A comprehensive picture of women's employment in the industry in the
1920s and 1930s is provided by two contemporary studies. The *New Survey
of London Life and Labour* reported the increase in women in the London
engineering and metal trades, from one in fifty in 1891 to one in five in
1929. Women were concentrated in 'virtually new industries', and the
research confirmed that 'the greater part of this work has been done by
female labour since its inception, although it provides employment for men
in the capacity of skilled maintenance engineers and as general labourers'
(Llewellyn Smith, 1931, p. 134). In lamp-making, men were supervisors
and maintenance staff; young women worked in teams at rotating tables
on the assembly. They were paid on a group piece rate, earning between £2
and £3 per week. The job could be learned in two or three weeks, and the
reporters considered it 'suitable' for women as the operations were fine,
requiring 'good eyesight and neat fingers' (p. 165). The work could be
hazardous, however, because of flying glass particles, indicating that the
protective impulse towards women demonstrated by men and the state
was somewhat selective in its application.

In the electrical instruments sector, women did 'light' work such as
assembling telephones or winding coils. In wireless production, the picture
was as in America: women were involved in 'earlier and simpler stages' but
'as the set nears completion it is taken over by male assemblers' (p. 168).
Women worked in battery production preparing zinc sheets, shaping and
soldering them, while men dealt with heavier zincs, prepared carbons and
fitted terminals. Women sealed the batteries with tar and wax. The
researcher's comment on these jobs is revealing as to the way women's
industrial employment was developing: 'the female labour is to some
extent interchangeable with other factory occupations, such as jam
making' (Llewellyn Smith, 1931, p. 170).

A similar picture emerges from Plummer's 1937 study of British
industry. In cable-making he noted that the lighter machines were
operated by women, the heavier by men of varying degrees of skill.
Women's work in batteries he considered to be 'easily learnt' requiring
little more than a 'combination of care and quickness'. Women were
banned under the Factory Acts from much of the work on accumulators
because of the use of lead, but did some packing and assembly tasks. In the
radio and motor accessory trades there was 'much light repetition work
with automatic or semi-automatic machinery, and a good deal of assembly

of small and light parts, all of which lends itself to the employment of female labour' (Plummer, 1937, pp. 59, 60, 67). Young girls, in particular, were found in many of these jobs. Glucksmann notes that in the period 1930–5 71 per cent of these women workers were under twenty-four (Glucksmann, 1986, p. 26).

This pattern persisted through subsequent decades; by the 1960s women were 42 per cent of employees in telecommunications, radio and electronics. They continued to predominate in unskilled and semi-skilled tasks, while men performed heavier, more skilled work. The industry was highly advanced technically and more amenable to rationalisation than other British industries of that period; thus the proportion of repetitive, fragmented tasks was great, providing many 'female' jobs for assemblers, wirers and inspectors (Wild and Hill, 1970).

In the 1980s the industry is highly complex, with an array of different products and processes. The Census categorisation of industrial orders lists no fewer than seventeen sectors, ranging from telegraph and telephone to batteries and accumulators, from domestic electrical appliances to electronic components. The total number of women employed has fallen considerably in the past decades, from 324,000 in 1961 to 217,000 in 1981, reflecting the trend to de-industrialisation, a general decline in British industry along with further processes of rationalisation and accompanying labour displacement. Women constitute 34 per cent of the work force as a whole, but the specific nature of women's employment is indicated by the fact that in the Census category of 'repetitive' assembly women outnumber men four to one.

Internationally, similar patterns have been observed in these highly advanced industries. Herzog's account of German pieceworkers is an evocative response to the monotony and poor conditions of 'women's work' in the electronics industry, working, for example, on television tubes and vacuum cleaners (Herzog, 1980). Reporting on the Australian 'whitegoods' industry (refrigerators, cookers and so on) Game and Pringle found that 60 per cent of workers were women. There were three job areas: skilled service and maintenance work, making components and unskilled assembly. Women's work was mainly in the labour-intensive assembly sector, and on light component work. Game and Pringle explained how the sex-typing of jobs was justified: 'management tried to convince us that, in these otherwise unpleasant jobs, women like the company of other women. Yet they were so tied to the spot, and the pace of work so fast, that they scarcely had time to say hello to each other' (Game and Pringle, 1983, p. 37). As so often, discrimination is explained as a matter of preference.

In a recent study of the electronics industry in the Irish Republic, which is dominated by foreign-owned firms, chiefly American, Murray and Wickham (1982) noted the concentration of women in the 'non-craft' jobs.

Unskilled work in microelectronics appears to be a worldwide growth area for female employment. Some 300,000 women are estimated to work in microchip assembly and manufacture in South East Asia, for example, and in California's famous Silicon Valley assembly is done by women (Science Policy Research Unit, 1982). The multinational companies involved in this industry seem to prefer a feminine work force. Grossman's well-known paper 'Women's Place in the Integrated Circuit' (1980) shows how paternalist employers in Malaysia have played upon themes of femininity and family membership to bind their workers to their pressurised, low-paid and unhealthy jobs (the young microchip assemblers become 'granmas' in their twenties, wearing spectacles as their sight deteriorates from peering at the minuscule circuitry).

Two major features, then, have characterised the industry in recent decades. First, like all others we have so far studied, it is marked by a very high level of sex-typing and sex-segregation. Both Purcell (1982) and Cavendish (1981) have reported how, in the electrical components factories they observed, there was a multitude of different jobs, all strictly assigned to one sex only. The second feature is the confining of women to monotonous, pressurised, low-skilled assembly work. Women in this industry are closely implicated in current processes of capital restructuring, as indeed Glucksmann claims was the case in the interwar period on which her study focuses.

Glucksmann draws our attention to the tendency of historians to associate women's employment with declining and backward industries. Bythell's work on the sweated trades (1978), for example, makes this connection, and Osterud's study of hosiery (1977) associates women's employment with less mechanised homebound work, men's with factories and technical advance. The case of the new industries, which I have surveyed in this chapter, invalidates such associations. In two of the areas discussed here, women were almost immediately brought in to highly mechanised jobs, in industries which were to set the pattern for technological advance. Rather than regarding these jobs as feminised we can see them as having been designated as feminine from the start.

However, I would dispute Gluckmann's claim that this marked a radical new step in the development of capitalist production relations, and associated gender relations. Nor can I accept her verdict that these gender divisions were generated internally by the production system itself, without reference to family relationships or to gender relations beyond the work sphere. On the contrary, if we locate the new industries within the historical process described in the previous chapters, we can see marked continuities with nineteenth-century work practices. In the traditional industries women had become confined to certain types of job which were seen as demonstrating the characteristics of 'women's work': little need for training, repetition, handling of 'lighter' machines, no technical knowledge required, cleanliness, call for dexterity and concentration, low mobility and so forth. Such jobs became more numerous with the advance of mechanisation, and the period 1880–1900 is perhaps the key period for the assigning of these as 'women's work', although in some cases development started earlier. Women's confinement to these jobs had many causes; men's desire to retain the best-regarded and most interesting tasks, management's desire to crush union strength and use cheaper female labour, Victorian squeamishness about sex and notions of propriety, cultural conventions and expectations about gender hierarchy in part at least formed in the family. Complex negotiations arising from all these factors culminated in the consolidation of sex-typed job structures. We can, for example, see all the above factors at work in the transitional case of the tobacco industry.

In newer industries like food processing and electronics, there were no traditional work customs to maintain, no militant male unionists to cling to the 'core' jobs, but as the new labour processes were designed there was a framework of existing expectations and definitions of what was 'suitable' work for either sex. Employers could then easily slot men and women into the new jobs on the basis of these definitions, thereby exploiting the profitability of cheap female labour in the fragmented, mechanised jobs which, as they claimed, 'only women would take'. Capitalist motivation here met no opposition from existing male or patriarchal interests, as it had in the traditional industries; but the allocation of meanings and characteristics to jobs, the notions of what types of jobs were 'skilled', 'heavy', 'responsible', had already been accomplished in the context of patriarchal relationships and male priorities within the traditional industries, which themselves had been heavily influenced by past patterns of household labour. Thus, as so often, it is misleading to detach an analysis of sex relations at work from an understanding of sex relations in the society as a whole and their historical evolution.

C

The Tertiary Sector: Professions and Service Industries

In our survey of extractive and of manufacturing industries we have seen that in virtually all cases jobs have tended to be sex-typed (although patterns of sex-typing are often fluid over time) and that it has been the norm for men and women to work apart, often in separate physical environments. When we turn to the service sector, on the face of it segregation and sex-typing are less apparent. Jobs such as teaching, office work and shopwork evoke images of a mixed work force working in a common space, and in the professions in particular it is considered that entry and subsequent progress are both determined on the basis of merit, so there is no reason why both sexes should not fare equally. When we probe beneath the surface, however, we find that sex-typing and segregation, though less rigid and visible, are not entirely absent. In many cases women and men are clustered in different areas within a service occupation or profession: even where they work side by side, nominally at the same work, men and women may be performing a different package of tasks. Since employment in these occupations is proportionally increasing, and since some of them are already among the major employers of women, it is highly significant for the future of gender relations in our society that segregation, even if in a muted form, is found in these jobs also.

The service area most studied by sociologists and historians interested in women's work has been clerical work, which is currently one of the major employers of women: in 1980 31 per cent of all employed women were clerical workers. Studies such as those by Holcombe (1973), Anderson (1976), McNally (1979), Barker and Downing (1980), Davies (1982), Crompton and Jones (1984), Zimmeck (1986) and Walby (1986) demonstrate how women are concentrated into jobs sex-typed as female (secretary, typist, keyboard operator, filing clerk, etc.), while men occupy the highest grades (especially those connected to promotion ladders within the organisation); women are lower paid and often work part time. Since so much information is already available on office work I have chosen to concentrate on three less studied and less familiar areas: retailing, medicine and teaching. The pioneering research of Lee Holcombe on the employment opportunities available for 'Victorian Ladies' has been an essential starting point for my survey; as the cases will show, her book documents the expansion of women's employment in these occupations in the Victorian period. The inferior status of women in comparison to men at that time ensured their consignment to areas seen as less challenging, less responsible and, as such, more fitted to the female personality. My argument will be that this continues to characterise their participation today.

11

SHOPWORK

In many societies women have had a major role in retailing. In tribal and agrarian societies women are often responsible for the marketing of produce, both foods and manufactured goods. Although Boserup points out that in some societies development has led to men monopolising trade (Chinese societies) and that in others shopwork is seen as 'unfit' for women for religious reasons (Islamic societies), in other traditional societies retailing, especially of clothing and foodstuffs, has become something of a woman's work; this was particularly so in Europe (Boserup, 1970; Hanawalt, 1986). In pre-industrial England this was a 'trade' into which women could penetrate in their own right. Studies of fourteenth-century Shrewsbury and London and of Tudor Salisbury show that there were many women acting as hucksters, peddlers, fishwives and pudding-wives, regraters (who bought market goods and resold them elsewhere for a profit) and other retailers. Women were commonly working as brewers and bakers in these periods, although in certain victualling trades they were fewer in number; grocery, for example, was a trade in which only a sprinkling of women was recorded (Lacey, 1985; Hutton, 1985; Wright, 1985). Female servants were also often employed as assistants in retailing businesses. Since no technical knowledge was necessary it was reasonably easy for women to gain access to the trade. As Alice Clark says 'the woman who was left without resources turned naturally to keeping a shop, or to the sale of goods in the street, as the most likely means of maintaining her children' (Clark, 1982, p. 198).

With the advent of capitalist systems in industry, retailing remained an area of business from which middle-class women were not excluded. Keeping a small shop or family business was not regarded as unsuitable work for women. Many owned shops and stall in their own right, while thousands more helped their husbands as part of a family business, aided by children and perhaps servants of either sex. Women were especially likely to be found in certain types of shops whose products had feminine associations, such as millinery or corsetry. According to the 1851 Census there were more female than male shopkeepers in England and Wales (14,026 to 12,900). Only towards the end of the century was there a decline in female proprietors as retailing became seen as a less than 'genteel' occupation for ladies; even then there must have been many distressed 'gentlewomen' like Miss Matty of *Cranford*, with her little shop selling tea, who found it a useful way of surviving in adversity, as also on a lesser scale did many working-class women who augmented the family budget by selling pies or lemonade.

Shopkeeping at the beginning of the nineteenth century was still very much what it had been in the pre-industrial epoch and still considered a trade. Often the business of selling was closely linked to the production of the commodities sold, as in the case of baking and shoemaking. In this trade, just as in others, an apprenticeship system operated. Boys were taken on to learn all aspects of the business; making of products where relevant, techniques of purchase and selection, preparation and storage, along with stock-keeping and book-keeping. The apprentice would have a good chance of progressing to run his own business in the future (Jefferys, 1954).

The classic example of this was grocery, which retained its trade structure right up to the end of the century and even into the twentieth, although new methods of food production began to erode the system from the 1850s. Grocery, as stated, had been a male specialism since medieval times. Grocery apprentices, always male, learned a variety of skills. These included: 'the blending of tea, the mixing of herbs and spices, the curing and cutting of bacon, the cleaning and washing of dried fruits, the cutting and millgrinding of sugar and the roasting and grinding of coffee' (Jefferys, 1954, p. 2). Twisting paper into 'pokes' or folding it in packets was another aptitude the young apprentice must acquire, along with boning hams and cutting salt. Storing and preserving the goods in the days before refrigeration was also a crucial element of training.

Apprenticeship, however, was not confined to these male-dominated trades. Girls might also be taken on to learn millinery or dressmaking. Margaret Bondfield (1948) describes how, as late as 1887, she was taken on by a draper where she learned to deal with trousseaux and layettes, to trim and embroider gowns. Such places were prized as they provided girls with skills which could be sold to employers, at home or in the factory, but also offered the distant hope of one day owning one's own business.

From mid-century, however, the structure of the retailing industry began slowly to change, with the advent of the larger type of shops, the chain store, the department store and so forth. These shops created new ever-expanding field of female employment. In 1851 the Census recorded only 1742 women working as shop assistants (though this figure is misleading, as it excludes the large numbers of family members and domestic servants involved in this activity). However, the 1850s and 1860s saw the arrival of a different breed of shopwomen, young girls employed deliberately because of their sex and femininity. In this new female occupation, in a manner different from the others we have so far surveyed, glamour and female appearance were to become an important part of employment qualifications. Georgiana Hill, an early commentator on women's work, summarised the trend between 1860 and 1900 as follows:

> The elegantly-attired damsel, with her elaborately dressed hair, who serves the public with drapery, flowers and ornaments, and makes the homely buyer in unpretentious array feel at a complete disadvantage, came in with the plate-glass fronts, the electric lamps, the gorgeous showrooms, in which the modern shopocracy delights. (Hill, 1896, p. 191)

Feminine allure was an important part of the blandishments with which the emerging consumer society began to woo it customers.

Women were associated from the beginning with these new experiments in retailing. In 1831 the Manchester Bazaar was set up, an arcade composed of small stalls. One of the objects of the enterprise was, it was stated, 'to give employment to industrious females' who were given premises on the second floor while men worked on the first. Themes of both femininity and respectability, which came to characterise the female shop assistant as opposed to her factory or farm sisters, were emphasised in the rules of the bazaar, which called for 'propriety of demeanour and dress': 'females will not be allowed to have their hair in papers or to wear bonnets' (quoted Adburgham, 1964, p. 20). Nor were they to eat, drink or gossip while at work!

A more significant development, however, was the growth of the department store. Bainbridges had established one in Newcastle before 1850, although the successes of such stores in Paris is supposed to have given the major boost to the development of the West End stores such as Selfridges and Debenhams. There is some indication that, in the grander of these, male shop assistants were employed at first. A satirical article in *Punch* portrayed the complaint of the fashionable lady: 'I should like to see myself in a shop with pert minxes waiting on me' (quoted Whitaker, 1973, p. 62).

In these early and perhaps rather exclusive stores 'solemn gentlemen in black' acted as 'shopwalkers' escorting ladies through the premises, while others helped them to chairs and ministered to their needs (Adburgham, 1964, p. 146). But as the stores expanded to cater for wider markets women entered them in certain capacities. The tasks of the assistants in these stores were very different from those of the skilled apprentice in the small shop. Jobs were limited, for example, to stock control, cashiering, selling to customers or window-dressing and display. Just as in manufacture, in fact, capitalist expansion of retailing meant fragmentation, routinisation and specialisation of the assistants' work. Skill requirements were also being eroded by the development of prepackaged forms of food and other goods. For example, tobacco retailing was originally a skilled job, which called for experience and expertise in blending tobacco mixture, keeping it moist, packing up small weights; the advent of prepackaged tobaccos and cigarettes degraded the job and paved the way for it to become one of the most female-dominated areas of shopwork.

In 1861 only 19 per cent of shop assistants were recorded as being women; by 1911 the proportion had grown to 31 per cent and was to increase still further. The spread of women's employment was gradual, reflecting the uneven nature of the industry's development, as many small shops continued on the old lines. But contemporary observers shared with later historians a strong sense of the direction of the change. Several reasons were given for it. Holcombe, in her valuable study of Victorian white-collar women workers, imputes the change to the cheapness of female labour, as did many male shopworkers at the time. Shop assistants' wages were anyway low and women might often earn only 50 per cent of male wages. In the 1870s in Scotland women were earning £40 to £50 per annum as opposed to men's £50 to £80. Young girls in particular were used. Holcombe reports that in 1884 almost 50 per cent of shop assistants were under twenty-one years of age. Paid low wages, often obliged to live in cramped unhealthy conditions and made to work excessively long hours (75 to 94 per week), such young women must have appeared an easily exploitable work force. Nevertheless, there is evidence that many girls were drawn to shopwork, preferring it to the alternatives available (especially farmwork and domestic service) because it promised them at least the *prospect* of greater freedom and independence from both parents and employers, along with the excitement of life in the city (Holcombe, 1973, p. 111; PP 1876 xxx, p. 693; Hellerstein et al., 1981).

Another major reason for the employment of women was the growing association of shopping with glamour, luxury and charm. This applied particulary in the clothing and footwear sectors. Lady Jeune, apparently an assiduous shopper, made comments indicating how successful this strategy might be for the 'shopocracy':

> The other reason for the increased temptation to spend money is the large numbers of women which are now employed. Women are so much quicker than men, and they understand so much more readily what other women

want; they can enter into the little troubles of their customers; they can fathom the agony of despair as to the arrangement of colours, the alternative trimmings, the duration of a fashion, the depths of a woman's purse, and, more important than all, the question of the becomingness of a dress ... to the wearer. (quoted Adburgham, 1964, p. 236)

Here, also, Victorian ideas of propriety played an important role, as two Dundee drapers explained in 1876:

Changes that are gradually taking place in the nature of the drapery trade, shoe trade and etc. demand more female labour than formerly ... A great deal more of the goods are made up now than they used to be, and it is much more suitable for females to sell made-up garments to ladies than for males, and in the shoe trade the same; it is much more a question of fitting on than of purchasing in the shop now ... I think that a gentleman would soon find that his male labour in putting on shoes to ladies and such things as that, would not be so suitable as his female labour. (PP 1876 xxx, pp. 797–8, 800)

This turnaround from the aristocratic preferences of the 1860s was confirmed in the 1890s. One man told the investigators of the Labour Commission that in his shop 'it would be impossible to replace women by men, many of the articles being such as women would only buy from women' (PP 1893–4 xxxvii, p. 4).

Women were perhaps also more easily made to submit to the harsh conditions and strict discipline of shop life which persisted through to World War I. The lives of shop assistants were tightly controlled. In a kind of degraded version of the apprenticeship system, many shops required their assistants to live on the premises or in their boarding houses. Young people were jammed in rooms with up to five or six beds, sometimes having to sleep two to a bed; food was often insufficient and of very poor quality, furniture was minimal and toilet facilities inadequate and unhygienic. In such conditions illness was common, and many cases of tuberculosis were recorded. Predictably, a major concern to those who investigated this system was the potential for immorality and the incitement of newcomers to sexual experiments, although the sexes were, it hardly needs saying, carefully segregated in the accommodation. For the young people themselves the lack of privacy was a great hardship.

Inside the shop too, conditions were poor; assistants had to work very long hours, both in small shops and in stores where the assistants had to remain behind after customers to tidy and set out stock often until eight, nine or ten in the evening. Only in 1899 did a clause of the Shop Act demand the provision of seats for assistants – one per three women; before then assistants were frequently forbidden to sit down, and it was reported in the 1890s that many girls suffered from varicose veins. Rules were strict, with fines and dismissals common for trivial offences, for example for talking, wearing flowers at work, bringing a newspaper to work or allowing customers to get away from the shop without buying anything! One shop in Holloway had no fewer than seventy-five such rules (Whitaker, 1973).

As women were drawn into certain sectors of the industry, a pattern of segregation began to develop between different areas and departments. In the 1890s it was reported that men still remained numerically dominant in ironmongery, jewellery, butchery, fishmongering, hairdressing and in chemists and music shops; women were dominant in bakery, confectionery and ice cream, newsagents and tobacconists, millinery, fancy goods and china goods, in fruiterers and where refreshments were served; in footwear and hosiery women and men were employed in equal numbers (though, as we have seen, labour would be sex-specific according to the sex of the customer), and bookselling was also mixed (PP 1893-4 xxxvii, p. 310). Thus, while shopwork might have (and still has) the image of an occupation where men and women work together, very many Victorian shopworkers were in departments with their own sex only.

Holcombe comments that men continued to be employed where training was necessary (in chemists and butchers, for example), where the cost of goods was high (as in jewellery or wine), where work was rough and heavy (as in ironmongery or furniture) and where the clientele was largely male (for example tailors and sports shops). Women, by contrast, were used where work was light and untrained, where the customers were female and where the pay was low. Nor did women often achieve promotion to the better posts in the shop hierarchy, such as those of floor managers, buyers or window-dressers.

The restructuring of the retailing industry during the nineteenth century, then, brought with it a complex pattern of changes in the way women were utilised within it. Holcombe considers the increasing employment of women to be part of the proletarianisation of the profession. This is certainly in part true; employers exploited the cheapness of women's labour, which was associated with the decline of apprenticeship. But this interpretation misses some of the complexities: it overlooks the extent of women's previous involvement in shopwork (this was not a straightforward case of feminisation) and it also underplays the extent to which men continued to predominate in many areas. These changes did not involve a simple replacement of men by women, but rather the elaboration of a new sexual division of labour within the industry. Also significant was the way in which women's employment was linked to the burgeoning culture of consumerism, through associations of glamour, luxury and romance, and it was in precisely these most consumerised sectors that women's employment was most marked. The privilege given to economic factors by Holcombe throughout her account of women's professions leads her to neglect more gender-specific elements which were important in the historical process of change.

It is important not to exaggerate the rate of this change. In certain areas women's participation did rise rapidly in comparison to men's; for example, between 1881 and 1891 the number of women in drapery shops rose from 29 for every 10,000 employed women to 40, while men's employment stayed stable at around 57–8 per 10,000. But at the end of the same decade boys still appear to have been going into shopwork in larger numbers than girls: in London 3584 boys leaving elementary school entered shopwork as opposed to 577 girls; in a less developed area, Leicester, the disparity was still greater, 127 boys to 14 girls (PP 1894 lxxxi, Pt I, p. 10; PP 1899 lxxv, pp. vii, 54). Such figures indicate how persistent the old small shop sector was with its established systems.

Nor was the employment of women unresisted. In her fascinating autobiography, *The Pit Village and the Store*, Linda McCullough Thew describes how she was taken on as the first-ever girl assistant in the local co-operative grocery store, a prize shop job, as hours and pay were firmly under union control (as one young girl said 'me mammie says if you can get a job in the store you're made for life'). Male employees fiercely resented her presence, seeing it as a threat to their skill and status: 'it's a great mistake. It won't work. Grocering is a man's job. It's a skilled job. Takes years of training. No girl, or woman either for that matter, is up to it.' The men made her life as unpleasant as they could, reducing her to nightly tears, till they became resigned to her stay. She summed up the situation: 'looking back, it is easy to see that several things contributed to my unhappiness during those early days as a store lass. Naturally the men would be of one accord when they saw (or thought they saw) their livelihood threatened and their metier as grocers undermined. It was a man's job; it could not be done by a woman' (McCullough Thew, 1985, pp. 125, 138, 145).

The spread of women in the more modernised sectors seems to have accelerated in the twentieth century. In 1908, among the London stores, one-third of Harrods' staff were women, while the figure for Derry and Toms was two-thirds. By 1919 Sir Woodman Burridge, Harrods' manager, reported that 3500 out of the 6000 employees were women (PP 1908 lix, Vol. I, pp. 209, 296; PP 1919 xxxi, p. 146).

During the war women had predictably taken over men's jobs; yet it was clear that conventional ideas about the sexual division of labour had not changed greatly. Burridge claimed that in prewar days only men had dealt with perishable goods 'as they could handle the goods with greater efficiency'; a man, he believed, had 'greater interest in, and knowledge of, his trade'. Window-dressing, another task seen as requiring talent, and some strength, was also a male preserve. The retailing union NUSAWC (National Union of Shop Assistants, Warehousemen and Clerks) reported that there was a 'fairly clear line of demarcation' between men's and women's work. This was not dissimilar to that reported in the 1890s: men outnumbered women in grocery, meat, fish and poultry, furniture, heavy drapery and wholesaling, which was virtually a male monopoly; women predominated in lighter drapery, women's wear, confectionery and bakeries. Most supervisors' jobs were held by men. A similar account was provided by representatives of the co-operative shopworkers' union who stated that women were 'practically monopolising' the sectors of drapery and footwear where 'women and children had to be waited on'. However, in luxury fabrics men still prevailed, as 'skill and knowledge were required for estimating and advising upon these expensive fabrics'. As McCullough Thew's story confirms, grocery in the co-operative stores was still a male job based on a seven-year apprenticeship. Heavy packing and handling requirements (in days when home delivery of goods was still standard) helped to keep it male, though the union did concede that there was room for women in some jobs calling for 'skill, method and brains'; this, of course, was a socially progressive organisation (PP 1919 xxxi, pp. 146, 148, 150).

It was debated whether after the war men would reassume the heavier and 'more responsible' jobs or whether women would retain them. Since women who had risen to supervisory and management posts in the war years had apparently filled them with great competence, the possibility of expansion of women's employment in these areas during the 1920s and 1930s became a real one.

Reports from the 1930s confirm that changes were in progress. The *New Survey of London Life and Labour* found that women buyers now outnumbered men. Women were increasingly reaching higher-level posts. In London, women now made up 50 per cent of shop assistants (though in the retail trade as a whole they were only 40 per cent). However, the pattern of segregation was little changed: where 70 per cent of employees in drapery and clothing were female, in the meat trades it was only 8 per cent (Llewellyn Smith, 1933). Diana Smith's study of employment in Croydon, based on 1931 Census figures, shows that women had penetrated more fully into grocery and bakery, but were still largely absent from the meat trades, fishmongery, ironware and furniture. Men continued to work in areas which could be defined as having a 'craft' element, where processing as well as selling was still part of the job (Smith, 1982).

The continued modernisation of the trade offered new types of jobs to girls. For example, most cashiers were young women. This job was seen as quite discrete from selling, described as being 'a class apart'. Girls, too, were being used as lift operators: 'her function was not merely to operate the lifts, for she must be a mine of information to customers as to the departments in which goods are to be purchased, and she must therefore be of a good type with good voice and address' (Llewellyn Smith, 1933, p. 141). As the nature of jobs changed, more emphasis was being placed by managers on the personality of the assistant, rather than expertise, experience or strength. Mechanisation (for example, bacon-cutting machines), continued to render old skills unnecessary, and new forms of packaging also simplified the job. Less physical effort was required of the salespeople. Changed products, too, could alter labour requirements. Whereas in the nineteenth century chemists normally employed male assistants, the spread of mass-produced cosmetics and luxury toiletries brought women into this branch, although qualified dispensers still were male. Sweets and chocolates were by now described as 'primarily a girl's trade'. These examples indicate the close link between the employment of women and the glamorisation of shopping, where the femininity and attractiveness of the young girl was an ever more valued asset. In drapery, where women now outnumbered men three to one, it was said that 'neat and good clothes are essential ... both for men and women. Moreover, good appearance, a suitable height and absence of noticeable accent are among the employer's stated requirements' (Llewellyn Smith, 1933, p. 177).

The sex composition of the work force may also have been affected by the fact that the changing structure of the industry made it more difficult for a young saleman to move into setting up his own business, as competition increased and capital costs grew much greater. This may have encouraged young men to look elsewhere for a career. However, the *New Survey* investigators noted the large numbers of small businesses still in existence and here, they claimed, there was 'no barrier of age and sex'; married couples in particular might find an agreeable niche here, though the researchers reported a deep sense of gloom as to the future viability of the small shop (Llewellyn Smith, 1933, p. 164).

Despite these trends, the most striking feature of the decades between 1880 and 1950 is how firmly the pattern of segregation persisted once established. The 1946 Equal Pay Commission noted how considerable this segregation was, with men still dominating in meat and fish, in ironmongery and all heavy work. In grocery men were said to deal with actually handling provisions, women with wrapping. The exclusion of women from butchery and fishmongery was ascribed to requirements of strength and the 'unpleasant nature of the work'; yet women on farms had been cutting up meat and gutting poultry for centuries, and processing fish, as we saw earlier in the book, has been a typically 'female' job on the production side of the industry! Much more significant is the fact that these jobs retained their associations of craft and training. The Commission, although it was committed to taking seriously the idea that women and men should receive equal pay for like work, nonetheless referred to men as 'more valuable employees' (PP 1945-6 xii, pp. 78-9).

A slightly different pattern of segregation evolved in North America. As in pre-industrial Britain, women in colonial America were extensively involved in retailing and running businesses. But as stores expanded the first assistants taken on were young men, 'on the theory', according to Wertheimer, 'that women customers preferred to be waited on by men' (Wertheimer, 1977, p. 156). One store manager indeed claimed to use 'the handsomest men he could obtain ... because he had noticed that ladies ... liked to gossip and even flirt with them' (quoted Baker, 1964, pp. 64–5). The dynamics of sexuality, thus, worked differently here.

Accordingly, few women were employed as assistants before the Civil War, although one or two larger establishments (following the example of department stores in Paris and England) did take on girls and women, such as Macy's in New York. During the Civil War, however, women were pulled into retailing, and remained there after the war, when the spread of larger shops helped to increase their numbers. Many young girls were taken on as runners, cash girls, sweepers and cleaners, hoping to reach the elite jobs of cashier, stock girl or sales clerk. The increase in numbers of women saleswomen between 1880 and 1900 was striking, from 7500 to 142,000, a rise of 1800 per cent! Three-quarters of these were young girls, aged between fourteen and twenty-five. Yet despite this increase women only accounted for 23 per cent of sales workers, and were concentrated in the larger cities where the new large stores were located (Baker, 1964, p. 65; Wertheimer, 1977, p. 158). Here, managers were finding the benefits of cheaper and more biddable female labour in the freer urban environment. One large store manager put it succinctly in 1889: 'we don't want men ... we wouldn't have them even if they came at the same price. Give me a woman every time ... Boys smoke and lose at cards and do a hundred things that women don't' (Hellerstein et al., 1981, pp. 373–4).

The name 'sales clerk' makes clearer then our British terminology the way in which this work held white-collar status. This made it attractive to ambitious young women, and numbers increased in the twentieth century, despite the low pay and poor conditions, similar to those in British shops. By 1980 women made up nearly 70 per cent of retail clerks and 83 per cent of cashiers, though in the sales business as a whole they were only 49 per cent, reflecting continued under-representation at higher levels (United States Bureau of the Census, 1988). Some shops specialising in goods for women customers, as in Britain, were found when surveyed in 1950 to be staffed almost entirely by women. As in Britain, women had gained access to higher-level jobs, holding 85 per cent of such jobs in personnel departments, two-thirds of those in publicity and over 50 per cent in merchandising, according to the Woman's Bureau (Baker, 1964, p. 247). Although this occupation has continued to exploit young girls for very poor wages, it is also significant as being one of the few non-professional areas in which women's careers are possible.

Although I have no detailed information on patterns of segregation between sectors, it seems clear that segregation exists, although not on exactly the same lines as in Britain, perhaps because the industry lacked the craft ethos where workers were identified as 'clerks' rather than 'artisans'. Baker reports that in 1950 women dominated in general stores and those selling cheap merchandise; while men virtually monopolised shoe selling (to both men and women) and the retailing of automobiles (Baker, 1964). Caplow, however, noted the link between the sex of sales staff and the customer:

> The prevailing pattern is that salesmen serve male customers and saleswomen serve female customers. Where the customers are mixed in gender, the salesforce follows the majority. An exception is made for very heavy or very valuable commodities which are commonly sold by men. In a normally organised department store, there will be men in the sports-goods department, women to sell curtains and dishware, men to sell hardware ... wedding silver and furniture. (Caplow, 1964, p. 232)

Men have claimed for themselves areas dealing with more valuable goods and calling for greater responsibility.

In Australia the pattern of segregation was similar to that in Britain. Prior to the appearance of department stores in the 1880s, the industry was divided between small family businesses (in which women played their characteristically important role) and larger specialist firms similar to wholesalers which men monopolised. Women were welcomed enthusiastically by managers into the new stores as assistants, but their employment was confined to certain areas and male unions fought to keep them out of 'male' specialisms. in 1938 a clear division of labour was noted. Men were allocated 'heavy work' (carpets, furniture, hardware), but much of the segregation was based on the idea of sexual propriety. Thus men predominated in all areas of men's clothing and footwear, as well as in areas where customers were generally male (sports goods, saddlery, wireless, cars and bicycles). Women predominated in women's wear and baby wear, in toiletry, jewellery, florists and bakery. Game and Pringle argue that this segregation was often linked to the feminine or masculine connotations of the consumer goods involved. As in Britain, grocery was seen as a skilled trade reserved for men. Some areas which were less clearly defined employed both sexes.

As in Britain and America, after World War II women spread more generally through retailing, especially as with the postwar boom men found they could make better careers in other occupations. The current restructuring of the industry has since then further eroded the old division of labour. Women have been used to fill the new jobs in the supermarkets and may do so in the wholesaling sector as it becomes automated. In the supermarkets women are on the checkouts and work as 'night fillers' restocking the shelves, also filling the many clerical roles which the new type of retailing has created. Bagging and parcel pickup, two mobile and possibly heavier jobs, are characteristically performed by boys. In fast-food shops, boys process the food in the kitchens while young girls dole it out in the front, reflecting the prevailing view that they are better at dealing with the public. Many women, too, are being employed in the proliferating part-time jobs in the industry, especially in the supermarkets. Although the old lines of status and gender divisions are being erased, a clear new pattern of gender ascription is now emerging (Game and Pringle, 1983).

Similar changes are currently under way in Britain. In the industry as a whole women outnumber men; 1981 Census figures show one and a third million women workers, as opposed to 918,000 men. In the catchall category of salesman (*sic*), assistants and shelf-fillers (i.e. the bottom tiers of the hierarchy) women outnumber men six to one. However, there are over twice as many men as women among representatives and agents, and women are a tiny minority among bakers and butchers.

Traces of the old pattern of segregation then, persist. Webb, in an interesting study of a department store, found that men still held most top positions in the hierarchy (management, training, stock control and so forth), and dominated in departments with expensive or bulky consumables (furniture, electronics), while women, more visible on display at counters, were predominant in female clothing (Webb, 1982). However, perhaps more significant than these continuities are the changed patterns of employment brought by the continued development of the industry. As in Australia, women are found in the new supermarket jobs, as store clerks, shelf-fillers and, above all, as cashiers. The latest point-of-sale automatic cash tills have removed many of the elements of variety and discretion from the cashiers; machines can read off all the details from the barcodes on the goods, 'ring up' the price automatically, calculate change and even weigh the goods; the human input becomes purely manual, reducing the cashier to an assembly-line worker (Huws, 1982). Women predominate in these mindless and pressurised jobs; according to the 1981 Census there were 69,500 women on checkout and cash tills, with no men at all. Since then some firms have taken on young boys, especially for weekend shifts. There is, indeed, some suggestion that, as blue-collar opportunities for male school-leavers drastically diminish, shopwork may be redesignated as a male career. If this happens, it is likely that young men will be taken on as full-time trainees, with access to career ladders into high positions, while women are used for the ever-increasing part-time labour force; between 1971 and 1975 106,000 full-time jobs were lost, to be replaced by 171,000 part-time ones (Huws, 1982, p. 77).

The other area of expanded work for women is in the booming mail order and warehouse sector. As well as creating many new office jobs for women, the sector employs many women 'picking' ordered goods from shelves. Cynthia Cockburn's *Machinery of Dominance* reveals the progressive deskilling of these jobs through computer technology. At first women moved freely around the warehouse, planning their own routes to fulfil orders; their mobility then became restricted by computerised assembly belts, with programmed instructions; finally women were isolated from companions, each at her own station beside a carousel from which she picked items. Women also worked as packers and stock clerks, while the men took the more mobile, less pressurised jobs of transport, assembly and maintenance. Such jobs were seen to require both physical and technical competence, characteristics which led to their being deemed 'man's work'. One man told Cockburn, 'no way I'd do the carousel work job myself. The boredom! You are always stuck in the same spot.' Another explained that he felt like his own boss when driving a truck, while he saw the pickers on the belt as being like robots (Cockburn, 1985, pp. 100–1). Managers perhaps would have been happy if the women had actually been robots!

As we have seen, although often producing low-paid jobs with poor conditions, retailing has been one area in which women have gained access to female careers (in 1981 there were 24,000 female sales supervisors compared with 10,000 men); it has provided women with jobs viewed as more desirable than factory work, with its connotations of dirt and roughness, and perhaps allowing more freedom, mobility and contact with other people than much low-level clerical work. But the next stage of capitalist development looks ominously set to change all that. Although the new shopping environment may bring to an end the pattern of segregated specialisms established in the late Victorian epoch, it presents women with tedious, degraded, machine-paced forms of work, many of which, being part-time, lack the fringe advantages historically associated with white-collar work. Men are likely to capture any career-type jobs with access to supervisory and managerial positions. In this case, at least, the microelectronics revolution is likely to deepen, not demolish, hierarchies of gender within the industry.

12

MEDICINE

We turn now to the professions, areas of employment which, in the 1980s at least, are seen as essentially open and undifferentiated by gender. In the 'higher' profession of medicine and law, however, it is commonly acknowledged that women are less well represented (numerically at least) than men. The history of these professions is one of male domination and female exclusion; women have only entered into them following determined campaigns by nineteenth-century feminists. Their victories were won against fierce and often hysterical opposition from men. Women now have access to the higher professions and, on the face of it, are able to do exactly the same work as men. Careful investigation, however, reveals that here, as in every other area we have investigated, elements of segregation are still at play.

It would be impossible in one brief chapter to do justice to all the aspects of women's involvement in the medical profession with its complex and highly differentiated structure of hierarchies. What I shall attempt to do in this chapter is to trace out one aspect of the division of labour; the split of the practice of medicine into two functions, 'curing' (largely performed by males) and 'caring' (overwhelmingly performed by females).

A number of influential studies, from Georgiana Hill's pioneering Victorian study *Women in English Life* (1896), to the work of Clark (1982) and of Ehrenreich and English (1979), have revealed the important role played by women as healers in pre-industrial societies. In medieval and Tudor Britain women of all social ranks were involved in both nursing and tending the sick and in administering healing techniques to them. Women learned techniques of healing, along with all sorts of herbal remedies, unguents, salves, potions and tonics, from older women, passing them on to their own daughters.

The Fussells show how the 'great lady' in each area might take responsibility for caring for those in her domain, counselling them in their illnesses. Such women would often write down recipes and curative procedures, carefully storing them for posterity (so that many such 'receipts' have indeed come down to us); this was part of their broader task of management within the aristocratic household. One such in the Civil War period was Lady Ann Halkett:

> In the summer season she vyed with the bee or ant in gathering herbs, flowers, worms, snails etc for the still or limbeck, for the mortar or boyling pan etc ... making preparations of extracted waters, spirits, ointments, conserves, salves, powders etc which she ministered every Wednesday to a multitude of poor infirm persons, besides what she dayly sent about to persons of all ranks who consulted her in their maladies. (quoted Hill, 1896, Vol. I, p. 191)

Lady Ann, with her weekly clinic, was quite clearly playing a role similar to that of the modern GP!

The farmer's wife, too, commonly possessed these skills. The *Country Farm* manual of 1600 exhorted her to be 'skilful in natural phisicke, for the benefite of her owne folke, and others when they shall fall out to be ill' (quoted Fussell and Fussell, 1985, p. 54). The wording emphasises how this skill was exercised not just within the family or the household but in the community at large, taking women into the public world. Lower-class women, equally, could gain the reputation of expertise in healing. Such were the 'wise women' who, as Hill (1896), Ehrenreich and English (1979) and Oakley (1976b) among others have shown, were in danger of being denounced as witches by male clerics and medical practitioners, because their prescribing of potions made them easily vulnerable to charges of magic.

In the pre-industrial epoch the distinction between nursing and healing, 'caring' and 'curing' was much less sharply drawn than is the case today. But, on the other hand, there was a clear and growing distinction between the academic branch of medicine, commercialised, based on 'science', training, theory and logic (in fact bearing the hallmarks of what we today consider to be a profession) and the practical 'empiric' form of medicine, based on experience and traditional lore, which the women described above were practising. In the theoretical branch male 'physicians' dominated, although in the early medieval period there are recorded instances of university-educated women doctors. Such women might become lecturers and, as late as the fifteenth century, the chair of anatomy at Bologna was held by a woman (Hill, 1896, Vol. I, p. 227). But the academic science of medicine, harking back to its Greek origins, had been organised and developed by men and the campaign by men to keep women out and to distinguish themselves from untrained practitioners grew in intensity from the fifteenth century.

In 1421 the universities of Oxford and Cambridge campaigned through Parliament for restriction of untrained practitioners. The Medical Act of 1512 was an attempt to bring this issue under church control, by requiring bishops to grant licences to practitioners. Although there is a record of a surgeon's licence being granted to a woman in 1568, this was a clear attack on women's involvement, specifying as it did curing activities of 'smiths, weavers and women'; the introduction of the church as arbiter helped foster the linking of women's healing work with sorcery and witchcraft (Leeson and Gray, 1978, p. 21). The witch-hunter's guide sponsored by the papacy, the *Malleus Maleficarum* of 1484, had already laid down a link between female medicine and witchcraft: 'if a woman dare to cure without having studied she is a witch and must die' (quoted Oakley, 1976b, p. 28).

The attack on women healers was carried out on two fronts. Attacks by the church and executions of witches may have helped deter many women from practice, while on the other side male bodies continued to press for restrictions of entry. Physicians remained the aristocrats of the medical world, while in the seventeenth century two groups of male practitioners, the barber-surgeons and the apothecaries, gained charters and organised themselves as guilds excluding women. A series of Medical Acts was passed to tighten academic professional control. Increasing use of scientific rhetoric and of medical technology (and particularly the medicalisation of childbirth, an area where female control was strong, through use of the forceps), along with the development of public hospitals, also helped to promote male power in the seventeenth and eighteenth centuries.

However, these developments failed to push women entirely from the field. For one thing there were insufficient medical men to cater for demand and their services were too expensive. In addition, as Faulkner and Arnold argue, early male medicine was far from impressive. The focus of academic endeavour was the classification of diseases and collation of symptoms, and treatment was often based on erroneous, if not downright dangerous, theorisation. Medical science, for example, saw water, light and air as injurious to health, while the female 'empirics' knew from experience the value of water for hygiene, of sunlight and fresh air (Faulkner and Arnold, 1985). In the eighteenth century, the age of 'Heroic Medicine' an array of procedures was used – bleeding by leeches, blistering, purging – which seem more designed to kill than cure the hapless patient! Sir Ralph Verney's advice to his wife in 1647, probably reflects popular feeling as to whose opinions to prioritise: 'give the child no phisick, but such as midwives and old women, with the doctor's approbation, doe prescribe; for assure yourselfe they by experience know better than any physition how to treat such infants' (quoted, Clark, 1982, p. 258).

Within the sector of academic male medical practice the now familiar division between curing and caring first began to manifest itself. Doctors, especially in hospitals, were assisted by nurses or their services supplemented by them, and where nursing was undertaken as a specialised task it had long been assigned to women. Not all nursing, of course, was under male supervision. From medieval times it had been an area of independent female employment. London hospitals in the fourteenth and fifteenth centuries employed women as nurses, while other women practised nursing as casual work, helping sick people in their homes or acting as wet nurses (Lacey, 1985; Wright, 1985).

Midwifery was the most prestigious (and profitable) form of nursing, and childbirth was an area in which women's wisdom and experience had established a near total monopoly. The presence of men at childbirth before the seventeenth century was a rarity, being considered unseemly, inappropriate and even unlucky. But the midwife's role went beyond childbirth. Wiesner (1986) points out that they were involved in a range of medical, social and even legal activities (administering medicine, helping the community in times of epidemics, counselling and welfare work, testifying in cases involving illegitimacy and infanticide, and so forth). This was one female profession which took women beyond the confines of the home and into the public sphere.

Midwives, like other women healers, came in for suspicion from the church, because of their association with feminine 'mysteries' especially the forbidden knowledge of methods of contraception and abortion; with access to such magical items as placentae and miscarried embryos, they also ran the risk of accusations of witchcraft. A licensing system was developed in the seventeenth century in an attempt to police this profession, but women retained dominance until the eighteenth century when it became the fashion for higher-ranking women to be attended by a doctor in childbirth; from then on the midwife began to lose her power and with it her social standing (Clark, 1982).

The eighteenth century, then, saw the slow crushing out of female skills and lore in medicine, although the process was not completed until the nineteenth century. Snell (1985) has found cases of eighteenth-century women apprenticed to surgeons or acting as surgeons and apothecaries in their own right. One such who caused a public stir in 1736 was Mrs Mapp or 'Crazy Sally' the 'bonesetter of Epsom': 'her bandages are extraordinary Neat and her Dexterity is reducing Dislocations and setting of fractured Bones wonderful. She has cured Persons who have been above 20 years disabled and has given incredible Relief in the most difficult Cases. The Lame came daily to her and she got a great deal of Money' (*Gentleman's Magazine*, August 1736). She had learned her craft from her father, a Wiltshire bonesetter. But the nickname given her and the public sensation surrounding her show that she and her like were a dying breed. Mrs Mapp bore witness to the last stand of empirical medicine before the coming of industrialisation brought with it the triumph of scientific techniques and the rationalisation, in the Weberian sense, of medicine, along with the consolidation of the doctor's profession. No longer would it be possible to say

> What signifies Learning, or going to School,
> When a Woman can do, without Reason or Rule,
> What puts you to Nonplus, and baffles your Art;
> For Petticoat-Practice has now got the Start.
>
> Dame Nature has giv'n her a Doctor's Degree,
> She gets all ye patients, and pockets the Fee.
>   (*Gentleman's Magazine*, October 1736)

In the nineteenth century 'petticoat-practice' came, temporarily, to an end. The development of the hospital and the spread of university education for men brought with it a sharp division of medical functions between curing and caring; curing roles were now firmly in male hands, and women's role in medicine in the first half of the century was a residual one. While they might practise traditional healing skills in the home, their only formal public role was in nursing. Novarra (1980) argues that 'tending the sick' is one of the six core female tasks. Certainly this task had been historically in Britain 'woman's work' and there was no attempt to take this away when medicine became professionalised. However, in the early nineteenth century the status of nurses seems to have fallen as the female link with curing was severed.

According to the 1851 Census, as well as 39,139 women working as servants carrying out nursing duties, another 25,466 were nurses outside of domestic service (plus a handful of men). Most of such professional nurses came from the labouring classes, and the work they carried out in hospitals, workhouses and asylums was as much domestic labour (cleaning and cooking) as medical care. At the top of the nursing hierarchy, which was similar to that current today, the matron, who acted as the housekeeper and co-ordinator, might come from a higher stratum; below her were sisters, nurses and ward nurses, the latter doing the most menial housework. Infirmary nurses were often drawn from the ranks of paupers to look after their own kind (Williams, 1980). Such women were denigrated as drunken, dirty, degenerate, greedy and ignorant: Dickens' Sairey Gamp may stand as an archetype for them. In her campaign to reform nursing and make it a fit career for middle-class women, Florence Nightingale lost no chance to promote this image of these 'fat drunken old dames' (Coburn, 1974, p. 136); 'they are all drunkards, without exception, sisters and all, and there are about two nurses the surgeon can trust to give the patients their medicine,' (quoted, Baker, 1964, p. 61) she reported of one hospital. But, as Vicinus (1985) indicates in her study of Nightingale's work, it was clearly in the interests of the reformers to downgrade the old system. No doubt many women performed well in gruelling and difficult conditions, and clients continued to appreciate the qualities of the old-style nurses as is shown in Flora Thompson's description in *Lark Rise* of

> The old woman who, as she said, saw the beginning and end of everybody. She was, of course, not a certified midwife; but she was a decent, intelligent old body, clean in her person and methods and very kind ... Complications at birth were rare; but in the two or three cases where they did occur during her practice, old Mrs Quinton had sufficient skill to recognise the symptoms and send post haste for the doctor. No mother lost her life in childbed during the decade. In these more enlightened days the mere mention of the old, untrained village midwife raises a vision of some dirty, drink-sodden old hag without skill or conscience. But not all of them were Sairey Gamps. The great majority were clean, knowledgeable old women, who took a pride in their office. (Thompson, 1946, pp. 119–20)

Nor did this tradition die out in the 1880s in the rural areas. Lill Digweed of Stretton-on-the-Fosse told Judith Cook about her mother, a midwife practising at the beginning of this century: 'She was never qualified, mind you, many of them weren't in them days, but she was really very clever at it ... The women around really trusted her' (Cook, 1984, p. 172). Among her clients was the lady of the local 'big house'.

The new system of nursing was influenced by the work of groups of nuns and other religious sisterhoods, and also by the efforts of pioneers like Elizabeth Fry; they attempted to raise the status of nursing by attracting recruits of higher social origin, who would raise the tone and bring new values into the work. Fry's Institute of Nursing Sisters, established in the 1840s, employed doctors to train 'ladies' as nurses. The essentially domestic duties involved in nursing were now redefined as *scientific* with stress on the medical aspects of hygiene, ventilation, regulation of temperature and so forth. All this was fully systematised and established as nursing orthodoxy by Nightingale, whose training school, opened in 1860, was to serve as the model for later such institutions, both here and abroad in countries like America and Canada (Vicinus, 1985; Williams, 1980).

It is difficult reading accounts of Nightingale's life and work not to sympathise with many of her aims. Deeply angry about the pointless, idle life led by many middle-class women, and herself in revolt from this as Elaine Showalter's interesting recent study shows, she sought to make nursing not just a respectable *job* for ladies, but a properly regulated middle-class *career*, to start it on the road to professionalism. To achieve this, she wanted to establish nursing as an autonomous female preserve, removing the administration of the profession and the training of nurses from male control, so that within the hospital doctoring and nursing would be organised as two separate structures, the latter managed by the powerful matron (Showalter, 1987; Vicinus, 1985). But this account of Nightingale's project shows how her brand of feminism, like that of many of her contemporaries, was predicated on the notion of differentiated male and female worlds. The new nursing profession, thus, reflected dominant Victorian thinking about sex roles. Two themes particularly emerge from the writing of Nightingale and her successors; the hospital as a reflection of family relationships and the subservience of nursing to the needs of (male) doctors.

Numerous commentators have remarked on the way family imagery and ideology have penetrated the world of medicine (for example, see Stacey et al., 1977; Gamarnikow, 1978; Leeson and Gray, 1978; Davies, 1980). In the hospital, consultants are patriarchs, matrons matriarchs. Nurses play a variety of feminine roles, wives (and more latterly girlfriends) to doctors, mothers to patients, mistresses of the house to the ward domestics. Patients are treated as children, handled with severity by the doctor-father, but given motherly if firm tenderness by nurses.

Such a view of appropriate sex roles was espoused by nurses and doctors alike. Nightingale emphasised that nursing was essentially an extension of mothering, seen as the natural, biological expression of femininity: 'every woman, or at least almost every woman, in England, has, at one time or another of her life, charge of the personal health of somebody, whether child or invalid – in other words, every woman is a nurse' (*Notes on Nursing*, 1860, quoted Hellerstein et al., 1981, p. 378). Indeed, the trained nurse could compensate for the deficiencies of the biological mother:

'The real fathers and mothers of the human race are NOT the fathers and mothers according to the flesh ... For every one of my 18,000 children, for every one of these poor tiresome Harley Street creatures, I have expended more motherly feeling and action in a week than my mother has expended for me in 37 years'. (quoted, Swindells, 1985, p. 79)

This view of nursing as something inherent in all women became the distinctive ideology of the profession, as the journal *Hospital* indicated in 1905: 'ability to care for the helpless is women's distinctive nature. Nursing is mothering. Grown-up folk when sick are all babies' (quoted Versluysen, 1980, pp. 181–2). Such attitudes were clearly compatible with the prevailing climate of (male) public opinion about medical practice; a speech in Parliament attacking female admission to medical schools reveals the strength of male prejudice:

God sent women to be ministering angels, to smooth the pillow, administer the palliative, whisper words of comfort to the tossing patient ... Let that continue to be women's work! Leave the physician's task, the scientific lore, the iron wrist and the iron will to men. (quoted Faulkner and Arnold, 1985, p. 101)

Improvements in treatment had brought the need for nurses to be trained in some aspects of medical knowledge, so that they could deal with aspects of patient care such as keeping charts, using thermometers, giving injections, conducting tests and so forth. Doctors, however, were at first resistant to Nightingale's attempts to raise the standard of nursing education, fearing that nurses might begin to question their servant role. It may, therefore, have been partly for tactical reasons that she so repeatedly addressed the theme of nurses being assistants to men, carrying out doctors' orders. Nursing, she declared, was 'the skilled servant of medicine, surgery and hygiene'; it must involve 'strict obedience to the physician's or surgeon's power and knowledge' (quoted Gamarnikow, 1978, p. 107). This was to become the deep-rooted orthodoxy of the profession: 'we nurses are and never will be anything but the servants of doctors and good faithful servants we should be, happy in our dependence which helps to accomplish great deeds' (*Hospital*, 1906, quoted Gamarnikow, 1978, p. 108). Doctors were happy to agree. The *Lancet* proclaimed, 'woman as a nurse is the natural help of man as a doctor. Woman as a doctor is a conceit contradictory to nature' (quoted Versluysen, 1980, p. 182).

If a woman doctor was seen as an anomaly 'contradictory to nature' so was a male nurse (if nurse equals mother equals woman) an anomaly, a contradiction in terms. However, there was one area where male nurses dominated: asylum nursing. Here the nurse was seen as much as a warder as a carer and bodily strength was seen as a prerequisite for a job which often involved the physical suppression of violent or disturbed patients. Women were also employed as asylum nurses, but they normally dealt only with women, being confined to the 'women's side' in the asylum. Perhaps propriety was also an issue, as one male nurse at the beginning of this century complained of the job entailing the bearing of 'obscene abuse' (Carpenter, 1980, p. 141). Male nurses were excluded from the self-governing processes of the reformed nursing profession and by the Nurses Act of 1919 were confined to a separate register. However, they continued to dominate in psychiatric nursing, although they had little chance until the formation of the NHS to penetrate other sectors of the nursing world (Stacey et al., 1977; Bellaby and Oribator, 1980).

The restructuring of nursing and subsequent consolidation of the sexual division of labour within medicine took place, then, while Victorian separatist ideologies of gender were at their most powerful. Curing and cleansing tasks (the latter having now been passed down from trained nurses to ward assistants) were firmly allocated to women, and nurses only had access to aspects of curative practice under the control of doctors. Their actions were dependent on the diagnoses and prescriptions of doctors and it was explicitly forbidden for any nurse, however inwardly critical she might be, to challenge a doctor's decision. Men, thus, attained a total monopoly of curing at this time, legitimated by male command and monopoly of science.

The only way for women to recommence curing practice was to gain access to doctor's qualifications. A few pioneer women, like Elizabeth Blackwell and Elizabeth Garrett, obtained medical degrees abroad and were able to practice in England, and in the 1860s and 1870s women began to campaign for admission to British medical schools. Male lecturers and students reacted with hostility, abuse, embargoes, and even violence to the prospect of female invasion, but finally women won admission to London University in 1878 and Edinburgh in 1886. In the same period women gained access to psychiatric medicine, although they did not find it easy to find posts in public hospitals, because of notions of propriety (Mackenzie, 1983). By 1911 there were 477 women doctors in Britain (382 of these being unmarried), rising to 1253 in 1921 (a rise from 2 per cent to 7 per cent within the profession) (Brittain, 1928; Elston, 1977).

During World War I many more medical schools admitted women, but the interwar period, with its reassertion of the doctrine of separate spheres, saw a resurgence of exclusionary policies in response to male students' dislike of female colleagues. In 1933 the Royal Dental Hospital decided to bar women (Goldsmith, 1946). Women, therefore, had to be highly talented and determined to fight their way into a profession in which they were clearly unwelcome. To do so meant inevitably having to accept its male ethos and culture, including the prevailing medical view of women as hysterics, neurotic and dominated by biological needs (see Foucault, 1976; Ehrenreich and English, 1976). As Mackenzie (1983) argues in her essay on psychiatry, the price of admission was an uncritical stance to the body of medical and psychiatric theory which had been developed by men.

Meanwhile nursing had become established as an important female career. In 1919 the Royal College of Nursing finally won its campaign for all qualified nurses to be registered and the profession to be self-regulating. However, the General Nursing Council formed to administer the new system had 16 male members out of 25, showing how hard it was for nursing to break free of male control (Goldsmith, 1946).

Nurses in the early twentieth century had poor salaries, but a wide range of jobs; they could specialise in midwifery, psychiatric work, or work with children or for the school service or the Poor Law; army nursing was seen as a 'plum' job. District nursing often drew upon middle-class women, but in all branches there were possibilities of promotion to a sister, an educator or a health visitor (Holcombe, 1973). At the top of the tree the matron was a powerful figure, presiding over a range of clinical, domestic and administrative tasks.

Male nurses were barred from the Royal College of Nursing in 1937, but the female domination of the profession began to break down in the 1950s;

the demands of the expanding NHS hospital system led to the employment of many extra orderlies and auxiliaries, some of whom were men. Male penetration into nursing was further aided by the restructuring of the NHS as a result of the Salmon Committee proposals of 1966. This established a new management system, with the objective of introducing a more business-like ethos and improved efficiency (Carpenter, 1977; Leeson and Gray, 1978). The implications of this for gender relations are spelled out by Carpenter in an interesting essay: 'in redefining "female" positions into strictly functional managerial ones they were made ripe for male capture ... Salmon transformed the image of men in nursing. They are now perceived to possess "managerial" traits. Their previous disadvantages make them potentially good administrators.' By contrast women are seen as 'naturally' good nurses but 'inherently unable to exercise administrative skills' (Carpenter, 1977, p. 180).

The changes instituted by the Salmon Report involved a further fragmentation of tasks within medicine, whereby non-nursing tasks (administration, co-ordination) were split off from nursing proper, the former going to men and the latter remaining with women. The immediate effect was a rapid increase of the number of men in top nursing posts. By 1970 men, although they have never been more than 10 per cent within the profession, held 33 per cent of top posts (Novarra, 1980). Carpenter found that between 1969 and 1972 the number of men in the top two grades (Principal Nursing Officer and Chief Nursing Officer) had increased eightfold.

Latest developments in the NHS are likely to increase this tendency, as attempts to 'modernise' and 'rationalise' the service bring increased fragmentation and specialisation of tasks; basic nursing, clinical and specialist nursing and management are increasingly being separated. Such tendencies may well further erode the autonomy of the nursing profession; where formerly a nurse was under the control of a sister and a matron, she is now more likely to be deployed as part of a team, where control is increasingly concentrated in the hands of a (normally male) consultant (Bellaby and Oribator, 1980).

It could be argued that this loss of female dominance in nursing has been counterbalanced by the increase in number of women doctors since the war, and that both developments are progressive, evidence of growing tendencies to sex equality and selection on the basis of talent and not gender. However, studies of women doctors reveal that not only are they in a minority but also they have failed to penetrate the top positions in the medical hierarchy.

On the eve of World War II women were only 15 per cent of medical students, but the war represented a gain for them; the figure rose to 25 per cent after the war, but then remained constant until the late 1960s. In the next decade it rose dramatically to 40 per cent, but Elston's informative survey of women in medicine revealed that only 20 per cent of practising doctors were women (Elston, 1977, p. 115). There is a high dropout rate of women qualifiers, which can partly be ascribed to the difficulty of reconciling medical work with the responsibilities of child care; hospital work involves long and irregular hours, making it unattractive to married women. A survey of 8000 women doctors carried out in 1962-3 showed that only 47 per cent were working full-time; 32 per cent had part-time jobs, while 19 per cent were not working at all (Leeson and Gray, 1978, p. 36).

Women, consequently, have not fared well in the hospital hierarchy. In 1974 there were only 4590 women among the 29,018 hospital doctors in England and Wales. Women constituted one-third of pre-registered house officers, one-half of post-registered house officers, but only one-fifth of registrars and one-tenth of consultants (Leeson and Gray, 1978, pp. 37-8). At the same time only 12 out of the 359 chairs in London medical schools were held by women and 42 of the 46 members of the General Medical Council were men. Women were only 14 per cent of GPs, although they were 54 per cent of local authority medical staff (Elston, 1977, pp. 121-125). Such work, falling more readily into the nine-to-five routine, is easier to combine with domestic responsibilities; but it must also be seen as part of a process which channels women into types of work seen as more 'suitable' for them and which (quite coincidentally!) are also of lower status within the profession. Such jobs include geriatrics, child psychology, mental handicap (all with clear connotations of women's assumed superiority in domestic 'caring') and also radiology and anaesthetics. In children's mental illness, for example, women constituted 60 per cent of registrars and 31 per cent of consultants in 1975; by contrast, in the high-status area of surgery women were only 3 per cent of registrars and less than 2 per cent of consultants (Elston, 1977, p. 128). Women are thus concentrated into what the *British Medical Journal* has referred to as 'less demanding' specialities (Leeson and Gray, 1978, p. 40). Yet at least one surgeon in America has provided a rationale for assigning surgical tasks to women: 'I suppose most people think that surgery is like being a butcher, but there is very little blood; there should not be any ... I think surgery is nearer dressmaking; you clip with scissors and you sew with a needle. It is a very delicate business, and small quick hands are an asset' (quoted, Baker 1964, p. 277).

The position in general practice is little better. In 1985 only 18 per cent of GPs were women. Lawrence's study of women GPs revealed that many of them felt dominated and disparaged by the male senior partners in group practices; she argues that, although women are generally successful at medical school, they are still disadvantaged in a professional culture controlled by men, in which men set standards and rules of how and what medical practice should be (Lawrence, 1987). A recent government-sponsored report has confirmed that an 'old boy mafia' serves to hold back women; a system of patronage and sponsorship, centred particularly on teaching hospitals, retards female careers (*Guardian*, 7 June 1988).

Women's advance as doctors, then, has been limited, and has done little to break down the sex hierarchies of the medical system or to destroy the sexual stereotyping which still characterises it. Within the health service today women are still largely responsible for cleaning and caring. The growth of the NHS has involved a huge increase in all sorts of jobs, most of which are assigned on the grounds of gender. In the 1970s there were 94,000 nursing auxiliaries in Britain, performing a range of 'unskilled', non-specialised caring tasks; 95 per cent were women. Two thirds of ancillary jobs (catering, cleaning, laundry and so forth) were filled by women (Leeson and Gray, 1978). In the minor medical professions women work in 'tending' jobs, like physiotherapy, occupational therapy and radiography, where handling patients is important. Hospital technicians are otherwise mainly men.

Accounts of hospital life by Neale (1983), Cockburn (1985) and Beechey and Perkins (1987) show the strength of sex hierarchies and stereotyping. Cockburn's study of radiographers reveals that male staff saw women as less gifted in using machinery, but better at dealing with patients. Men held most of the top scientific jobs in this area (as medical physicists). One such physicist explained, 'the men are more interested in "playing with toys". The whole thing is more *fun* to the men ... It's partly technical competence. But it is also an interest in *having* technical competence ... As a gross observation, as I see it, it is something to do with the way men and women are born' (Cockburn, 1985, p. 136). Similar stereotyping is revealed in Homans' study of NHS scientists; women were seen by the males as less reliable (especially in terms of their propensity to become pregnant!) and as having different talents; although the work they did was supposedly equal, Homans argued that men spent more of their time on administration and actual research, while women's daily routine included more clerical tasks and cleaning up after experiments, again echoing the old patriarchal order of men as directors, and women as assistants. This, in turn, leads to the attitude that women are less important. As one male bluntly put it, 'if it were possible to have two absolutely equal people ... one male and one female, you would appoint the male' (Homans, 1987, p. 94).

Neale's description of the hospital world stresses how hierarchies of class, gender and race are intricately linked. At the top are the consultants, 'prima donnas' in his phrase, treated virtually as gods. Nurses continue to be cast as mothers to patients, assistants, secretaries and mistresses to doctors; sexual innuendo and flirting between doctors and nurses are an important part of hospital culture. Yet the legacy of Nightingale's Victorianism ensures that the nurse's sexuality is carefully controlled, disguised by a demure uniform: 'a nurse is set up as an embodiment of all that is best in women. And she is therefore passive.' Technicians and porters (with more mobile, less controlled work patterns) are male; at the bottom of the tree, cleaners are women, typically black. Each grade is immediately identifiable to others within the hierarchy by its uniforms and men's jobs are normally two or three grades higher than comparable jobs done by women (Neale, 1983, pp. 11, 13, 17). Beechey and Perkins similarly found 'a strict form of job segregation' between male and female ancillary workers, men being porters and women domestics (Beechey and Perkins, 1987, p. 86); in the lowest Grade One (cleaners and catering) there were no men at all. The male job of window-cleaning was assigned to Grade Three!

Thus, in the modern British health service women are kept in their (traditional) places; despite the public adulation given to nurses, those 'natural' female skills are poorly rewarded in economic terms. Devaluation of female skills applies at all levels. Rosser and Davies' work on NHS administration reveals how women who actually *do* important administrative work are *recorded* as clerical or secretarial workers (with consequently lower salaries); and here, too, the skills shown by these women in managing the human sides of departments are seen as a 'natural' extension of motherliness (Rosser and Davies, 1987).

In other countries women have not been so thoroughly excluded from curing tasks. Between 30 and 40 per cent of Chinese doctors are women; in Poland it is 46 per cent, in the Soviet Union 74 per cent (although in these countries too, men tend to occupy the highest-status posts and specialisms) (Leeson and Gray, 1978, p. 43). In America, however, the story is, if anything, more dismal than in Britain.

The early history is similar. In colonial America, with a severe lack of trained doctors, women practised healing in the family, aided by extra infusions of folk knowledge from the African slaves and Indian populations. Midwifery was a full-time prestigious female job. Women were more involved in the commercialised sector than their British counterparts. Matthaei records examples of the numerous ointments and patent medicines marketed by women, such as Nurse Tucker's cure for 'the Piles, Rheumatism, strains, all kinds of Pains, Ring-Worm, Moths, Carbuncles, Sun-burning, Freckles, and chopping of the skin; and women that are likely to have Sore Breasts, if they apply in Time' (Matthaei, 1982, p. 60).

The nineteenth century saw attempts to exclude untrained practitioners, but in such a huge and geographically developing society it was less easy for the trained elite to monopolise. In what were known as the 'irregular' sections (what we might now label alternative medicine) some women continued to practise and to receive instruction, although campaigns against them grew fiercer. In 1871 the President of the American Medical Association (which excluded women up till 1915) declared than a woman doctor was a 'monstrous production', echoing his

British colleagues (Ehrenreich and English, 1979, p. 58). Women were kept out of hospitals, and in 1900 were only 6 per cent of the profession. Nor has their number since increased to the same extent as in Britain. Women were only 7 per cent of doctors in 1960 and, despite the successes of feminism in promoting women's rights, were still less than 18 per cent in 1986, while only 4 per cent of dentists were women (United States Bureau of the Census, 1988; Matthaei, 1982).

Lorber's study of American women physicians shows that their position is very similar to that of their British sisters. Despite increased numbers of female entrants in the 1970s, women are pushed into traditionally female specialisms (pediatrics, family and community medicine, psychiatry, anaesthesiology) and fail to reach top posts. Just as in Britain women suffer from lack of sponsorship from powerful seniors and teachers and are excluded from male networks. Where medicine is more commercialised than in Britain this is a severe handicap: women cannot make the contacts needed to get into prosperous high-status medical business. Domestic responsibilities further restrict their social activities and they must fight against prevailing stereotypes which portray them as less fitted to be doctors than men: 'the stereotypical physician embodies supposedly manly characteristics – rationality, objectivity, technical authoritativeness and aggressiveness in the face of emergencies' (Lorber, 1984, p. 1).

As in Britain, women tried to make nursing a female profession. Many women took up nursing work during the Civil War and in the 1870s Nightingale-style training was developed. By 1890 40,000 women were working as nurses and midwives, but the majority had received no formal training and were very poorly paid. The links with domestic service remained stronger than in England, and persistent shortages have led to the employment in great numbers of 'semi-skilled' nurses (known as 'practical nurses', similar to British 'enrolled' nurses) and of auxiliaries and aides. Baker shows how tasks have been shared between the different groups; professional (i.e. registered) nurses work mainly as administrators, organisers and teachers, practical nurses perform the actual bedside caring work and domestic work is carried out by the various auxiliary grades (Baker, 1964; Wertheimer, 1977).

A major difference from Britain was the total crushing out of the traditional female skill of midwifery. The story is traced by Ehrenreich and English: in 1900 50 per cent of babies were still delivered by midwives, but higher-class women were switching to the new type of childbirth provision, medicalised and controlled by doctors. The doctors of the AMA then mounted a devastating attack on female midwifery as barbaric and unscientific, and simply refused to allow practice under licence, as was the British system. By 1930 midwives had been almost entirely eliminated. Ehrenreich and English suggest that the greater commercialisation of American hospitals may have provoked this attempt to establish a male monopoly over childbirth, a potentially profitable business.

Matthaei points to the contrast between the male-controlled physicians' profession, and the almost entirely female (95 per cent in 1986) nursing profession. Whereas the male professions maintain their power by monopolising abstract knowledge, through strong organisation and the principle of self-control, female professions have tended to establish themselves under the control of hierarchical male authorities. Inevitably this limits their power, and brings with it a culture of servility and deference to men. A quotation from the *Canadian Nurse* neatly encapsulates the relation between the two branches of medicine: 'she owes to the attending physicians absolute silence regarding their professional demerits or blundering. No nurse who has not learned the lesson of implicit obedience to authority and practised it until it has become a habit of life is fitted to command others' (quoted Coburn, 1974, p. 157). Leeson and Gray comment in the English context, 'decisions are made by the men doctors and the subservient women ward staff exercise authority over the patients on their behalf, as if they were fathers, mothers and children respectively' (Leeson and Gray, 1978, p. 12). As in Britain, American schools of nursing endorse these attitudes of subservience (Wilson, 1971).

It remains to be seen whether the switch from the paternalist model to a more bureaucratic one (occurring in other countries besides Britain) will destroy this traditional division of labour. Continuing technological advance, such as the greater use of machines for diagnosis and treatment, and the installation of automatic monitoring consoles in wards, is also likely to bring further specialisation and changes in the division of labour. In Australia and Canada a new category of 'nurse practitioners' is being developed to fill in gaps in the service, and there is currently talk of trying this out in Britain; but, unless there is a major change of attitudes among the male medical authorities, such a reintegration of curing and caring tasks is likely to be conducted firmly under the control of male doctors.

This male profession (like its companions, the law and the church) shows little sign of conceding complete parity to women. It is apparent that women face resistance or practical difficulties in entering jobs in these professions, and that their exclusion from such jobs is backed up by complacent male ideologies of sex differences in personality and aptitudes. Women continue in the main, to take subsidiary roles, and the NHS is organised on the basis of elaborate hierarchies of gender and race. The crucial axis of power is the definition of what constitutes correct professional practice and the control of scientific knowledge. Women have made little inroad into the professional bodies which organise their activities. Thus the medical profession, like others, is still marked by both horizontal and vertical segregation.

13

TEACHING

We turn finally to teaching, an area where, at least, it seems that segregation and sex-typing are at a minimum. In today's schools women and men work side by side teaching, by and large, the same subjects. Only in specialist 'boys'' and 'girls'' subjects (such as woodwork, technical drawing, cricket and rugby on one side, needlework, typing, netball and hockey on the other) is there pronounced sex-typing, and there is some possibility that this will begin to break down following the Sex Discrimination Act of 1976.

However, although horizontal segregation is low in the teaching profession, vertical segregation is by no means absent. In each branch of teaching men tend to rise to the higher positions, and the higher status of the area the more marked is the male dominance; in British universities, for example, in 1986 women constituted only 17 per cent of full-time academic staff and only 3 per cent of professors; while only 15 per cent of men remain at the lecturer level for their whole career, this is true of 48 per cent of women (Lovenduski, 1987).

I hope to show that this is related to two views of the nature of the teaching task which have been present since the origin of the school system, assigning men and women different attributes as teachers, which in turn are linked to ideas of male and female characters as differentiated. These views were particularly strong in nineteenth-century Britain, but linger on today, lying behind, for example, the concentration of women in primary teaching and the domination of men in the university sector.

One of these two views emphasises very strongly the link of teaching with child care and child bearing. This view seems to have been common in pre-industrial times, both in Britain and America. Accordingly, the 'care of children's education' was seen as a female duty (Fussell and Fussell, 1985,

p. 84). Part of bringing up children successfully and equipping them for adulthood is to teach them the form of behaviour, knowledge and skills which will be necessary in their various future social roles; teaching, then, becomes inseparable from socialisation. It is this logic, possibly, which leads Novarra (1980) to see education as one of the 'six tasks' almost universally assigned to women.

In pre-industrial societies the bulk of this teaching was done by mothers within the home, or, among the higher ranks, by governesses and tutors (according to the sex of the children and the wealth of the household) engaged for the purpose. But where small schools were set up in Britain and America for young children of the lower strata they were often run by women; these schools, disparaged by their critics as 'dame schools' with low educational standards, were common by the eighteenth century. Higher up the social hierarchy single women and widows with a little capital might set up boarding schools of a more select nature for young ladies. As Vicinus tells us, these were run on the lines of an enlarged family, with a small number of pupils (15 to 20) who all worked in one class with the mistress; such schools were often of 'few academic pretensions and many social ones' (Vicinus, 1985, p. 165). One woman involved in this line of work in the seventeenth century was Hannah Woolley, who was orphaned at fourteen and straightaway became mistress of a 'little school', before going on to become a governess and eventually to marry a schoolmaster with whom she jointly ran more schools. As a teacher Woolley offered her clients a wide range of accomplishments, ranging from the useful (writing and arithmetic, 'all manner of Cookery', 'making Salves, Oyntments, Waters, Cordials') to the decoratively pointless ('rocks made of Shell or in Sweets', 'Feathers of Crewel for the corners of Beds', 'making Sweet Powders for the Hair') (Stuart, 1933, p. 183).

As the Woolley example indicates, there were also many schoolmasters in Britain (although apparently they were less common in America) and this is an indication of the competing version of the teaching role. This was the academic view of teaching, concerned with the acquisition and passing on of specialised, complex and often rather esoteric forms of knowledge; it was fostered by the universities, and medieval universities like Oxford and Cambridge were by and large a male stronghold. The link of learning and universities with the church strengthened that male monopoly, although studies of medieval and Tudor women indicate that there were numerous learned women among both the religious orders and the laity; nuns, aristocratic ladies and even a few noted female scholars. European universities (especially in Italy) did also admit female students and appoint female professors in the medieval and Renaissance periods. However, specialised academic learning became increasingly a male preserve, just as did academic medicine. Where the aim of teaching was instruction in specialised knowledge, such as classical language, philosophy or theology, it would be entrustesd to men. Thus schooling for the sons of the nobility was carried out by male tutors and masters, and 'grammar schools' for the higher and middle classes were also staffed by men. This tradition, of course, carried on into the nineteenth-century public schools, and was strengthened by the growing emphasis given to team sports and physical training, along with a notion that pupils in these schools were having their characters built as 'leaders of men'. In this more exalted sphere of education women would not be considered competent as this comment by one Renaissance scholar shows:

> It neither becometh a woman to rule a school ... Because a woman is a frail thing, and of weak discretion and may lightly be deceived ... Therefore a woman should not teach, lest when she hath a false opinion or belief of anything, she spread it into her hearers. (quoted Tickner, 1923, p. 105)

Such education, however, was the domain of a tiny minority of the elite, and the dominant form of teaching was the female one, with the education of children seen as an extension of motherhood. As education for the mass of the populace slowly developed from the late eighteenth century onwards, many women worked as teachers, both privately and as employees of the church voluntary societies and later on of the state when it began to support church schools. Asher Tropp in his influential study of the teaching profession describes the majority of teachers in the first half of the nineteenth century as 'men (*sic*) who had tried other trades and failed' (Tropp, 1957, p. 10); however, the 1851 Census recorded twice as many women teachers as men (71,966 to 34,378).

Among administrators and educational reformers there was growing concern over the standard of teaching and of schools, since at this date no qualifications or certificates were needed to teach or establish a school; thus, the quality of schools varied greatly, some providing education at the most minimal level. The majority of teachers were of working-class origin, which may also have worried paternalist reformers. Kay Shuttleworth's pupil-teacher scheme, introduced in 1846, marked the beginning of government attempts to raise standards of teaching and police the system. Men were in the majority among the recruits at first, the proportion of women, however, rising fairly rapidly from 32 per cent to 46 per cent between 1849 and 1859 (Tropp, 1957). It was hoped to attract recruits of higher social origin, but Widdowson, in her detailed examination of women elementary school teachers, argues that the early start to a pupil-teacher's working life (at age thirteen) was incompatible with middle-class lifestyle and custom (Widdowson, 1983). Some in the educational world were, indeed, opposed to the entry of middle-class recruits on these grounds. One witness to the Newcastle Commission (which investigated state-aided schools) considered that 'the rough coarse work of these schools, the publicity, and the low associations, must render the office of teacher extremely repulsive to those who have been brought up as ladies' (quoted, Hollis, 1979, p. 92). Another participant in this debate declared that middle-class girls 'would marry the Clergyman or the Squire or their sons in nearly every parish they went to', thus invalidating the use of public money for their training (Hollis, 1979, p. 91). Nonetheless, by the 1860s and 1870s lower-middle-class girls were starting to enlist as teachers, partly encouraged by the expansion of teacher training colleges and perhaps partly driven to it by lack of 'respectable' career alternatives. By the end of the century teaching was a major female occupation (Widdowson, 1983).

The immediate impact of government-sponsored teacher training was an encouragement to the employment of males in schools aided by state grants; in 1872 whereas three-quarters of all teachers were women they constituted only 51 per cent of teachers in grant-aided elementary schools. But by 1870 the number of girl pupil-teachers was greater than that of boys and the following three decades saw a dramatic feminisation of the state-aided sector, the proportion of women rising to 70 per cent in 1896 and by 1913 to 75 per cent, remaining on or around the three quarters mark up till World War II (figures from PP 1945-6 xi, p. 22; Holcombe, 1973, p. 203). During the last quarter of the century teaching was one of the nine occupations in which the employment of women had increased relative to population increases (nursing was another), whereas the proportion of men relatively declined (PP 1894 lxxxi, Pt II, p. 3). Holcombe calculates that between 1875 and 1914 women's employment in elementary teaching expanded by 862 per cent (Holcombe, 1973, p. 34). Figures for elementary school leavers for 1899 show that the proportion of boys going to be teachers was about 1 per cent in most of the major urban regions, while percentages were much higher for girls, ranging from 3 per cent in Yorkshire to 6 per cent in the South East, South West and East Midlands (PP 1899 lxxv, p. viii). This period, then, saw a clear consolidation of female numerical dominance in the profession. It is likely that the general rise in working-class wages at this time made teaching a less attractive proposition for working-class boys.

As Hellerstein et al. (1981) argue, elementary schoolteaching was seen as highly compatible with the domestic destiny ascribed to women in Victorian ideology; for young women, teaching was viewed as an apprenticeship for motherhood; the middle-class teacher could serve as 'a mother to her pupils, a model of Christian behaviour, and her house will be an example of domestic comfort and efficiency' (Widdowson, 1983, p. 31). Most women gave up teaching on marriage as they were expected to do. An article in *The Schoolmaster* in 1874 presents arguments which were to be rehearsed for many decades:

Married women teachers are unjust to the families of the teachers themselves ... their children are neglected ... It is an injustice to the school ... she has not the same incentive to work as one who is single, for she has her husband to fall back upon. Young women, fresh from college, or wishing to change their situations, complain of this unfair competition. (quoted, Hollis, 1979, p. 93)

However, this was a career which offered the chance of an independent life to any who might not wish to enter or be likely to succeed in the marriage market. In her discussion of teaching, Horowitz Murray (1984) points out that many woman teachers and governesses had dependants (elderly parents, sisters, young relatives) helplessly relying on their support. For the school boards the appeal of such women was the cheapness of their labour and their apparent capacity to put up with poor conditions.

The expansion of women's employment in teaching, however, placed them firmly within the lower ranks of the developing educational hierarchy, which Hellerstein et al. argue reproduced the structure of the patriarchal family, with the female schoolteacher under the direction of a male administrator. Not only that, but women were discriminated against within the ranks of teachers in various ways. First, they were less likely than men to be certificated and trained: in 1875 70 per cent of male teachers but only 57 per cent of women teachers were fully qualified, with the gap widening by 1914 to 66 per cent and 32 per cent respectively (Holcombe, 1973, p. 36). Women were thus the bulk of uncertificated teaching staff, drafted in because of shortages, who would receive only 50 or 60 per cent of the certificated teachers' salary. The lowest grade of all were the 'supplementary' teachers, who were only required to be over eighteen, vaccinated and accepted by an inspector. In 1907 there were 18,437 women supplementary teachers and only 195 men; they earned the pathetic salary of £20 to £30 per annum (Widdowson, 1983, p. 58).

Secondly, even where they were of the equivalent grade to men, women were paid less, earning from two-thirds to three-quarters of a man's salary. For example, in 1905 male headteachers were earning an average of £160.5 per annum, women £109.7, male assistant teachers were earning £114.5, women £83.7 (PP 1919 xxxi, p. 66). It is an interesting reflection of the contemporary estimation of women's worth that a female head was likely to earn less than a male assistant!

Finally, though, as Holcombe points out, in the early days virtually every certified teacher could expect to become a head, the expansion of the system, the growing size of schools and the development of departmental structures within them, meant that women became less likely to reach higher posts. In 1914 women, while constituting 70 per cent of elementary assistant teachers, were only 56 per cent of head teachers (men being only 33 per cent of assistants but 44 per cent of heads). A clear pattern of segregation based on sex-typing was developing, as is revealed in the 1919

Report on Women in Industry. In elementary schools, infants' and girls' departments were staffed by women with women heads. Women were permitted to teach boys up to standard III, but higher classes for boys were taken entirely by men. In mixed schools, therefore, headteachers tended to be male. Women largely staffed special schools (where the work was likely to be as much tending and caring as instruction). At secondary level proportionally fewer women were employed. In 1914, for example, there were more male teachers (6609) than female (6321) in state-financed secondary schools (Holcombe, 1973, p. 57). Most secondary schools were single sex, and so had headmasters or headmistresses respectively; in 1914 there were 668 male heads and 349 female (PP 1919 xxxi, pp. 20–1).

The important thing about this pattern of employment was that it was firmly linked to a view of differentiated capacities of men and women. Quoted in the Report is the comment of the Education Officer for the London County Council: 'men could not take the place of women in an infants' department or girls' school, nor could a woman look after the boys' organised games or bring the same experience as could men in the training of the boy's character which was as essential as the teaching of knowledge' (PP 1919 xxxi, p. 21). Such a view appears to have been shared by some women. One wrote to The Schoolmaster (indicative title) to protest against the idea that women might be employed as school inspectors; 'the woman's nature is too small for the work of judging, it is too exacting towards its own sex, it is too much turned on details to the exclusion of generalities, and it is too concentrated on parts, to be able to grasp a clear view of the whole' (quoted Hollis, 1979, p. 93).

Thus we can see that where the teacher's role was conceived as a 'sort of substitute mother' (Deem, 1978, p. 110) women were considered the proper occupants; whereas the teaching of boys was considered to require different attributes, particularly that of the authoritarian father, considered to be possessed by men. The taking of responsibility in a large school was also seen as more aptly done by men. However, other factors worked against the total exclusion of women from top posts. One was simply economics: especially in the rural areas 'local authorities often appointed a headmistress for reasons of economy, in spite of the preference of local opinion for a male teacher because of his wider usefulness in the parish' (PP 1919 xxxi, p. 21). Nor was it easy to attract men to a job with poor pay and heavy responsibilities (the above quotation points to the broader role the teacher was expected to play in a small community) in isolated social conditions.

Another factor was the changing class background of female recruits, while their male counterparts continued to be of lower-class origin. By the end of the century lower-middle-class women were still predominating, but women from higher-middle-classs backgrounds were joining the service, a trend which became established in the early twentieth century

(Widdowson, 1973; Vicinus, 1985). From the 1870s the attempts to attract more 'genteel' women had persisted, led by campaigners who were aware of the grossly limited opportunities facing unmarried women from the respectable classes, like the hapless Madden sisters in Gissing's *The Odd Women* who lived a life of near starvation, driven to depression and drink. Governessing remained one 'suitable' job for such near-destitute women, despite the awful conditions, low pay and contemptuous treatment from pupils and employers alike which governesses often experienced (see Hollis, 1979; Horowitz Murray, 1984). Governesses' pay ranged from £10 to £100 per annum, according to the establishment, but most were giving up their liberty for £20 to £30. From the 1890s, however, employment of this kind was on the wane, as the school system expanded. Such women might now turn to teaching with its better pay and greater independence, particularly as the establishment of high-quality girls' secondary schools and the opening up of higher education for women provided new possibilities of high-level teaching careers and produced a new type of entrant. According to Vicinus, large numbers of female university graduates became teachers (50 per cent of the early students of Newnham College, Cambridge, for example).

Vicinus' fascinating study describes how, in the closing decades of the nineteenth century, these careers attracted dedicated single women, who were often motivated by high ideals and prepared for a life of altruistic self-sacrifice and service to the community. Agnes Maitland, the principal of Somerville College, Oxford, spoke in praise of the 'often beautiful unselfishness of tutors and lecturers not long since students themselves' (quote Vicinus, 1985, p. 136). Teaching was seen as a moral vocation, for which little material reward was expected. This was to be an enduring attitude among some women teachers. Ida Rex, speaking of her experience in Hackney in the interwar period, explained how 'teaching was looked upon as a type of social work in the East End ... It wasn't the money that you got, it was helping children ... The Headmistress was one of the old English really dedicated women who had come from a very good family and was really doing it from a point of view of, not so much a career, but as her social work for the country' (Hackney WEA, undated, p. 25).

By contrast Vicinus describes how these attitudes began to be challenged by other women who *were* concerned with teaching as a career and its status, demanding a better level of professional recognition and treatment. For example, Sarah Burstall, headmistress of Manchester High School for Girls, declared 'parents have to realise that the teacher is an expert professional and is entitled therefore to the deference shown to the skilled professional opinion of the doctor, lawyer or architect' (quoted Vicinus, 1985, p. 175). The determination of these women helped to prevent teaching, as a female-dominated profession, from sinking to the level of nursing. Widdowson argues that the influx of higher-class women during this period helped, on the contrary, to upgrade it. Such women were also more drawn to union activity than any of the female groups we have so far studied. In 1911 the National Union of Teachers (NUT) elected its first female president (Holcombe, 1973).

These women, at least, had access to important career posts, such as principals of women's training colleges (posts reserved by legislation for women), teachers at women's university colleges, or headmistresses of the newly reformed girls' boarding schools. Despite the low pay, this was becoming a profession which offered women real opportunities.

However, prospects for woman teachers in the early twentieth century were poorer then for men. Women recalling their teaching work in the early part of the century made that clear to Judith Cook. Kate Roberts was the first female to graduate in Wales (in 1904, with a first-class honours degree) but reported that 'however well qualified you were, you started in the primary schools, as I did'. She started work earning £60 a year and only in World War I did she get a secondary post. Edith Breedon, too, recalled that men always took priority (Cook, 1984, pp. 76, 159). Ida Rex was another who only moved into teaching older children when the men had gone to the front; she was then able to teach science and geography as a specialist teacher to boys large and small. Altogether some 13,000 extra women were employed during World War I apparently without great detriment to the service.

In the interwar period, however, the old pattern of sex-typing was reaffirmed on the grounds of differing capacities. The actions of some male teachers reinforced these divisions. Campaigns by groups of women teachers and feminists, such as the Equal Pay League, for parity with men had met with strong opposition from male members of the NUT. A motion on equal pay at the 1904 NUT conference provoked a 'hideous outburst of rage and yells of scorn and contempt and bitter hostility' as its (male) proposer recalled (quoted Partington, 1976, p. 10). When the NUT conceded to female pressure on equal pay in 1919, the National Association of Schoolmasters (NAS) was formed as a breakaway union in protest. The NAS persistently opposed policies of sexual equality; for example, in 1926 it passed 'amid cheering' a resolution 'declaring opposition to any assistant master serving under a headmistress' (Brittain, 1928, p. 65). Throughout the 1930s it campaigned against equal pay and against women teaching boys aged over seven (Oram, 1983). Partington's useful study provides ample instances of its assertion of male superiority and sexual differentiation; members argued that it was 'impossible for a man to serve under a woman and retain his self-respect and manhood' and that they could not 'feminise 700,000 boys without feminising the nation'. Boys should be taught by men, girls by women; and women who matched male achievements were derided as monstrosities: 'no woman could train a boy in habits of manliness. It was true that one occasionally met the woman who could "manage boys as well as any man". Such a one might be an admirable proprietress of a Wild West Saloon, but they had no room for her in our boys' school' (quoted Partington, 1976, pp. 36, 41).

Although the NUT's counter-campaign was unsuccessful, the rates of women's pay did rise slowly, from about 75 per cent of men's rates in 1914 to 80 per cent in 1945. Despite this slight improvement in women's position, the Report on Equal Pay demonstrates the continued social commitment to segregated teaching roles: 'for the very young children of either sex, woman, qua woman, is the best teacher, even though men of higher teaching qualifications may be available ... For the older boys, men, because they are men, are the best teachers, even though women of higher teaching qualifications may be available' (PP 1945-6 xi, p. 147). Thus, in 1938 there were only 27 women heads of boys' schools and 19 of senior mixed schools, while conversely there were no male heads in infants' or girls' only departments (p. 24). Nearly half way into the twentieth century little had changed from the 1890s; women continued to monopolise the teaching of small children and to be little involved in teaching boys aged over eleven.

The interwar period was also the epoch of the marriage bar. As we have seen, it was already established custom for most women teachers to retire after marriage. Ida Rex reported this to be the social norm before the 1914 war on the grounds that women couldn't 'manage both things at once', a position with which she agreed (Hackney WEA, p. 29). Linda McCullough Thew (1985) reports that in her childhood teaching was viewed as a job for life, incompatible with marriage, partly because of the requirement of lengthy training; such an image was a deterrent to young girls eager for romance and marriage. Shopwork offered better hope of a husband. The 1911 Census recorded that only a tiny minority (7 per cent) of female reachers were married, but possibly in areas where women's rights were more of an issue the picture was different. According to Widdowson, London County Council figures showed that in 1908 39 per cent of London headmistresses and even 23 per cent of female assistants were married (Widdowson, 1983, p. 65).

Official disapproval of married women teachers found its expression in the marriage bars imposed by some LEAs in the early decades of the century, these becoming more widespread in the 1920s and 1930s. The war had increased the proportion of married women to 15 per cent, and in her study of the marriage bar Oram argues that the hardening attitude was caused by a backlash, reasserting male power in face of the apparent ease with which women had occupied male posts. Clearly, a contributory factor was the recession, bringing the spread of male unemployment and worries about public expenditure, which made it easy to rally popular support for the exclusion of married women. Consequently, these two decades saw a reaffirmation of the Victorian ideology that only single women had a right to jobs, while women who were prepared to leave babies to go and teach were seen as bad mothers and inherently unfit for the teaching role of 'substitute mother'! Economic reasons (the costs of maternity leave, high rates of absenteeism among married women) were also raised, but it is hard to resist Oram's conclusion that these were merely excuses to back up a discriminatory policy with its roots in patriarchal ideology. The result of all this was that the proportion of male teachers rose, from 22 per cent to 29 per cent between 1922 and 1938 (Oram, 1983). According to Vicinus, this also served to undermine the image of teaching as a good, independent career for women, as it ran the danger of appearing as 'a dumping ground for old maids' (Vicinus, 1985, p. 209).

World War II again led to women standing in for male teachers, as 20,000 men left to fight, but, as the Equal Pay Commission findings and conclusions quoted above demonstrate, this did not bring an end to sex-typing or established social views on the teacher's role. Despite evidence that other countries had institutionalised equal pay for teachers in state schools (Soviet Union, France) or were moving towards it where work was similar (America) the Commission refused to recommend it. In general, it considered men's work to be of more 'value' than women's because of men's greater physical attributes. As this was hardly relevant to teaching, they resorted to the argument that equal pay would have a detrimental effect on wage levels in the service and might drive men from teaching; such a finding was no doubt pleasing to a (Labour) government with no desire to finance increased costs within its education service.

Perhaps it is unsurprising that the immediate postwar years brought a shortage of women teachers. While the numbers of male teachers more than doubled between 1945 and 1951, the number of women decreased, although the 'baby boom' heralded the need for an increase in the provision of infant education. Women, it seemed, were more attracted by expanded opportunities elsewhere, and many continued to leave teaching on marriage, although the marriage bar had been outlawed by the 1944 Education Act. A special recruitment campaign was launched which did entice more young women into teacher training, but the proportion of women steadily decreased to 62 per cent in 1955, thence to 57 per cent in 1964 (Partington, 1976). Equal pay was finally granted in 1955, not being fully implemented until 1961; subsequently the proportion of women rose again. With improved pay and prospects, teaching once again appeared as a good career for the middle-class girl. In Tropp's opinion, it was 'the most convenient occupation for the middle-class married woman, and ... the most profitable investment for a girl whose aspirations include marriage and motherhood' (Tropp, 1957, p. 263).

However, government statistics for 1985 show how extraordinarily persistent the pattern of vertical segregation and differentiated sex roles have proved to be; 61 per cent of assistant teachers in state-sector schools in Great Britain are women, but only 40 per cent of head teachers. Virtually no men are employed in state-run nursery schools (11, as opposed to 1676 women) and women strongly predominate in primary schools (132,015 compared to 37,576 men). However, at secondary level, there are more male teachers than women. Men are more likely to be well qualified (56 per cent of male teachers in England and Wales were graduates, as opposed to 37 per cent of women). At almost every level in the profession they rise to higher posts. Only in nursery and infant schools do female heads predominate; in junior schools with infant departments there were well over twice as any male heads, and 80 per cent of schools with juniors had men as heads. In the primary sector as a whole, women make up 78 per cent of teaching staff but only 45 per cent of head teachers. In the secondary sector only 16 per cent of schools have headmistresses, many of these being all-girl schools; only 14 per cent of comprehensives are headed by a woman. Women are 29 per cent of deputy heads in secondary schools, at the level of second masters and mistresses they predominate slightly (54 per cent), but they make up only 20 per cent of other senior teachers. Moreover, not only do women fail to rise to the very top, they also stick at the bottom. In primary teaching only 9 per cent of men are in the lowest grade as opposed to 35 per cent of women and at secondary level the figures are 19 per cent and 40 per cent respectively (Statistics of Education, 1985).

Behind this pattern of lower female achievement, many elements are discernible. An important contributory factor is the tendency of women to leave the profession altogether for motherhood, or to have their careers interrupted by spells of full-time child care. Acker (1987) suggests that the promotional structure of the profession is biased towards men, since long uninterrupted periods of service are an important criterion. She also reviews material which suggests that women are less ambitious, but studies of this kind indicate that career aspirations are realistically geared to the current situation; thus women in the infant sector are most likely to aspire to a headship and women in the secondary sector least likely. Some women may also feel that the extra responsibilities associated with a senior post are too grave to be easily combined with family responsibilities.

But not all women are married or have children and it seems clear that differential achievement also reflects the extent to which women and men are *still* assigned different roles in teaching. In Deem's words:

> Maternalistic and pastoral roles are often played by women teachers and paternalistic and authoritarian roles by men teachers. Many primary schools implicitly recognise the similarity between their relationships and structure and that of the family, even referring to their organisation of pupils as 'family' groupings. Mothers are frequently seen as the model for teachers of young children and fathers seen as the model for teachers of older children. (Deem, 1978, p. 112)

The allocation of pastoral duties to senior mistresses in large comprehensive schools may explain why women fare better at this level. Partington's study shows that this post has historically held low prestige, sometimes lacking real authority or responsibility. As the figures above suggest, women are generally considered less suitable for posts of responsibility, which is seen as less compatible with female character and aptitudes. Deem provides evidence of those attitudes elsewhere in her study of women in education. For example, R. R. Dale, a leading researcher of the 1970s into secondary schooling, holds views about male and female characteristics extraordinarily similar to those of the nineteenth-century commentators quoted earlier in the chapter: 'the female personality may not be ideally suited to the traditional class teaching situation ... where there is some need for dominance, which comes more naturally to a man'. He suggests that the 'male and female mind' take different approaches to problem solving and considers that 'it is generally accepted that the feminine mind takes great care of detail and if anything is over-conscientious (which leads to fussiness) ... in a mixed school the men of the staff would keep such a process in check' (quoted Deem, 1978, pp. 49, 74, 122).

Evidence confirms that these stereotypes are also held by schoolchildren, for whom the ideal 'good teacher' is a youngish married man, accessible but firm (Deem, 1978, p. 22). Stanworth's interviews with schoolchildren revealed that most felt that men were better teachers, using criteria ranging from better discipline to greater academic proficiency and knowledge of their subjects. Women were seen as insufficiently authoritarian; by comparison men were held to command greater respect, particularly from rowdy and trouble-making male pupils; 'they tend to handle a class better and you pay more attention to them ... I've had quite a few women teachers and they will let the class go' (quoted Stanworth, 1983, p. 34).

This problem of the relation of women teachers to adolescent boys may be a real barrier to the breakdown of sex-typing in teaching. However, it is not altogether clear to what extent such differences in effectiveness are real or simply imagined on the basis of stereotypes. Not all female teachers are incapable of controlling a class, nor can there be any reality in the children's claim that they are less academically competent than their male colleagues. Deem suggests that the problem rises from the fact that adolescent males have strongly internalised social values which emphasis male superiority and power over women (and Stanworth's accounts of the boys' contemptuous attitude to their female peers would confirm this); the boys will exploit this sense of superiority to mount a challenge to the school system which many of them reject. Thus, the 'discipline problems' of female teachers reflect social attitudes which hold women in lower esteem than men.

For Deem and Acker, differences in male and female teachers' achievements are related as much to discrimination and ideological constructions as to any real difference in aptitudes. This can be demonstrated more clearly if we consider the position of women teaching in higher education. Women were late entrants to the ranks of university teachers, gaining grudging acceptance from the 1890s on. Margherita Rendel (1980) has used university yearbooks to calculate proportions of women academics between 1912 and 1951, which rose only from 5 per cent to 12 per cent. Recent statistics show little dramatic improvement in women's position. While girls perform as well, if not better, in school examinations than men, they are slightly under-represented as undergraduates (for example, they were 43 per cent of full-time university students in 1986). There is a slight fall-off at postgraduate level (38 per cent in 1986), but as the figures cited at the beginning of this chapter show there is a dramatic decrease in the proportion of women as we move up the teaching hierarchy. Women fare a little better in public sector higher education, making up 24 per cent of the 1986 full-time teaching staff, but this reflects the proportion of 'non-advanced' and vocational work in this sector (nursery nursing, catering, commercial work, primary teaching and so forth). As in the universities, women are concentrated at the bottom of the hierarchy; 48 per cent of them are found at the lowest lecturer grade as opposed to 27 per cent of men, while only a handful rise to top posts (a mere 8 per cent of principal lecturers are women, for instance). In part, this may reflect the absence of women from the male-dominated disciplines of science and technology and their concentration in arts and social science subjects, where competition for teaching posts is more severe; but even in these areas, where women outnumber men as undergraduates, they are clearly in the minority as teachers.

McAuley (1987) argued that the ethos and culture of higher education militates against women; in polytechnics, for example, science and technology are the most highly valued subjects and women's lack of participation in these helps to confirm their inferiority. McAuley believes, too, that the socialisation of boys has fitted them better for the highly competitive world of research, whereas the co-operative and caring values developed in female socialisation are less regarded and may lead to the channelling of women into pastoral work. Success in teaching results in women acquiring heavier teaching loads and becoming more committed to this work than men; this very success, ironically, handicaps them for promotion where teaching counts for little compared to research achievements and administrative experience. Deem (1978) points out that, in addition, women lack the 'sponsors' who often help young male academics establish themselves in the early stages of their careers, as we also saw to be the case in the medical profession. Domestic ties, too, make it difficult for women to be involved in the circuits of conferences and paper-giving by which academic reputations are established. Indeed, a 1968 survey revealed that over half of women academics are unmarried, and an even higher proportion are childless (Williams et al., 1974); like the pioneers of women's education, such women may see motherhood and career success as incompatible.

Studies of women teachers in America and Canada reveal some similarities with the British case. In America teaching was perhaps even more clearly construed as a female profession. In the colonial period women, particularly single women, employed themselves taking in children as boarders, running 'dame' schools for local children or perhaps rather grander establishments for 'young ladies'; those mentioned by Matthaei laid on the same kind of training 'accomplishments' as did Hannah Woolley: Mrs Hiller's boarding school offered 'Wax-work, Transparent and Filigree Painting upon Glass, Japanning, Quill Work, Feather Work and Embroidering with Gold and Silver' (Matthaei, 1982, p. 59). In the rural areas in particular the general shortage of male labour helped open up such opportunities for women.

As in Britain, the teaching of children was seen as a natural part of motherhood, and Matthaei describes how the expansion of education and women's part in it during the nineteenth century was part of a 'social homemaking' movement whereby feminine and motherly attributes were expanded into the public sphere. Leading feminists saw this as a special mission for women. According to Catherine Beecher, 'our Creator designed women to be the chief educator of our race and the prime minister of our family state and our aim is to train her to this holy calling' (quoted Matthaei, 1982, p. 179). Emma Willard emphasised the suitability of the female temperament for such work: 'nature designed our sex for the care of children ... She has given us, in a greater degree than men, the gentle arts of insinuation, to soften their minds, and fit them to receive impressions; a greater quickness of invention to vary modes of teaching to different dispositions; and more patience to make repeated efforts' (quoted Matthaei, 1982, p. 179).

Local school boards, as in Britain, were happy to employ women since they would work for only a half, or even a quarter, of men's wages and apparently shared the feminist perception of women's capacities. The Boston Board of Education in the 1840s considered women 'incomparably better teachers for young children than males ... the whole forces of the mind are more readily concentrated upon present duties' (Baker, 1964, p. 56).

The need for teachers in an expanding society with high proportions of immgrants was great and women fulfilled that need; Wertheimer tells us that in the decades from 1830 to 1860 a quarter of native-born American women had done some kind of teaching work. By 1880 two-thirds of elementary teachers were women (many untrained and very low paid), a figure which rose to 73 per cent by 1900 (Wertheimer, 1977; Lewenhak, 1980). Of these 92 per cent were single. Women were expected to resign on marriage and teaching was again seen as a preparation for motherhood rather than a career. For many of the social homemakers the work was a mission requiring altruistic self-sacrifice, as in Victorian England. Young women following this vocation would not only receive limited material rewards, but might also expect an extremely high level of control by their employers and the sacrifice of their desires and personal freedom. Wertheimer reproduces the Massachusetts School Board rules from the 1900s, which include the following:

Do not get married.
Do not keep company with men.
Be home between the hours of 8 p.m. and 6 a.m.
Do not loiter downtown in ice cream stores.
Do not get into a carriage with any man except your father or brother.
Do not dress in bright colours.
Do not wear any dress more than two inches above the ankle.

(Wertheimer, 1977, p. 248)

Setting an example of purity and sobriety was seen as an integral part of the 'substitute mother' teacher's role.

A study of New York schools in 1910, reported by Wertheimer, suggests that patterns of segregation were found, as in Britain, but that the shortage of manpower enabled women to get further into high school (secondary) level; 14,751 of the 15,333 teachers were women. Nearly all elementary teachers were female, the few males being concentrated in high schools, and superintendents and principals were men (p. 243). Although equal pay was granted for high school work in 1912, women were much more likely to be confined to the lower, less remunerative grades.

Teaching in America became *par excellence* the career for middle-class women, a profession lacking the status and remuneration of the traditional male professions. Because of this, it was always difficult to attract males into it. After World War II, only 15 per cent of elementary and high school teachers were men. An attempt to raise the status of the profession by encouraging graduates to enter training in 1952 raised the proportion of males to 25 per cent in 1960. These were, predictably, concentrated at secondary level, where they made up half the teaching staff.

The greater advance of women into secondary level teaching at an earlier period than in Britain made it more difficult to exclude them from higher education. There were already fifty women's colleges in America before the Civil War (although few of these gave accreditable degrees) and thus teaching opportunities in colleges and universities were more numerous than in Britain. By 1922, 25 per cent of college and university teachers were women, in 1939 23 per cent (a figure never equalled in Britain). Academic work was not particularly well paid and its status was not comparable with other male professions, which may have helped women gain greater access, although Baker argues that the success of the women's rights movement was also a factor. In 1986 women were 36 per cent of academics (Baker, 1964, pp. 281–4; United States Bureau of the Census, 1988).

An interesting essay by Graham on teaching in Canada reveals similar trends. Before 1940 most education was rooted in the family, with the familiar emphasis on the natural propensities of women as teachers. Although the state education system initially employed a lower proportion of women than in Britain (only a quarter in 1861) over the century women came to outnumber men by five to one. Women were preferred to men by the state because of their cheapness, which, as in Britain and America, was justified by ideologies of female sacrifice, with emphasis being put on the teacher's role as moral standard-bearer and exemplar for youth. Women teachers faced poor conditions, arduous training, social isolation and strict control over their personal lives. Thus the idea of teaching as an inherently female occupation was fostered both by economic considerations and by ideologies of gender. Sir Fred Clarke, Chairman of the Department of Education at McGill University in the 1930s, explained this in words which reek of professional male condescension: 'if education is a ritual of the school, a thing of puerilia and "keeping out of mischief" then it is really a nursery concern and women are its proper hierophants' (quoted Graham, 1974, p. 200).

Clearly, between societies and cultures conceptions of the teacher's role will vary greatly; but where it is viewed (as in Britain, America and Canada) as a 'nursery concern' it is likely to evolve as a highly feminised profession. Where the state is the major source of funding, economic considerations may also encourage the employment of women; and even when equal pay is conceded, salaries are likely to be kept down by the employing state, so that the overall status of the profession remains low.

Traditionally male professions, like law and medicine, are characterised by high social standing, very high material rewards and chances to expand into a wider sphere of social influence. Male professionals have managed to monopolise bodies of knowledge and expertise which are defined as highly specialised and too complex to be accessible to the laity, and which are deliberately kept arcane and obscure by the use of specialised vocabulary and discourse. Finally, they are characterised by very strict gate-keeping and limitation of access, with lengthy (and often expensive) training an absolute necessity. By contrast, female professionals have lower status, lower rewards and are seen as less central to social leadership. Although they do require training and mastery of a body of knowledge, entry to training is easier and special categories of entrants are frequently admitted without training, such as uncertificated teachers and nursing auxiliaries. Scarcity thus, paradoxically, works to the disadvantage of these professions, while it benefits doctors and lawyers who can use their male power to exploit it. The knowledge of the female professionals is seen as less specialised and difficult and is less compartmentalised from the rest of the life of the laity.

When men enter the female professions they are able to exploit their gender to rise rapidly up the hierarchy to top posts. By contrast, ideologies of altruism, female sacrifice and maternalism make it difficult for women in the professions to mount campaigns which might make their work commensurable with that of male professionals, so that the Royal College of Nursing is still clinging to its 'no-strike' rule in 1988. Thus, while professional work provides women with the best career chances and puts them on a closer footing with men, nurses and teachers, just like their counterparts in industrial and clerical work, are nonetheless subjected to ideologies of male superiority and to processes of sex-typing which confine the majority to subordinate positions in the hierarchy.

Part III

CONCLUSION

14

GENDERED JOBS AND SOCIAL INEQUALITY

We are now in a position to draw some conclusions. Despite occupational, regional and national variations we have seen common patterns emerge from the case studies. In all cases for which evidence exists it points to a sexual division of labour in pre-industrial societies, often linked to household systems of labour. In these societies 'women's work' was of two types. They were either to be found in specialist women's trades (such as midwifery or spinning) or, more commonly, they worked within the household economy, engaged in a wide variety of tasks, but often acting as assistants to men in whatever the family business might be. In such cases, whatever was seen as the core task was taken by the man.

Both these versions of 'women's work' persisted into the industrial period. The studies show conclusively that the impact of capitalism (whether in its industrial or pre-industrial phase) was to increase segregation and to destroy or marginalise women's traditional skills. However, capitalism is characteristically dynamic; accordingly, the sexual division of labour was fluid and changeable as new work processes and technologies were introduced. In every case, however, new patterns of segregation and sex-typing replaced the old, in line with the contemporary ideologies of masculinity annd femininity.

From the case studies is has emerged that the 1880s and 1890s were perhaps the key period in laying down the patterns of segregation and sex-typing on which the current sexual divisions in employment are founded. Partly this is because these decades witnessed a massive expansion of capitalist production; this above all was the era in which capitalism entered its consumerist phase, bringing with it, as I have argued, a specific new use of women's labour in service industries such as saleswork and clerical work. The glamorised image of the female worker appeared for the first time. But this was also the era in which the nineteenth-century ideology of domesticity achieved, in the epoch of high Victorianism, its most polished version. It must also be significant that this was the period in which there occurred in America, according to the pioneer work now being done under the rubric of men's studies, a 'crisis of masculinity' (Brod, 1987, Kimmel, 1987a, 1987b). The onslaughts of mass production and the end to the expansion of the 'frontier' made redundant the old version of masculinity, based on notions of men as tough, pioneering breadwinners, while men feared loss of authority and status as women left the home to work. One way to offset the threat was to ensure that segregation at work served to maintain women in an inferior position.

By the beginning of the twentieth century this pattern of segregation was well entrenched as was shown in the government surveys of women's work which have been quoted in the case studies (PP 1919 xxxi; PP 1929–30 xvii). This was precisely documented in a survey of women's work in Birmingham published in 1906 (Cadbury et al., 1906). The researchers found that in manufacturing trades there were few instances of men and women doing the same work, and even where they appeared to be doing so there were in fact differences in quality and quantity. They concluded that women did different work from men, did inferior work (which men often refused to do) and were paid less (one-third to one-half of men's wages). In white-collar work men's and women's work was more similar (clerical work, teaching, shopwork), but it was still taken for granted that women should be paid less. As we have seen, this type of pattern has persisted over the century, despite the temporary disruptions of the two wars, with little change except in the professions.

As discussed in chapter 10, Glucksmann (1986) has seen the new industries of the interwar period as the birthplace of contemporary gender divisions within capitalist production. But this underestimates the continuities in the social definitions of men's and women's jobs and the extent to which the gender parameters of mechanised mass production were being set in America in the 1880s, subsequently to be exported to Britain and the rest of the world.

We can see, then, that family relationships and work arrangements, capitalist development and social definitions of masculinity and femininity have, indeed, all been intertwined in the cases we have studied, thus confirming Barrett's view that 'the gender divisions of social production in capitalism cannot be understood without reference to the organisation of the household and the ideology of familialism' (Barrett, 1980, p. 186). We will now examine each of these (family relations, capitalist production, ideology), more fully.

The Origins and Maintenance of Segregation and Sex-typing

As I have argued in chapter 3, the pre-industrial family was patriarchal. Despite the importance of women's economic contribution to the household unit, their work was framed by male authority and household requirements. Although a few took female careers and became independent craftswomen, the majority of married women worked in subordination to men's needs. Many worked with their menfolk in a family business and here they often took on the roles and tasks which, however important they really were, were conventionally *seen* as subsidiary. Women were *seen* as assistants and 'helpmeets' to men. Patriarchy did not preclude an appreciation of the complementarity of male and female economic activities; and, as I argued in chapter 2, the informality of the household economy meant that there was a flexibility in the sexual division of labour which permitted greater varieties than under the new system of production which was to supplant it.

Industrial capitalism brought many changes to the family, but not an immediate end to patriarchy. Mann (1986) has described this epoch as one of 'neo-patriarchy' but the continuities are so marked that the name change seems unnecessary. For a start men clung on to their political and public supremacy in their persona of head of household, with women still lacking a political and public voice (see Alexander, 1984). Middle-class women by and large had their economic roles constricted and, becoming confined to the home, fell more firmly under male control. Indigent women of the middle classes, especially those who failed to find a husband, escaped this but were often forced into demeaning and ill-paid forms of work subject to the tyranny of employers. As this book has shown, in some industries household working systems continued well into the nineteenth century and Mark-Lawson and Witz (1988) are surely right to see these as an alternative type of patriarchal control strategy to the trade unions' exclusionary strategies which we have also seen so frequently in evidence. Once the household systems broke down, many working men took up the call for politics which would permit them to keep wives at home, under their patriarchal control as in the middle-class family. Although many working-class women, especially single girls, did 'go out' to work, thus escaping supervision by fathers and husbands, they were nonetheless usually subject to male authority when at work and in most homes, as the work of Burnett (1984) and Sarsby (1988) indicates, the word of the father was still law. Indeed, in many working-class homes, young girls were still required to hand over their wage packets to their parents, and to accept their parents' decisions about when they left school and what jobs they should take, right up until World War II. Although mothers often took charge of such arrangements they themselves were subject to male decisions (sometimes violently enforced) and in running the household they shaped things to fit the father's activities and requirements, always seen as the first priority. As Matthaei (1982) suggests, women's work through the nineteenth century continued to be framed in terms of either the family's or society's needs. It was only men, historically, who could take account of their own personal bents, needs and satisfactions.

However, by the end of the nineteenth century patriarchy had, more generally, come under attack. Middle-class feminist campaigners were fighting their way back into economic life. The legal backing of patriarchy was beginning to crumble as the Married Women's Property Act of 1882 paved the way for women's rights and female suffrage. In their famous (or infamous!) book *The Symmetrical Family* (1973) Willmott and Young argued that these developments, along with increased labour market opportunities for women and improved contraceptive technology, have culminated in the twentieth century in the appearance of the symmetrical family, where sex roles are less differentiated, with both spouses going out to work and men sharing in domestic work, and power is equalised. But more recent studies of the family hardly sustain such a view.

If families are no longer strictly patriarchal they are still transmitters of sex inequalities. The ideals of the family wage, the male breadwinner and the full-time mother are nourished within the family and as Hartmann has argued (see chapter 2) these ideals are highly supportive of segregation. Despite Willmott and Young's curious findings, more recent surveys of domestic labour (including Oakley, 1976a; Martin and Roberts, 1984; Collins, 1985) have shown that women still bear the brunt of housework and child care and, most importantly, bear responsibility for it. This is perhaps even more true of America than Britain (see Gerson, 1987; Meade-King, 1988). If married women go out to work, it is up to them to make alternative arrangements to cover housework and child care. This, in turn, restricts their entry into employment. Jobs have to fit in with their domestic duties (part-time work, perhaps, located near to the home, homeworking in some cases). Their careers are broken to look after young children, typically at the key stages in which male colleagues are starting on the promotion ladder; as a result their chances of promotion and of further training are limited. Exhausted by the burden of looking after children and bearing responsibility for the home on top of a full-time job, women lack the energy to perform as well as men or to engage in the social and political wheeler-dealing essential for success in competitive jobs. All this traps women in a vicious circle of dependence, as Hartmann (1981) argues. Domestic responsibilities prevent them from getting jobs which pay as well as men; it then becomes rational for the person with lower economic prospects to become the domestic worker, full time if necessary; this further limits their prospects. And so on.

Modern marriages may be 'companionate' rather than 'patriarchal', in Stone's terminology, but by and large I would argue, families remain 'androcentric'. Arrangements within them are still moulded to the requirements of men. Families move around the country because of men's career choices and potentials. Women fit their choices in round this. Although most men in the 1980s no longer express hostility to the idea of their wives going out to work, as they have so often done in the past, there is often an implicit assumption that a wife can only take on a job if she can arrange matters so that the everyday management of the home is not disrupted. Modern families, as many have pointed out (for example, Anderson, 1980; Gittins, 1985), are extremely variable and flexible in their form and in their internal arrangements. But, where there is an adult male within them, economic choices revolve upon him. Family arrangements now, just as in pre-industrial societies, promote and support segregation in work.

Segregation and sex-typing, then, predate capitalist industry. Many of the gender arrangements of early capitalist production sprang directly from the patterns of work that existed in the pre-capitalist economy. However, capitalism has had a crucial role in maintaining, consolidating and reconsructing patterns of segregation and sex-typing. The employment of women in jobs designated as 'women's work' was a key part of the development of a degraded capitalist labour process. This served two purposes for capitalist employers. Women could be employed more cheaply, because of the lower social value already put on their work, thus leading to the accumulation of more profit. In addition the use of female labour helped in the struggle to break the control of male workers which was founded in their knowledge of and mastery over traditional craft techniques. When men fought back by claiming that certain jobs must remale 'male', this only served to deepen segregation, a process I have defined elsewhere as 'resegmentation' (Bradley, 1987). Women were driven into low-paid female jobs, thus posing less threat to the male workers while simultaneously satisfying the desire of capitalists for cheap labour. At times, as the case studies reveal, capitalist employers and trade unions colluded in maintaining sex-typing, as patriarchal ideologies and interests overrode class divisions. Notions of skill and technology and their different application to the sexes have been used to ensure that technological change confirms the allotment of prime jobs to men, while women are pushed into the mindless machine-minding jobs produced by mechanical advance and 'rationalisation'.

Barrett (1980) is right, I think, in her view that there is no *logical* necessity within the capitalist dynamic for sexual divisions to be created or maintained. Capitalism thrives on dividing the work force, but there are other ways of doing this, as the example of South Africa shows. Equally correctly, Hartmann (1981) has pointed out the flexibility of capitalist production, its ability to adapt to circumstances and make use of whatever is at hand in the search for profit. The attempt made by, for example, Young, to show that capitalist production must *necessarily* be founded on gender divisions and the marginalisation of women, that these are 'an essential and fundamental characteristic' of capitalist production relations (Young, 1981, pp. 58, 61), is therefore mistaken. However, since sex divisions are the most fundamental and primary within human societies apart from age divisions (in the sense that being derived in part from biology they inevitably predate those that are purely cultural) and since family relations and social ideologies have so persistently emphasised gender differences, there can be no doubt that historically capitalist production has *always* developed, in each and every case, on the basis of sex-typed jobs. The statistics in chapter 1 illustrate the consistency of segregation in capitalist nations around the world. However, though capitalist production must historically be seen as gendered and although the reproduction of capitalist production relations means the reproduction of gender divisions, this does not mean that an end to capitalism will bring an end to sex-typing. As the examples of Russia and China discussed in chapter 1 show, family relationships together with ideologies of gender will ensure that segregation continues unless those, too, change. Since we have argued that gender relations must be seen as separate from economic ones (although everywhere interpenetrated with them and acting upon them and being acted upon by them) there is no justification for the claim that socialism (even 'true' socialism) would, by itself, bring an end to sexual inequality, as long as socialism is defined as a type of economic arrangement.

A contrasting view comes from Elshtain, whose work was discussed in chapter 3. She believes that it is possible to achieve sex parity within a framework which accepts that men and women are different and will thus be found doing different things. To my mind such an account seriously overlooks the way in which gender relations are interpenetrated by capitalist relations. In a type of production system based on the assumption that hierarchies are necessary and that people at different levels in the hierarchy should be rewarded differently, any type of visible difference (gender, ethnicity) is prone to be seized upon and incorporated into the hierarchies of work. To this extent Marxists are right in their assertion that capitalism promotes racial and sexual divisions. For example, the Confederation of British Industry is currently campaigning for the abolition of British anti-discrimination legislation on the grounds that having to pay women as much as men makes British industry 'non-competitive'. While this book has been trying to ram home the message that stratification is gendered, we must not forget that the converse is equally true: as Mann says 'gender is stratified' (Mann, 1986, p. 56).

Throughout the case studies I have emphasised the importance of gender ideologies. The ideology of domesticity and of separate spheres (see chapter 2) is usually seen as emerging within the family as a response to the disruptions brought by industrialisation, which destroyed traditional family roles and required in particular the specification of new social functions for women. I hope this book has also clearly shown that social meanings of masculinity and femininity were also negotiated *within the workplace itself* in the course of the changes and conflicts described above. Despite the doctrine of 'separate spheres' many women took part in economic activity inside and outside the home and would continue to do so. Therefore it was necessary to establish notions of 'suitable' work for women and of the proper type of work environment in which this should take place. Moral panics involving the constant reiteration of these notions drove women out of some jobs (mining, farmwork and fishing) and into others (nursing, shop work and food processing). Thus ideas about feminine and masculine nature and behaviour were highly involved in the gendering of jobs and resulted in the formation of gendered work cultures. Matthaei has emphasised this strongly in her study of sex-typing in America; she also makes the point that such definitions were not simply imposed on male and female workpeople, but that, as the case studies suggest, they shared in their construction: 'a basic force behind sex-typing of jobs was the workers' desires to assert and reaffirm their manhood or womanhood and hence their difference from the opposite sex' (Matthaei, 1982, p. 194).

This continues to be a 'force' today in steering boys and girls into 'appropriate' career choices, especially in the teenage phase when sexual identity appears very fragile. Gendered work cultures then continue the process, helping to perpetuate notions of distinct sexual identities as has been well documented by Cockburn; as she says, work-based gender ideologies specify

> What a man 'is', what a woman 'is', what is right and proper, what is possible and impossible, what should be hoped and what should be feared. The hegemonic ideology of masculism involves a definition of men and women as different, contrasted, complementary and unequal. It is powerful and it deforms both men and women. (Cockburn, 1986, p. 85)

The case studies have shown that employers have used the perception that women prefer working with women, men with men, to justify both sex divisions and discriminatory practices. But it should be emphasised that this perception appears basically correct. Both women and men have accepted the idea that it is more pleasant to work among your own sex. Many men prefer male exclusivity at work and have fought over the years to keep women out and developed ways to keep them in their place when they get in. Fine (1987) has demonstrated some of the tactics used by males against women seen as intruders in their cheerful and companionable male environments. Women are considered potentially disruptive and are made to feel outcasts unless they are prepared to join in the male culture with its swearing, boozing and sexist banter. Equally many women seem prepared to accept social definitions of what they can or cannot do and are happy to find themselves in a feminised work environment. Only a minority have rejected prevailing expectations. Here again ideas of the skills specific to each sex and of the different aptitudes of men and women with regard to technology are at play and are largely accepted; in this way sex distinctions are seen as necessary and unavoidable.

Gendered work cultures are still well entrenched today. As we have seen, many female work groups in factories and offices 'bring home into' the work environment, both domesticating it (making boring work more tolerable, making the office a pleasant, sociable and cosy place to be in) and also being domesticated by it (as once again the 'inbuilt' domestic orientation of women is emphasised and made visible to men). Women in the traditionally female professions have no need to import the home into work, for, as we have seen, it is already there! Hospitals and schools mirror family relationships and in them women practice their 'inbuilt' feminine skills for the public good. As long as most comprehensive schools are headed by men, while men teach boys football, women teach girls netball, men teach physics and woodwork, women teach English and domestic science, it is hardly surprising that overt messages of sex equality put forward by teachers in lessons make little impression.

The position of the minority of women who enter male-dominated trades and professions is rather different. They are faced, by contrast, with the problem of fitting into a male occupational culture. As Spencer and Podmore have pointed out, this presents them with a double bind; if they take men on in their own terms, they are denying their femininity, which may diminish their private status as women; if they assert their femininity they risk being labelled as inferior and inadequate workers. American women, too, it is reported, face the same dilemma (Prather, 1971; Meade-King, 1988); in one researcher's words 'the fear of a threat to femininity through successful achievement is the result of cultural learning so prevalent as to affect most women' (Laws, 1976, p. 46). However, in the work context, the former choice seems preferable, and many individual women succeed conspicuously in such jobs by outplaying the men at their own games of toughness and competitiveness. Yet even these women may privately confess to feelings of isolation and vulnerability. The setting up of female support or 'networking' groups is one way that some women have tried to counterpoise some element of female culture to the male work environment.

Scott's survey of several contemporary societies, both more and less industrialised, revealed that in all of them 'notions that women constituted a special category of labour persisted even where they could no longer be differentiated from men in terms of their supply characteristics' (Scott, 1986, p. 181). Women and men are viewed by employers in terms of their 'appropriateness for a job, rather than their actual abilities to do it' (p. 160). Thus even when the conditions of the labour market change, when production processes require different abilities, when family relations are in flux, gender ideologies persist. They must be seen as having, as it were, a life of their own. Without doubt they are one of the most important props for continued segregation and sex-typing.

If gender ideologies are to be considered as having their own independent reality, this does not mean of course that they will not alter in form over time as work and family relationships change. But I am arguing that there should be no expectation that they will directly reflect those changes. Thus current gender ideologies seem to me without doubt to be descended from the Victorian ideology of domesticity and of separate spheres. In consequence, as others have argued, these ideologies can legitimately seen as patriarchal, even in a society where families are no longer strictly governed by patriarchy. This returns us to the issue of patriarchy and its relation to work. Walby has recently developed an account of phases of patriarchy, arguing that the private family-based form characteristic of pre-industrial and nineteenth-century societies has been replaced by a public form in which patriarchal control is maintained by work relations and the state:

> Private patriarchy is based upon the household, with a patriarch controlling women individually and directly in the relatively private sphere of the home. Public patriarchy is based in sites other than the household, although this still may be a significant patriarchal site. Rather institutions conventionally regarded as part of the public domain are central in the maintenance of patriarchy. (Walby, 1988, p. 5)

Walby believes that private patriarchy reached its peak in the mid-nineteenth century in middle-class families and that there has been since a movement away from it, largely as a result of feminist politics.

We may go further than Walby has and assert that many, if not most, contemporary families in Britain and America are no longer patriarchal in the strict sense; they may more aptly be described as 'androcentric'. The power of the father in the family now receives little social and legal sanction (although social security regulations are one exception here, giving support to Walby's view of the state). However, most social institutions are shaped around male definitions, priorities, requirements, preferences; men run most of them, if not all; the political and social ideas that rule our epoch come from men; in sum society revolves round men, is literally 'androcentric'.

Walby is correct in seeing the work sphere as crucial in maintaining male supremacy; and Prather has argued for America too, that 'the concept of work is defined in masculine terms' (Prather, 1971, p. 19). Work relations are a paramount example of 'androcentrism'. For example, the arrangements of the traditional working week, nine to five and the weekend off, fit well the with male life routine (work all day, home for meal cooked by wife, evening at the pub or in front of the television, weekends spent in the garden or at sporting functions). It fits *not at all* with the life routine of the woman responsible for feeding and clothing children and taking them to school. On her free days she wants to be able to go to the shops and banks, not football matches. Yet part-time work, flexible hours or job-sharing schemes which fit with her requirements are seen as inferior forms of working and carry penalties in terms of deprivation of rights and benefits. Promotion prospects too, are based on assumptions of a normal male career, as the case studies demonstrate. Companies often require employees to move round the country to gain promotion, a thing impossible for most married women. Even in the traditional female profession of teaching, promotions have usually to be gained by moving to a new school or college, which again handicaps women and may well be one reason why, it is claimed, women do not apply for top posts. There are even some companies which require their managers to have a non-employed wife, so that she is available for entertaining and can give him the domestic support necessary to ensure his total dedication to the firm. The assumption, of course, is that *all* managers *must* be male. No company would dream of asking that a female manager have a non-employed husband! Social rituals of work, trade union activities and so forth reflect male timetabling and interests and priorities. We could go on ad infinitum. Finally, on top of this, it is at least feasible to argue (with Walby) that not only are current work arrangements androcentric, they are also correctly described as patriarchal at least if we apply the analogy of the household and authoritarian father to the enterprise or organisation. As we have seen in chapter 1, all over the world, men give orders, women obey. The patriarch may have lost his seat in the drawing-room; he is still comfortably lodged in the office or behind the boardroom table.

Feminism, Legislation and Possibilities for Change

This study has highlighted the extraordinary staying power and resilience of gender segregation and sex-typing in employment. Is there any hope of change? In her admirable study of sex-typing in America Matthaei (1982) suggests that changes in relations between the sexes in the family and rising aspirations among women are finally breaking down segregation at work. I am somewhat less sanguine.

There has been a persistent strand in (predominately male) sociological historical thought which suggests that processes of social and economic change, 'progress', will inevitably in the end do away with sexual divisions. This has taken many forms. The 'Whig view of history' has it that the spread of civilisation and enlightenment will sweep away all unjust social divisions. Functionalist sociologists have argued that the need of a progressive industrial economy for highly skilled labour and a socially mobile population will eventually make all kinds of 'non-rational' divisions redundant (this view is still very much with us today at a more popular level). Marxists believe the march of socialism (if not halted) will bring an end to other types of social inequity once class barriers have crumbled. The latest version of this can be found within the array of writings on 'postindustrialism', 'post-Fordism' or 'postmodernism' as it has variously been called.

The basic premise of all these is that the latest technological developments (particularly information technology) are bringing about a total revolution in the world of work, and indeed in social relations in general. In this 'new' type of society all our working lives will be transformed and this brings the chance to overcome sex inequalities. Robots and computers will remove the need for mindless machine-tending jobs. The computer will break down the distinction between the home and the office. The pace of change will require a new brand of 'flexible' worker possessed of 'flexible' skills, prepared to change careers and move around the country many times in his or her working life. New patterns of working ('flexible' hours, job-sharing, etc.) will enable the individual to fit work in better to other needs and activities. In this brave new future world men and women will work co-operatively in creative, skilled, fulfilling jobs, while the fragmented politics and culture of postmodern society will ensure that every type of social interest group has its rights recognised and its needs catered for.

Pages and pages of this kind of stuff have been churned out! Is it utter tosh or is there some truth in it? Certainly what we know of the impact of the 'microelectronic revolution' to date hardly supports the optimistic scenario. As we saw in chapters 10 and 11, the new jobs created by new technology for women are typically degraded and highly automated, located in highly pressurised and tightly policed environments, low-paid and often part-time (see Huws, 1982; Science Policy Research Unit, 1982; Gill, 1985). They are also firmly sex-typed. What none of the postindustrial forecasters are able to do is to explain how we get from the here of sex-typing and segregation to the there of sex parity and co-operation. This is because all share a deterministic view of change as following automatically from technological and economic requirements, ignoring the realities of power. Dominant social groups of whatever kind do not yield their privilege, prestige and power voluntarily. They will manipulate their advantage to ensure that whatever changes occur remain compatible with their own continued supremacy. It is here that gender ideologies (quite ignored in most of these types of account) come in so handy for elite groups. If change comes about, then, it will not be automatic but will result from the political actions of the groups involved; the most salient being the state, feminist campaigning groups – and men.

This book has already pointed to the failure of anti-discrimination legislation to break down segregation both in Britain and America, although it appears to have been rather more successful in the latter, at least in the higher echelons of the economy. Critics explain this failure in two ways. Either the existing legislation has been badly designed and ineptly enforced and should be reformulated; or legislation *in itself* is doomed to fail unless accompanied by real changes in social attitudes and institutions; it cannot cope with the real issues at the heart of segregation (male power, the profit motive, the family division of labour and so forth).

There is truth in both positions. Studies in America and Britain suggest the need for careful monitoring of legislation and for an effective active watchdog body (the Equal Opportunities Commission is judged to have so far been inadequate in enforcing change on reluctant employers). The American experience suggests that legislation involving some kind of positive or affirmative action programme (for example specification of quotas of women employees and dates to achieve them by) may be necessary to overcome that reluctance, although the general climate of opinion in Britain seems set against that approach (Gelb and Palley, 1982; Stamp and Robarts, 1986). There is a need, too, to work for the abolition of existing discriminatory legislation (the Factory Acts) and its replacement with new protective legislation controlling hours and conditions for *both* sexes. However, what can be done within this kind of framework is I believe, fairly limited, especially within the parameters of a legal system based on individual contracts and presenting conflict as a matter of individual grievances. Inevitably, such a system can do little to overcome structural and collective inequities. Moreover, anti-discrimination legislation must by its nature operate only within the sphere of work. As Jackson (1984) has argued, it is thus totally ineffective to transform family arrangements which are so crucial an underpinning to segregation and sex-typing. Randall, too, believes that any sex equality policy which ignores the impact of family responsibilities on women's economic chances is doomed to failure (Randall, 1987).

This being the case, it seems to me that the crucial area in which women should be campaigning for state action is that of child-care facilities. This is born out by the examples of both Russia and America where nursery provision in one case and tax concessions on child care expenses on the other have made a significant difference in helping married women to maintain career jobs (see Lapidus, 1978; Dex and Shaw, 1986). In America, for example, Dex and Shaw report that 57 per cent of women are now returning to work soon after childbirth as opposed to 30 per cent of British mothers. There are many possibilities here: provision of nurseries and creches by the state itself or requirement that employers should make provision; better maternity benefits and paternity benefits as in Scandinavia, another area with a better than average profile; arrangements such as those made already by some companies (banks, GEC) for firms to hold open jobs for women leaving for childbirth for several years while ensuring that they are kept up to date with relevant job developments; tax concessions on child care and so forth.

Governments of recent years have not exactly been rushing forward to 'burden' employers with the expenses of such reforms or to fund them themselves. However in Britain in 1989 there has been an upsurge of official interest in child-care provision, following an outburst of media publicity over the 'demographic timebomb'. Falling birth-rates in the 1960s and 1970s, especially among lower social class groupings, will lead to a shortage of labour force recruits of school-leaving age in the 1990s, according to the forecasters. There will be a need for married women to return to work to make up for the shortfall. It is assumed, therefore, that the British government will have to rethink its policies on child care. Moreover, the equally well publicised 'skills shortage', especially of highly trained technical and computer personnel, will also provide an impetus to free women from the burdens of domestic responsibility to undertake appropriate training.

The predictions of social and economic forecasters are not always correct, and a cynic might point to a potential counter-tendency in the continued displacement of labour through automation and the advance of information technology; this could reverse the trend of the late 1980s and bring a new rise in unemployment and fall in demand for labour. Nevertheless, child care has been brought to the political agenda and women should be quick to take advantage of this. The Tory government in the late 1980s, with its disdain for the 'nanny state', is unlikely to want to fund the provision of state nannies! The indications point, rather, to possible tax relief both for workers using private services and for employers who pay for workplace nurseries, with some possible back-up system, such as child-care vouchers, for low-paid workers.

So far, however, government and employers have been content to let working mothers (and fathers) find their own solutions to child-care problems. While some large and progressive firms and organisations may be prepared to fund nurseries as part of their labour recruitment policy, the high cost of such provision may put it beyond the reach of the expanding small-firm sector; such costs clearly conflict with capitalist imperatives, the continued pressure for international competitiveness, higher profits and a reduced bill for labour. If women can be persuaded to work without provision of nurseries and creches, employers are likely to drag their feet. A much more rational and effective solution would be the provision of state-funded or -aided neighbourhood nurseries, as in Denmark or in Russia, for example. If this is to be achieved further campaigning by women themselves will be necessary. The thrust for change will have to come from women's groups and their representatives in parliament or other decision-making bodies. Walby (1988) is quite right to see feminist politics as very largely responsible for the improved position of women in Britain and America this century (rather than ascribing this to the necessary developments of either capitalism or industrialism). Women will have to go on fighting both to maintain that improved situation and to advance upon it.

However, one of the problems with the feminist movement historically has been that it has always drawn the bulk of its impetus from women of the middle-class elite. Working-class women activists, in trade unions for example, have tended to see their primary political loyalty in class terms. This has meant that women have done better in pushing their way into middle-class male occupations (especially in America) than in desegregating working-class jobs. Indeed, it can be argued that in the USA in the past two decades there has been a clear polarisation among women. Middle-class women in the professions and especially in the business world have pushed their way into the economic elite. They can then use their high salaries, along with tax relief, to pay for domestic help. Such a trend can also be observed in the prosperous parts of Britain, where a rise in the employment of maids and nannies has been reported. Middle-class women, relieved from domestic responsibilities, are then in a position to compete for top posts with male colleagues and attack vertical segregation. At the other end of the class structure, however, working-class women remain trapped in low-paying sex-typed jobs, struggling to find employment which can be fitted in with household demands. In future women will need to attack the bastions of male exclusivity on both fronts if sex-typing is to be destroyed and the process of class polarisation among women halted.

Even this will not suffice unless men, too, can be persuaded or forced to change their expectations and behaviour. Let us not mince words here. This will not be easy. Studies have repeatedly revealed how the attitudes of men (managers, male workers, trade unions, husbands) reaffirm gender stereotypes: women cannot do certain jobs, women are unsuitable for jobs requiring toughness and responsibility, men will not work under a woman, marriages are better if a wife can stay at home, it is the woman's responsibility to run the home etc. (see, among numerous examples, Bass et al, 1971; Hunt, 1975; Cockburn, 1985; Braybon and Summerfield, 1987). Studies of the construction of masculinity reveal how deep-rooted the processes of male socialisation are (Brod, 1987; Kimmel, 1987a). The analysis of gender must not let men off the hook.

It needs to be recognised that the movement of women into 'men's jobs' will not end sex-typing unless at the same time men enter 'women's jobs'.

The case studies have revealed how unwilling men have been historically to do this, unless it has implied taking over a female occupation and redefining it as male (as happened with spinning, with obstetrics and nursing management, with social work, for example). Back in 1968 Gross noted that the entry of men into a job does not make women leave it, while men turned their backs on an occupation once women had become identified with it. While men raise the status of a job, women's jobs are inevitably considered inferior. Consequently, men resist becoming typists, filing clerks, cleaners and sewing machinists. To change this means attacking male attitudes about masculinity at a very basic level and can perhaps only be achieved through education. Stamp and Robarts (1986) give some heartening indication of the way schools can begin to break down gender stereotyping within the curriculum, though this will self-evidently be a slow and laborious process as long as the other media of socialisation (families, the mass media in particular) continue to promote Action Man and Sindy Doll images of the sexes. The other positive hope must be for a concerted attempt by trade unions to fight for an upgrading of *all* types of work so that there are no jobs seen as so ill-paid and demeaning that they are 'only fit for women'. Unfortunately there is considerable evidence of entrenched sexism in trade unions (see for example, Boston, 1980; Beale, 1982; Charles, 1983a). But in a period of rapid change and job redesign there is at least a possibility of moving beyond traditional prejudices. Certainly, without some kind of revolution in 'the hearts of men', the 'second industrial revolution' is likely only to replicate what we have seen to be the outcome of the original one: the rapid establishment of new gender hierarchies with men grabbing the best of the new jobs for themselves.

Gendered Jobs, Sociology and History

Finally, we must turn to the prospects for the further understanding of gender segregation in sociology and history. The study of gender, and specifically the study of women, is now firmly established on the agenda of both disciplines. An important topic for further research, I would suggest, is the functioning of gender stereotypes and ideologies in every area of social life. In particular, we need to know more about the circumstances, both now and in the past, in which women and men either accept or challenge prevailing definitions of masculinity and femininity. Such research should look not only at the experiences of women, although much still needs to be uncovered in this area, but also at men. The study of masculinity is still in its infancy. Interesting work is being done in the new area of 'men's studies', but it is perhaps regrettable that this should be developing as an endeavour separate from 'women's' or 'gender' studies.

Many women have expressed apprehension that scarce resources may be directed away from those areas into men's studies, and see this as yet another attempt by men to steal the limelight and prioritise their own concerns. While I think these fears may be misplaced, it is certainly important that such work is integrated into a broader 'gender studies' approach and indeed into orthodox disciplinary frameworks. The understanding of gender relations is central to the understanding of social life in general and should be part of the main body of concerns of both sociology and history.

Clearly this has strong implications for theories of stratification in general. A major theme of this book has been that while class and gender are irreducible to one another and must be seen as analytically separate, neither can be satisfactorily understood without the other. Surely only the most diehard of class theorists can now seriously maintain that it is possible to analyse classes without taking gender into account? Most class theorists take either the labour process or the labour market as a core element in class formation and this study (like many other recent contributions) has argued that historically both of these have to be seen as gendered. It follows that any account of class relations in industrial capitalist societies which ignores the fact that the 'working class has two sexes' is likely to be seriously flawed. Such accounts will be unable to represent with any adequacy the nature of class consciousness and consequently of class action.

This is particularly true when considering the political aspects of class. For example, Goldthorpe's account of the 'mature' working class facing the heterogeneous, fragmented middle class (1980) ignores the likely effects of sexual divisions in weakening the political maturity of the former. Perhaps it is invidious to pick on Goldthorpe, for I would argue that *no* existing account of class politics in contemporary Britain, Marxist, Weberian or whatever, has yet seriously confronted the significance of gender and sexual segregation. The Marxist tendency to try and incorporate gender as being simply one of several forms of division (class 'fractions') within the working class is as unsatisfactory as it would be to argue that class is merely significant as a form of internal division within the female sex!

Lockwood (1986), by contrast, asserts that gender is not an essential part of the system of stratification *at all*. The crux of his argument seems to be that women do not manifest a group identity through common collective action and therefore cannot be seen as a social collectivity as is a class. Even were this true, and it is clearly disputable, it fails to recognise that non-action may be just as significant in terms of social outcomes as action, a curious lacuna for a Weberian. As Mann says 'the differential impact of gender in modern employment relations may reduce the impact of traditional (predominantly male) collectivities like class' (Mann, 1986, p. 56). The actions and non-actions of women, both in their own right as a discriminated group, and as part of class groupings, have to be taken into account in understanding the performance of classes as social actors. Yet historians and sociologists of all persuasions continue to write about the behaviour of the working class as if it were entirely composed of males.

Despite the well-known methodological difficulties involved, women must be included in empirical studies of class, while in more abstract types of analysis the ways in which gender relations interact with class must be grasped. Mann (1986) points out that the import of studies of gender (as of studies of racial and ethnic divisions) is that stratification is far more complex than the old sociological models allowed for. He believes we should investigate a number of different and distinct 'nuclei' of stratification without automatically assigning primacy to any of them (class and gender, the two I have been discussing, among them, along with race and ethnicity). Future sociology must work along these lines if it is to overcome what Mann calls a serious theoretical crisis in stratification analysis.

Conclusion

As Cockburn has argued, the culture of masculism deforms both men and women. As individuals we are all trapped and constrained by gender stereotypes. Because I have emphasised the way in which sex-typing of jobs has pushed women into inferior places in the hierarchy and into economic dependency, that does not mean that men, too, do not suffer from the pressures of having to live up to ideas of masculine behaviour which may be alien to them as individuals. In interpersonal and emotional terms, sexual stereotypes have intervened between men and women, barring the way to free and supportive relations between the sexes. We are still struggling to come to terms with the conflicts within marriage and within families that arise from differentials in male and female experience, expectations and power.

Politically, divisions between the sexes have weakened the working class. Male trade unionists have wasted their energies trying to preserve the sexual status quo when they could have worked jointly with women to obtain better material rewards and working conditions for the whole class. Middle-class women have, of course, fared better and many share the capitalist and masculist assumptions of their menfolk; however, their own experiences of discrimination and inequity have also led some of them in the past to adopt a more critical view of the societies they live in, and may continue to do so in the future. The channelling of middle-class women into public sector occupations and professions and into jobs concerned with 'the production of people' may also lead some to question the masculist, capitalist assumption that profits are more important than people (as long as they are not all suborned into competing to prove that they can be more deadly than the male). A leavening of masculine culture with views of the world derived from feminine experience would not, of course, remove class or other inequalities from our societies. But it might offer glimpses of alternative values and be a step on the road towards a juster society in which segregation would be transcended, so that there would no longer be any such thing as 'men's work' or 'women's work'.

AFTERWORD

Since the manuscript of this book was completed the Conservative government has put forward proposals to end the ban on women working underground in mines. Developments of this kind initiated by the more socially
progressive governments in the countries of Northern Europe, such as
Denmark and Sweden, have led some European feminists to talk of a new
era of state feminism. I would be hesitant to apply this label to Britain. The
proposal to allow women to return to the mines is motivated less by
concern to bring an end to sex segregation than by a dogmatic
commitment to the ideal of the perfectly free market, unhampered by any
restricting legislation. However the New Right devotion to individual
liberty does open up a space in which those committed to sex equality can
work.

I believe we should respond to these opportunities with wary optimism.
Wariness relates to the motives of capitalist entrepreneurs in the current
economic situation and to the priority given by governments to their
perceived needs. This book has shown how the initial process of industrialisation was founded upon the exploitation of the cheap labour of women
and children. Only when the organised male-led labour movement had
gained sufficient political strength to challenge unchecked capitalist
imperatives did the pattern of sex-typing we know today solidify, as men
reclaimed for themselves the prime labour market consideration. Once
again, entrepreneurs are responding to the challenge of the 'second
industrial revolution' of the information era by attempting to construct a
new phase of capitalist expansion on the base of the cheap labour of
women and young people. The potential difference, this time around, lies
in the possible response of a reconstructed and revitalised labour
movement. The call this time should not be for the restoration of male

privilege and sex segregation in the labour process and the labour market, but for a fairer distribution of employment chances and juster rewards for labour for all, regardless of sex, race or age. It is for this that all those interested in the cause of sex equality should now be campaigning, through all available political channels and pressure groups, but above all within the trade unions. Therein lies the hope for the future.

H. B. May 1989

BIBLIOGRAPHY

Books and Articles

Acker, S. (1987), 'Primary School Teaching as an Occupation' in Delamont, S., *The Primary School Teacher*, Lewes: Falmer Press.

Adburgham, A. (1964), *Shops and Shopping*, London: George Allen and Unwin.

Alexander, S. (1984), 'Women, Class and Sexual Differences in the 1830s and 1840s', *History Workshop Journal* 17, pp. 125–49.

Allen, S. and Wolkowitz, C. (1987), *Homeworking: Myths and Realities*, London: Macmillan.

Allen, V. (1981), *The Militancy of British Miners*, Shipley: Moor Press.

Anderson, B. (1987), 'The Life Course of Soviet Women from 1905–1960' in Millar, J. (ed.), *Politics, Work and Daily Life in the USSR*, Cambridge: University Press.

Anderson, G. (1976), *Victorian Clerks*, Manchester: University Press.

Anderson, M. (1980), *Approaches to the History of the Western Family 1500–1914*, London: Macmillan.

Ardener, S. (1975), *Perceiving Women*, London: Malaby Press.

Ashby, M. (1961), *Joseph Ashby of Tysoe 1859–1919*, Cambridge: University Press.

Atkinson, D., Dallin, A. and Lapidus, G. (1978), *Women in Russia*, Brighton: Harvester.

Attwood, L. and McAndrew, M. (1984), 'Women at Work in the USSR' in Davidson, M. and Cooper, C. (eds), *Working Women: an International Survey*, Chichester: John Wiley.

Baker, E. (1964), *Technology and Woman's Work*, New York: Columbia University Press.

Bamberger, J. (1974), 'The Myth of Matriarchy: Why Men Rule in Primitive Societies' in Rosaldo, M. and Lamphere, L. (eds), *Women, Culture and Society*, Stanford: University Press.

Banks, O. (1981), *Faces of Feminism*, Oxford: Martin Robertson.

Barker, J. and Downing, H. (1980), 'Word Processing and the Transformation of the Patriarchal Relations of Control in the Office', *Capital and Class* 10, pp. 64–99.

Barrett, M. (1980), *Women's Oppression Today*, London: Verso.

Barrett, M. and MacIntosh, M. (1980), '"The Family Wage": some Problems for Socialists and Feminists', *Capital and Class* 2, pp. 51–72.

Barron, R. D. and Norris, G. M. (1976), 'Sexual Divisions and the Dual Labour Market' in Allen, S. and Barker, D. L. (eds), *Dependence and Exploitation in Work and Marriage*, London: Longmans.

Bass, J., Krusell, J. and Alexander, R. (1971), 'Male Managers' Attitudes towards Working Women' in Fidell, L. and Delameter, J. (eds), *Women in the Professions*, London: Sage.

Beale, J. (1982), *Getting it Together*, London: Pluto.

Beauvoir, S. de (1953), *The Second Sex*, London: Jonathan Cape.

Becker, G. (1957), *The Economics of Discrimination*, Chicago: University Press.

Beechey, V. (1977), 'Some Notes on Female Wage Labour in Capitalist Production', *Capital and Class* 3, pp. 45–66.

Beechey, V. (1986), 'Women's Employment in Contemporary Britain' in Beechey, V. and Whitelegg, E. (eds), *Women in Britain Today*, Milton Keynes: Open University Press.

Beechey, V. and Perkins, T. (1987), *A Matter of Hours*, Cambridge: Polity.

Bellaby, P. and Oribator, P. (1980), 'The History of the Present – Contradiction and Struggle in Nursing' in Davies, C. (ed.), *Rewriting Nursing History*, London: Croom Helm.

Bellaby, P. (1986), 'Life Cycle in 3-D', unpublished paper presented at BSA Annual Conference.

Beller, A. (1982), 'Occupational Segregation by Sex: Determinants and Changes', *Journal of Human Resources* 17, pp. 371–91.

Bennett, A. (1954), *Clayhanger*, Harmondsworth: Penguin (first edn 1910).

Board of Trade (1946), *Working Paper Reports: Hosiery*, London: HMSO.

Bondfield, M. (n.d., ?1948), *A Life's Work*, London: Hutchinson.

Boserup, E. (1970), *Women's Role in Economic Development*, New York: St Martin's Press.

Boston, S. (1980), *Women Workers and the Trade Union Movement*, London: Davis Poynter.

Bradley, H. (1986a), 'Technological Change, Management Strategies, and the Development of Gender-Based Job Segregation in the Labour Process' in Knights, D. and Willmott, H. (eds), *Gender and the Labour Process*, London: Gower.

Bradley, H. (1986b), 'Work, Home, and the Restructuring of Jobs' in Purcell, K., Wood. S., Waton, A. and Allen, S. (eds), *The Changing Experience of Work*, London: Macmillan.

Bradley, H. (1987), 'Degradation and Resegmentation: Social and Technological Change in the East Midlands Hosiery Industry 1800–1960', Ph.d. thesis, University of Durham.

Branca, P. (1975), *Silent Sisterhood*, London: Croom Helm.

Braverman, H. (1974), *Labor and Monopoly Capital*, New York: Monthly Review Press.

Braybon, G. (1981), *Women Workers in the First World War*, London: Croom Helm.

Braybon, G. and Summerfield, P. (1987), *Out of the Cage*, London: Pandora.

Brittain, V. (1928), *Women's Work in Modern England*, London: Noel Douglas.

Brod, H. (1987), *The Making of Masculinities*, London: George Allen and Unwin.

Brown, J. (1970), 'A Note on the Division of Labor by Sex', *American Anthropologist* 72:5, pp. 1073–9.

Brownmiller, S. (1976), *Against Our Will*, New York: Bantam.

Bruegel, I. (1979), 'Women as a Reserve Army of Labour: A Note on Recent British Experience', *Feminist Review* 3, pp. 12–23.

Burchill, F. and Ross, R. (1977), *A History of the Potters Union*, Ceramic and Allied Trades Union: Hanley.

Burke, G. (1986), 'The Decline of the Independent Bal Maiden: The Impact of Change in the Cornish Mining Industry' in John, A. (ed.), *Unequal Opportunities*, Oxford: Basil Blackwell.

Burnett, J. (1984), *Destiny Obscure*, Harmondsworth: Penguin.

Burton, A. (1976), *The Miners*, London: Futura.

Byatt, I. (1979), *The British Electrical Industry 1875–1914*, Oxford: Clarendon Press.

Bythell, D. (1978), *The Sweated Trades*, London: Batsford.

Cadbury, E., Matheson, M. and Shann, G. (1906), *Women's Work and Wages*, London: T. Fisher Unwin.

Caplow, T. (1964), *The Sociology of Work*, New York: McGraw Hill.

Carpenter, M. (1977), 'The New Managerialism and Professionalism in Nursing' in Stacey, M. et al. (eds), *Health and the Division of Labour*, London: Croom Helm.

Carpenter, M. (1980), 'Asylum Nursing before 1914: A Chapter in the History of Labour', in Davies, C. (ed.), *Rewriting Nursing History*, London: Croom Helm.

Cassell's Great Industries of Britain, (1873), London: Cassell.

Cavendish, R. (1981), *Women on the Line*, London: Routledge and Kegan Paul.

Chamberlain, M. (1983), *Fenwoman*, London: Routledge and Kegan Paul.

Chapkis, W. and Enloe, C. (1983), *Of Common Cloth*, Amsterdam: Transnational Institute.

Chapman, S. (1967) *The Early Factory Masters*, Newton Abbot: David and Charles.

Charles, L. (1985), 'Introduction' in Charles, L. and Duffin, L. (eds), *Women and Work in Pre-Industrial England*, London: Croom Helm.

Charles, L. and Duffin, L. (1985), *Women and Work in Pre-Industrial England*, London: Croom Helm.

Charles, N. (1983a), 'Women and Trade Unions in the Workplace', *Feminist Review* 15, pp. 3–22.

Charles, N. (1983b), 'Trade Union Censorship', *Women's Studies International Forum* 6:5, pp. 525–33.

Chevillard, N. and Leconte, S. (1986), 'The Dawn of Lineage Societies' in Coontz, S. and Henderson, P. (eds), *Women's Work, Men's Property*, London: Verso.

Chodorow, N. (1978), *The Reproduction of Mothering*, Berkeley: University of California Press.

Christensen, J. (1977), 'Man Power and Woman Power: Technological Change among the Fanti Fishermen of Ghana' in Estellie Smith, M. (ed.), *Those Who Live from the Sea*, New York: West Publishing.

Clark, A. (1982), *Working Life of Women in the Seventeenth Century*, London: Routledge and Kegan Paul reprint (first edn 1910).

Coburn, J. (1974), '"I see and am Silent": A Short History of Nursing in Ontario' in Ontario Women's History Collective, *Women at Work 1850–1930*, Ontario: Canadian Women's Educational Press.

Cockburn, C. (1983), *Brothers*, London: Pluto.

Cockburn, C. (1985), *Machinery of Dominance*, London: Pluto.

Cockburn, C. (1986), 'The Relations of Technology' in Crompton, R. and Mann, M. (eds), *Gender and Stratification*, Cambridge: Polity.

Collins, R. (1985), '"Horses for Courses": Ideology and the Division of Domestic Labour' in Close, P. and Collins, R. (eds), *Family and Economy in Modern Society*, London: Macmillan.

Cook, J. (1984), *Close to the Earth*, London: Routledge and Kegan Paul.

Coontz, S. and Henderson, P. (1986), *Women's Work, Men's Property*, London: Verso.

Coyle, A. (1980), 'The Protection Racket', *Feminist Review* 4, pp. 1–12.

Croll, E. (1983), *Chinese Women Since Mao*, London: Zed.

Crompton, R. and Jones, G. (1984), *White Collar Proletariat*, London: Macmillan.

Dahlberg, F. (1981), *Woman the Gatherer*, New Haven: Yale University Press.

Dahlerup, D. (1987), 'Confusing Concepts – Confusing Reality: a Theoretical Discussion of the Patriarchal State' in Sassoon, A. S. (ed.), *Women and the State*, London: Hutchinson.

Dalla Costa, M. and James, S. (1972), *The Power of Women and the Subversion of the Community*, Bristol: Falling Wall Press.

Davidoff, L., L'Esperance, J. and Newby, H. (1976), 'Landscape with Figures: Home and Community in English Society' in Oakley, A. and Mitchell, J. (eds), *The Rights and Wrongs of Women*, Harmondsworth: Penguin.

Davidoff, L. and Hall, C. (1987), *Family Fortunes*, London: Hutchinson.

Davidson, M. and Cooper, C. (1984), *Working Women: An International Survey*, Chichester: John Wiley.

Davies, C. (1980), *Rewriting Nursing History*, London: Croom Helm.

Davies, M. (1982), *Woman's Place is at the Typewriter*, Philadelphia: Temple University Press.

Day, G. (1982), *Diversity and Decomposition in the Labour Market*, Aldershot, Gower.

Deem, R. (1978), *Women and Schooling*, London: Routledge and Kegan Paul.

Deem, R. (1980), *Schooling for Women's Work*, London: Routledge and Kegan Paul.

Deem, R. (1986), *All Work and No Play*, Milton Keynes: Open University Press.

Delamont, S. (1987), *The Primary School Teacher*, Lewes: Falmer Press.

Delphy, C. (1977), *The Main Enemy*, London: Women's Research and Resources Centre.

Dex, S. (1986), *The Sexual Division of Labour*, Brighton: Harvester.

Dex, S. and Shaw, L. (1986), *British and American Women at Work*, London: Macmillan.

Dodge, N. (1978), 'Women in the Professions' in Atkinson, D., Dallin, A. and Lapidus, G. (eds), *Women in Russia*, Brighton: Harvester.

Douglass, D. and Krieger, J. (1983), *A Miner's Life*, London: Routledge and Kegan Paul.

Dupree, M. (1981), 'Family Structure in the Staffordshire Potteries, 1840–1880', unpublished D. Phil. thesis, Oxford University.

Edwards, R. (1979), *The Contested Terrain*, London: Heinemann.

Ehrenreich, B. and English, D. (1979), *For Her Own Good*, London: Pluto.

Ehrlich, C. (1981), '"The Unhappy Marriage of Marxism and Feminism": Can it be Saved?' in Sargent, L. (ed.), *Women in Revolution: The Unhappy Marriage of Marxism and Feminism*, London: Pluto.

Eisenstein, Z. (1979), *Capitalist Patriarchy and the Case for Socialist Feminism*, New York: Monthly Review Press.

Elshtain, J. B. (1987), 'Feminist Political Rhetoric and Women's Studies' in Nelson, J., Megill, A. and Mclosky, D. (eds), *The Rhetoric of the Human Sciences*, Wisconsin: University Press.

Elston, M. (1977), 'Women in the Medical Profession: Whose Problem?' in Stacey, M. et al. (eds), *Health and the Division of Labour*, London: Croom Helm.

Engels, F. (1972), *The Origin of the Family, Private Property and the State*, New York: Pathfinder (first edn 1884).

England, P. (1982), 'The Failure of Human Capital Theory to Explain Occupational Sex Segregation', *Journal of Human Resources* 17, pp. 358–69.

Epple, G. M. (1977), 'Technological Change in a Grenada West Indies Fishing Community 1950–1970', in Estellie Smith, M. (ed.), *Those Who Live from the Sea*, New York: West Publishing.

Estellie Smith, M. (1977), *Those Who Live from the Sea*, New York: West Publishing.

Estioko-Griffin A., and Griffin, P. Bion (1981), 'Woman the Hunter: the Agta' in Dahlberg, F. (ed.), *Woman the Gatherer*, New Haven: Yale University Press.

Everitt, A. (1967), 'Farm Labourers', in Thirsk, J., *The Agrarian History of England and Wales, Vol. IV 1500–1640*, Cambridge: University Press.

Faulkner, W. and Arnold, E. (1985), *Smothered by Invention*, London: Pluto.

Felkin, W. (1967), *A History of the Machine-Wrought Hosiery and Lace Manufacture*, New York: Augustus M. Kelley reprint (first edn 1867).

Finch, J. (1983), *Married to the Job*, London: George Allen and Unwin.

Fine, G. (1987), 'One of the Boys: Women in Male-dominated Professions' in Kimmel, M. (ed.), *Changing Men*, London: Sage.

Firestone, S. (1979), *The Dialectic of Sex*, London: Women's Press.

Fox, A. (1958), *A History of the National Union of Boot and Shoe Operatives*, Oxford: Basil Blackwell.

Foucault, M. (1976), *A History of Sexuality Vol. I*, Harmondsworth: Penguin.

Frank, P. (1976), 'Women's Work in the Yorkshire Fishing Industry', *Oral History* 4:1, pp. 57–72.

Fussell, G. and Fussell, K. (1985), *The English Countrywoman*, London: Bloomsbury Books (first edn 1953).

Gamarnikow, E. (1978), 'The Sexual Division of Labour: The Case of Nursing' in Kuhn, A. and Wolpe, A. (eds), *Feminism and Materialism*, London: Routledge and Kegan Paul.

Game, A. and Pringle, R. (1983), *Gender at Work*, Sydney: George Allen and Unwin.

Gardiner, J. (1976), 'Domestic Labour in Capitalist Society' in Barker, D. L. and Allen, S. (eds), *Dependence and Exploitation in Work and Marriage*, London: Longmans.

Garson, B. (1977), *All the Livelong Day*, Harmondsworth: Penguin.

Gates, M. (1976), 'Occupational Segregation and the Law' in Blaxall, M. and Reagan, B. (eds), *Women and the Workplace*, Chicago: University Press.

Gelb, J. and Palley, M. L. (1982), *Women and Public Policies*, Princeton: University Press.

Gerson, K. (1987), 'What do Women Want from Men?' in Kimmel, M. (ed.), *Changing Men*, London: Sage.

Gill, C. (1985), *Work, Unemployment and the New Technology*, Cambridge: Polity.

Gillison, G. (1980), 'Images of Nature in Gimi Thought' in MacCormack, C. and Strathern, M. (eds), *Nature, Culture and Gender*, Cambridge: University Press.

Ginswick, J. (1983), *Labour and the Poor in England and Wales 1849–51*, London: Frank Cass.

Gittins, D. (1985), *The Family in Question*, London: Macmillan.

Glucksmann, M. (1986), 'In a Class of Her Own', *Feminist Review* 24, pp. 7–37.

Goldsmith, M. (1946), *Women and the Future*, London: Lindsay Drummond.

Goldthorpe, J. (1980), *Social Mobility and Class Structure in Modern Britain*, Oxford: Clarendon Press.

Goodale, J. (1980), 'Gender, Sexuality and Marriage: A Kaulong Model of Nature and Culture' in MacCormack, C. and Strathern, M. (eds), *Nature, Culture and Gender*, Cambridge: University Press.

Goodman, J., Armstrong, E., Davis, J. and Wagner, A. (1977), *Rule Making and Industrial Peace*, London: Croom Helm.

Graham, E. (1974), 'Schoolmarms and Early Teaching in Ontario' in Ontario Women's History Collective, *Women at Work 1850–1930*, Ontario: Canadian Women's Educational Press.

Gray, M. (1978), *The Fishing Industries of Scotland 1790–1914*, Oxford: University Press.

Green, F. (1927), *History of the English Agricultural Labourer 1870–1920*, London: P. S. King and Son.

Grieco, M. and Whipp, R. (1986), 'Women and the Workplace: Gender and Control in the Labour Process' in Knights, D. and Willmott, H. (eds), *Gender and the Labour Process*, London: Gower.

Gross, E. (1968), 'Plus ça change? The Sexual Structure of Occupations over Time', *Social Problems* 16, pp. 198–208.

Grossman, R. (1980), 'Women's Place in the Integrated Circuit', *Radical America* 14:1, pp. 29–49.

Gullickson, G. (1986), *Spinners and Weavers of Auffay*, Cambridge: University Press.

Hackney WEA, n.d., *Working Lives Vol. I*, Hackney: Centerprise.

Hakim, C. (1979), *Occupational Segregation by Sex*, Department of Employment Research Paper No. 9.

Hakim, C. (1981), 'Job Segregation: Trends in the 1970s', *Department of Employment Gazette* December, pp. 521–9.

Hall, C. (1979), 'The early Formation of Victorian Domestic Ideology' in Burman, S. (ed.), *Fit Work for Women*, London: Croom Helm.

Hall, C. (1980), 'The History of the Housewife' in Malos, E. (ed.), *The Politics of Housework*, London: Allison and Busby.

Hamilton, R. (1978), *The Liberation of Women*, London: George Allen and Unwin.

Hanawalt, B. (1986), *Women and Work in Preindustrial Europe*, Bloomington: Indiana University Press.

Harding, S. (1981), 'What is the Material Base of Patriarchy and Capitalism?' in Sargent, L. (ed.), *Women in Revolution: The Unhappy Marriage of Marxism and Feminism*, London: Pluto.

Harris, O. (1980), 'The Power of Signs: Gender, Culture and the Wild in the Bolivian Andes' in MacCormack, C. and Strathern, M. (eds), *Nature, Culture and Gender*, Cambridge: University Press.

Harrison, P. (1979), *Inside the Third World*, Harmondsworth: Penguin.

Hartmann, H. (1976), 'Patriarchy, Capitalism and Job Segregation by Sex', *Signs* 1:3, pp. 137–68.

Hartmann, H. (1981), 'The Unhappy Marriage of Marxism and Feminism: Towards a More Progressive Union' in Sargent, L. (ed.), *Women in Revolution: The Unhappy Marriage of Marxism and Feminism*, London: Pluto.

Head, P. (1968), 'Boots and Shoes' in Aldcroft, D. (ed.), *The Development of British Industry and Foreign Competition 1875–1914*, London: George Allen and Unwin.

Hellerstein, E., Hume, L. and Offen, K. (1981), *Victorian Women*, Harvester: Brighton.

Herzog, M. (1980), *From Hand to Mouth*, Harmondsworth: Penguin.

Hicks, E. (1981), 'Cultural Marxism: Nonsychrony and Feminist Practice' in

Sargent, L. (ed.), *Women in Revolution: The Unhappy Marriage of Marxism and Feminism*, London: Pluto.

Hill, B. (1984), *Eighteenth-Century Women: An Anthology*, London: George Allen and Unwin.

Hill, G. (1896), *Women in English Life*, London: R. Bentley & Sons.

Hilton, R. (1975), *The English Peasantry in the Later Middle Ages*, Oxford: Clarendon Press.

Hobsbawm, E. (1984), *Worlds of Labour*, London: Weidenfeld and Nicolson.

Holcombe, L. (1973), *Victorian Ladies at Work*, Newton Abbot: David and Charles.

Hollis, P. (1979), *Women in Public*, London: George Allen and Unwin.

Homans, H. (1987), 'Man-made Myths: the Reality of Being a Woman Scientist in the NHS' in Spencer, A. and Podmore, D. (eds), *In a Man's World*, London: Tavistock.

Horowitz Murray, J. (1984), *Strong-minded Women*, Harmondsworth: Penguin.

Hoskins, W. (1957), *The Midland Peasant*, London: Macmillan.

Hostettler, E. (1977), 'Gourlay Steell and the Sexual Division of Labour', *History Workshop Journal* 4, pp. 95–100.

Howell, M. (1986), 'Women, The Family Economy and the Structures of Market Production in Cities of Northern Europe during the Late Middle Ages' in Hanawalt, B. (ed.), *Women and Work in Preindustrial Europe*, Bloomington: University of Indiana Press.

Hudson, D. (1974), *Munby: Man of Two Worlds*, London: Abacus.

Humphries, J. (1977), 'Class Struggle and the Persistence of the Working-Class Family', *Cambridge Journal of Economics* 1:1, pp. 241–58.

Humphries, J. (1981), 'Protective Legislation, The Capitalist State and Working Class Men: The Case of the 1842 Mines Regulation Act', *Feminist Review* 7, pp. 1–33.

Humphries, J. (1983), 'The Emancipation of Women in the 1970s and 1980s', *Capital and Class* 20, pp. 6–27.

Humphries, J. (1987), 'The Origins of the Family: Born out of Scarcity not Wealth' in Sayers, J., Evans, M. and Redclift, N. (eds), *The Origin of the Family*, London: Tavistock.

Hunt, A. (1975), *Management Attitudes and Practices Towards Women at Work*, London: HMSO.

Hutchins, B. and Harrison, A. (1911), *A History of Factory Legislation*, London: G. Bell and Son.

Hutton, D. (1985), 'Women in Fourteenth Century Shrewsbury' in Charles, L. and Duffin, L. (eds), *Women and Work in Pre-Industrial England*, London: Croom Helm.

Huws, U. (1982), *Your Job in the Eighties*, London: Pluto.

Jackson, C. (1984), 'Policies and Implications of Anti-discrimination Strategies' in Schmid, G. and Weitzel, R. (eds), *Sex Discrimination and Equal Opportunity*, Aldershot: Gower.

Jefferys, J. (1954), *Retail Trading in Britain 1850–1950*, Cambridge: University Press.

John, A. (1984), *By the Sweat of Their Brow*, London: Routledge and Kegan Paul.

John, A. (1986), *Unequal Opportunities*, Oxford: Basil Blackwell.

Jones, M. (1961), *Potbank*, London: Secker and Warburg.

Jonung, C. (1984), 'Patterns of Occupational Segregation by Sex in the Labour Market' in Schmid, G. and Weitzel, R. (eds), *Sex Discrimination and Equal Opportunity* Aldershot: Gower.

Jordanova, L. (1980), 'Natural Facts: an Historical Perspective on Science and Sexuality' in MacCormack, C. and Strathern, M. (eds), *Nature, Culture and Gender*, Cambridge: University Press.

Knightly, C. (1984), *Country Voices*, London: Thames and Hudson.

Kimmel, M. (1987a), *Changing Men*, London: Sage.

Kimmel, M. (1987b), 'The Contemporary "Crisis" of Masculinity in Historical Perspective' in Brod, H. (ed.), *The Making of Masculinities*, London: George Allen and Unwin.

King, P. (1948), 'Task Perception and Inter-Personal Relations in Industrial Training' Pt 1, *Human Relations* 1:3, pp. 721–30; Pt 2, *Human Relations* 1:4, pp. 373–412.

Kitteringham, J. (1975), 'Country Work Girls in Nineteenth-Century England' in Samuel, R. (ed.), *Village Life and Labour*, London: Routledge and Kegan Paul.

Kowaleski, M. (1986), 'Women's Work in a Market Town: Exeter in the Late Fourteenth Century' in Hanawalt, B. (ed.), *Women and Work in Preindustrial Europe*, Bloomington: University of Indiana Press.

Kreckel, R. (1980), 'Unequal Opportunity Structure and Labour Market Segmentation', *Sociology* 4, pp. 525–50.

Kuhn, A. and Wolpe A (1978), *Feminism and Materialism*, London: Routledge and Kegan Paul.

Lacey, K. (1985), 'Women and Work in Fourteenth and Fifteenth Century London' in Charles, L. and Duffin, L. (eds), *Women and Work in Pre-industrial England*, London: Croom Helm.

Land, H. (1976), 'Women: Supporters or Supported?' in Allen, S. and Barker, D. L. (eds), *Sexual Divisions in Society*, London: Tavistock.

Lapidus, G. (1978), *Women in Soviet Society*, Berkeley: University of California Press.

Larguia, I. (1975), 'The Economic Base of the Status of Women' in Rohrlich-Leavitt, R. (ed.), *Women Cross-Culturally: Change and Challenge*, The Hague: Mouton.

Larwood, L. and Gutek, B. (1984), 'Women at Work in the USA' in Davidson, M. and Cooper, C. (eds), *Working Women: an International Survey*, Chichester: Wiley.

Laws, J. (1976), 'Work Aspiration of Women: False Leads and New Starts' in Blaxall, M. and Reagan, B. (eds), *Women and the Workplace*, Chicago: University of Chicago.

Lawrence, B. (1987), 'The Fifth Dimension – Gender and General Practice' in Spencer, A. and Podmore, D. (eds), *In a Man's World*, London: Tavistock.

Leacock, E. (1975), 'Class, Community and the Status of Women' in Rohrlich-Leavitt, R. (ed.), *Women Cross-Culturally: Change and Challenge*, The Hague: Mouton.

Leeson, J. and Gray, J. (1978), *Women in Medicine*, London: Tavistock.

Leibowitz, L. (1986), 'In the Beginning: The Origins of the Sexual Division of Labour and the Development of the First Human Societies', in Coontz, S. and Henderson, P. (eds), *Women's Work, Men's Property*, London: Verso.

Leicester Industrial Handbook (1946), Leicester: City Council.

Lévi-Strauss, C. (1969), *The Elementary Structure of Kinship*, Boston: Beacon.

Levine, D. (1977), *Family Formation in an Age of Nascent Capitalism*, New York: Academic Press.

Lewenhak, S. (1980), *Women and Work*, Glasgow: Fontana.

Lewis, J. (1984), *Women in England 1870–1950*, Brighton: Wheatsheaf.

Llewellyn Smith, H. (1931, 1933), *The New Survey of London Life and Labour*, Vol. II, Vol. V, London: P. S. King and Son.

Lloyd, C. (1975), *Sex, Discrimination and the Division of Labour*, New York: Columbia University Press.

Lockwood, Baroness and Knowles, W. (1984), 'Women at Work in Great Britain' in Davidson, M. and Cooper, C. (eds), *Working Women: An International Survey*, Chichester: John Wiley.

Lockwood, D. (1986), 'Class, Status and Gender' in Crompton, R. and Mann, M. (eds), *Gender and Stratification*, Cambridge: Polity.

London Feminist History Group (1983), *The Sexual Dynamics of History*, London: Pluto.

Lorber, J. (1984), *Women Physicians*, Tavistock: London.

Lovenduski, J. (1987), 'Hard Lessons for Dons of Inequality', *Guardian*, 15 December 1987.

Lukes, S. (1974), *Power: a Radical View*, London: Macmillan.

Lummis, T. (1985), *Occupation and Society*, Cambridge: University Press.

Lyotard, J. P. (1984), *The Postmodern Condition*, Manchester: University Press.

McAuley, A. (1981), *Women's Work and Wages in the Soviet Union*, London: George Allen and Unwin.

McAuley, J. (1987), 'Women Academics: A Case Study in Inequality', in Spencer, A. and Podmore, D. (eds), *In a Man's World*, London: Tavistock.

MacCormack, C. (1980), 'Nature, Culture and Gender: A Critique' in MacCormack, C. and Strathern, M. (eds), *Nature, Culture and Gender*, Cambridge: University Press.

MacCormack, C. and Strathern, M. (1980), *Nature, Culture and Gender*, Cambridge: University Press.

McCullough Thew, L. (1985), *The Pit Village and the Store*, London: Pluto.

McDonough, R. and Harrison, R. (1978), 'Patriarchy and Relations of Production' in Kuhn, A. and Wolpe, A. M. (eds), *Feminism and Materialism*, London: Routledge and Kegan Paul.

Macfarlane, A. (1978), *The Origins of English Individualism*, Oxford: Basil Blackwell.

McGrew, W. (1981), 'The Female Chimpanzee as a Human Evolutionary Prototype' in Dahlberg, F. (ed.), *Woman the Gatherer*, New Haven: Yale University Press.

Mackenzie, C. (1983), 'Women and Psychiatric Professionalisation 1780–1914' in London Feminist History Group, *The Sexual Dynamics of History*, London: Pluto.

Mackintosh, M. (1977), 'Reproduction and Property: A Critique of Meillassoux,' *Capital and Class* 2, pp. 119–27.

McNally, F. (1979), *Women for Hire: A Study of the Female Office Worker*, London: Macmillan.

Madden, J. (1975), 'Discrimination: A Manifestation of Male Market Power?' in Lloyd, C. (ed.), *Sex, Discrimination and the Division of Labour*, New York: Columbia University Press.

Malcolmson, R. (1981), *Life and Labour in England 1700–1780*, London: Hutchinson.

Mallier, A. and Rosser, M. (1987), *Women and the Economy*, London: Macmillan.

Mann, M. (1986), 'A Crisis in Stratification?' in Crompton, R. and Mann, M. (eds), *Gender and Stratification*, Cambridge: Polity.

Mark-Lawson, J. and Witz, A. (1988), 'The Family System of Labour in Nineteenth Century Coalmining: Familial Control or Patriarchal Domination?' paper presented to BSA Annual Conference.

Martin, H. and Roberts, C. (1984), *Women and Employment: A Lifetime Perspective*, London, HMSO.

Marx, K. and Engels, F. (1967), *Communist Manifesto*, Harmondsworth: Penguin (first edn 1848).

Matthaei, J. (1982), *An Economic History of Women in America*, Brighton: Harvester

Meade-King, (1988), 'Those who Made it Can't Take it' *Guardian*, 8 October 1988.

Middleton, C. (1979), 'The Sexual Division of Labour in Feudal England', *New Left Review* 113–14, pp. 147–68.

Middleton, C. (1985), 'Women's Labour and the Transition to Industrial Capitalism' in Charles, L. and Duffin, L. (eds), *Women and Work in Pre-Industrial England*, London: Croom Helm.

Middleton, C. (1988), 'The Familiar Fate of the Famulae: Gender Divisions in the History of Wage Labour' in Pahl, R. (ed.), *On Work*, Oxford: Blackwell.

Mies, M. (1986), *Patriarchy and Accumulation on a World Scale*, London, Zed, 1986.

Millar, J. (1987), *Politics, Work and Daily Life in the USSR*, Cambridge: University Press.

Miller, C. (1980), 'Farming, Farm work and Farm workers in Victorian Gloucestershire', unpublished Ph.D. thesis, Bristol University.

Millet, K. (1971), *Sexual Politics*, London: Sphere.

Mitchell, J. (1975), *Psychoanalysis and Feminism*, Harmondsworth: Penguin.

More, C. (1980), *Skill and the English Working Class*, London: Croom Helm.

Morgan, D. (1975), 'The Place of Harvesters in Nineteenth-Century Village Life' in Samuel, R. (ed.), *Village Life and Labour*, London: Routledge and Kegan Paul.

Murdock, G. and Provost, C. (1973), 'Factors in the Division of Labour by Sex: A Cross-Cultural Analysis', *Ethnology* 12:2, pp. 203–35.

Murgatroyd, L. (1985), 'The Production of People and Domestic Labour Revisited' in Close, P. and Collins, R. (eds), *Family and Economy in Modern Society*, London: Macmillan.

Murray, P. and Wickham, J. (1982), 'Technocratic Ideology and the Reproduction of Inequality: The Case of the Electronics Industry in the Republic of Ireland' in Day, G. (ed.), *Diversity and Decomposition in the Labour Market*, Aldershot: Gower.

Neale, J. (1983), *Memoirs of a Callous Picket*, London: Pluto.

New International Co-operative (1985), *Women: A World Report*, London: Methuen.

Newby, H. (1980), *Green and Pleasant Land?*, Harmondsworth: Penguin.

Novarra, V. (1980), *Women's Work, Men's Work*, London: Marion Boyars.

Oakley, A. (1976a), *Housewife*, Harmondsworth: Penguin.

Oakley, A. (1976b), 'Wisewoman and Medicine Man' in Oakley, A. and Mitchell, J. (eds), *The Rights and Wrongs of Women*, Harmondsworth: Penguin.

Oakley. A, (1981), *Subject Woman*, Harmondsworth: Penguin.

Ontario Women's History Collective (1974), *Women at Work 1850–1930*, Ontario: Canadian Women's Educational Press.

Oram, A. (1983), 'Serving Two Masters? The Introduction of a Marriage Bar in Teaching in the 1920s' in London Feminist History Group, *The Sexual Dynamics of History*, London: Pluto.

Ortner, S. (1974), 'Is Female to Male as Nature is to Culture?' in Rosaldo, M. and Lamphere, L. (eds), *Women, Culture and Society*, Stanford: University Press.

Osterud, N. (1977), 'The Sexual Division of Labour', *History Workshop Journal* 4, pp. 42–3.

Osterud, N. (1986), 'Gender Divisions and the Organisation of Work in the

Leicester Hosiery Industry' in John, A. (ed.), *Unequal Opportunities*, Oxford: Blackwell.

Pahl, R. (1984), *Divisions of Labour*, Oxford: Blackwell.

Parmar, P. (1982), 'Gender, Race and Class: Asian Women in Resistance' in Centre for Contemporary Cultural Studies, *The Empire Strikes Back*, London: Hutchinson.

Parr, J. (1986), 'Disaggregating the Sexual Division of Labour: A Transatlantic Case Study', unpublished paper.

Partington, G. (1976), *Women Teachers in the Twentieth Century*, London: NFER.

Phillips Bevan, G. (1876, 1877), *The Industrial Classes and Industrial Statistics*, Vol. I, Vol. II, London: Edward Stanford.

Pinchbeck, I. (1981), *Women Workers and the Industrial Revolution*, London: Virago reprint (first edn 1930).

Plummer, A. (1937), *New British Industries in the Twentieth Century*, London: Pitman.

Pollert, A. (1981), *Girls, Wives, Factory Lives*, London: Macmillan.

Porter, M. (1983), '"Women and Old Boats": the Sexual Division of Labour in a Newfoundland Outpost' in Gamarnikow, E., Morgan, D., Purvis, J., Taylorson, D. (eds), *The Public and the Private*, London: Heinemann.

Power, E. (1975), *Medieval Women*, Cambridge: University Press.

Pownall, P. (1979), *Fisheries of Australia*, Farnham: Fishing News Books.

Prather, J. (1971), 'Why Can't Women be More Like Men' in Fidell, L. and Delameter, J. (eds), *Women in the Professions*, London: Sage.

Purcell, K. (1982), 'Female Manual Workers, Fatalism and the Reinforcement of Inequalities' in Robbins, D., *Rethinking Social Inequality*, Aldershot: Gower.

Randall, V. (1987), *Women and Politics*, London: Macmillan.

Razzell, P., and Wainwright, R. (1973), *The Victorian Working Class*, London: Frank Cass.

Rendel, M. (1980), 'How Many Women Academics 1912–1976?' in Deem, R. (ed.), *Schooling for Women's Work*, London: Routledge and Kegan Paul.

Reyerson, K. (1986), 'Women in Business in Medieval Montpellier' in Hanawalt, B. (ed.), *Women and Work in Preindustrial Europe*, Bloomington: Indiana University Press.

Roberts, M. (1979), 'Sickles and Scythes: Women's Work and Men's Work at Harvest Time', *History Workshop Journal* 7, pp. 3–28.

Roberts, Y. (1984), *Man Enough*, London: Chatto and Windus.

Rohrlich-Leavitt, R. (1975), *Women Cross-Culturally: Continuity and Change*, The Hague: Mouton.

Rosaldo, M. (1974), 'Women, Culture and Society: A Theoretical Overview' in Rosaldo, M. and Lamphere, L. (eds), *Women, Culture and Society*, Stanford: University Press.

Rosaldo, M. and Lamphere, L. (1974), *Women, Culture and Society*, Stanford: University Press.

Rose, S. (1986), 'Gender at Work: Sex, Class and Industrial Capitalism', *History Workshop Journal* 21, pp. 113–31.

Rosser, J. and Davies, C. (1987), '"What Would We Do Without Her?" – Invisible Women in NHS Administration' in Spencer, A. and Podmore, D. (eds), *In a Man's World*, London: Tavistock.

Rowbotham, S. (1981), 'The Trouble with "Patriarchy"' in Feminist Anthology Collective (eds), *No Turning Back*, London: Women's Press.

Rubery, J. (1980), 'Structured Labour Markets, Worker Organisation and Low Pay', in Amsden, A. (ed.), *The Economics of Women and Work*, Harmondsworth: Penguin.

Rubin, G. (1975), 'The Traffic in Women: Notes on the "Political Economy" of Sex' in Rapp, R. (ed.), *Towards an Anthropology of Women*, New York: Monthly Review Press.

Saffioti, H. (1975), 'Female Labor and Capitalism in the United State and Brazil' in Rohrlich-Leavitt, C. (ed.), *Women Cross-Culturally*, The Hague: Mouton.

Saliou, M. (1986), 'The Processes of Women's Subordination in Primitive and Archaic Greece' in Coontz, S. and Henderson, P. (eds), *Women's Work, Men's Property*, London: Verso.

Samuel, R. (1975), *Village Life and Labour*, London: Routledge and Kegan Paul.

Sargent, L. (1981), *Women in Revolution : The Unhappy Marriage of Marxism and Feminism*, London: Pluto.

Sarbsy, J. (1985), 'Sexual Segregation in the Pottery Industry', *Feminist Review* 21, pp. 67–93.

Sarsby, J. (1988), *Missuses and Mouldrunners*, Milton Keynes: Open University Press.

Science Policy Research Unit (1982), *Microelectronics and Women's Employment in Britain*, University of Sussex.

Schmid, G. and Weitzel, R. (1984), *Sex Discrimination and Equal Opportunity*, Aldershot: Gower.

Scott, A. (1986), 'Industrialisation, Gender Segregation and Stratification Theory' in Crompton, R. and Mann, M. (eds), *Gender and Stratification*, Cambridge: Polity.

Scott, J. D. (1985), *Siemens Brothers 1858–1958*, London: Weidenfeld and Nicolson.

Scott, J. and Tilly, L. (1975), 'Women's Work amd the Family', *Comparative Studies in Society and History* 17, pp. 44–5.

Seccombe, W. (1974), 'The Housewife and her Labour under Capitalism', *New Left Review* 83, pp. 3–24.

Segalen, M. (1983), *Love and Power in the Peasant Family*, Oxford: Basil Blackwell.

Sharpe, S. (1976), *Just Like a Girl*, Harmondsworth: Penguin.

Sharpe, S. (1984), *Double Identity*, Harmondsworth: Penguin.

Shaw, C. (1977), *When I was a Child*, Firle, Sussex: Caliban (first edn 1903).

Shaw, S. (1970), *History of the Staffordshire Potteries*, Newton Abbot: David and Charles reprint (first edn 1829).

Shorter, E. (1976), 'Women's Work: What Difference did Capitalism Make?', *Theory and Society* 3:4, pp. 513–29.

Showalter, E. (1987), *The Female Malady*, London: Virago.

Slettan, D. (1982), 'Farmwives, Farm Hands and the Changing Rural Community in Trøndelag Norway', in Thompson, P. (ed.), *Our Common History*, London: Pluto.

Smith, D. (1982), 'Women in the Local Labour Market' in Day, G. (ed.), *Diversity and Decomposition in the Labour Market*, Aldershot: Gower.

Snell, K. (1985), *Annals of the Labouring Poor*, Cambridge: University Press.

Spencer, A. and Podmore, D. (1987), *In a Man's World*, London: Tavistock.

Stacey, M., Reid, M., Heath, C. and Dingwall, R. (1977), *Health and the Division of Labour*, London: Croom Helm.

Stamp, P. and Roberts, S. (1986), *Positive Action: Changing the Workplace for Women*, London: NCCL.

Stanley, L. and Wise, S. (1983), *Breaking Out*, London: Routledge and Kegan Paul.

Stanworth, M. (1983), *Gender and Schooling*, London: Hutchinson.

Stearns, P. (1972), 'Working-Class Women in Britain 1890–1914' in Vicinus, M.

(ed.), *Suffer and Be Still*, Bloomington: Indiana University Press.

Stone, L. (1979), *The Family, Sex and Marriage in England 1500–1800*, Harmondsworth: Penguin.

Strathern, M. (1980), 'No Nature, No Culture: The Hagen Case' in MacCormack, C. and Strathern, M. (eds), *Nature, Culture and Gender*, Cambridge: University Press.

Stuart, M. (1933), *The Girl Through the Ages*, London: Harrap.

Summerfield, P. (1984), *Women Workers in the Second World War*, London: Croom Helm.

Sutton, G. and Sutton, B. (1979), *C. and J. Clark 1835–1903*, York: William Sessions.

Swindells, J. (1985), *Victorian Writing and Working Women*, Cambridge: Polity.

Sykes, A. (1969), 'Navvies: Their Work Attitudes' and 'Navvies: Their Social Relations', *Sociology* 3, pp. 21–54, pp. 157–72.

Thom, D. (1978), 'Women at the Woolwich Arsenal 1915–1919', *Oral History* 6:2 pp. 58–73.

Thompson, F. (1946), *Lark Rise*, London: Guild Books.

Thompson, P. (1982), *Our Common History*, London: Pluto.

Thompson, P., Wailey, T. and Lummis, T. (1983), *Living the Fishing*, London: Routledge and Kegan Paul.

Thompson, P. (1983), *The Nature of Work*, London: Macmillan.

Tickner, F. W. (1923), *Women in English Economic History*, London: J. M. Dent and Sons.

Tiger, L. and Fox, R. (1971), *The Imperial Animal*, New York: Holt, Rinehart and Winston.

Tropp, A. (1957), *The School Teachers*, London: Heinemann.

Tunstall, J. (1962), *The Fishermen*, London: McGibbon and Kee.

Tusser, T. (1984), *Five Hundred Points of Good Husbandry*, Oxford: University Press, reprint (first edn 1580).

Versluysen, M. (1980), 'Old Wives' Tales? Women Healers in English History' in Davies, C. (ed.), *Rewriting Nursing History*, London: Croom Helm.

Vicinus, M. (1985), *Independent Women*, London: Virago.

Vogel, L. (1981), 'Marxism and Feminism: Unhappy Marriage, Trial Separation or Something Else?' in Sargent, L. (ed.), *Women in Revolution: The Unhappy Marriage of Marxism and Feminism*, London: Pluto.

Wainwright, H. (1984), 'Women and the Division of Labour' in Abrams, P. and Brown, R. (eds), *UK Society: Work, Urbanism and Inequality*, London: Weidenfeld and Nicolson.

Walby, S. (1986), *Patriarchy at Work*, Cambridge: Polity.

Walby, S. (1988), 'The Historical Periodisation of Patriarchy' paper presented at BSA Annual Conference.

Weathergill, L. (1971), *The Pottery Trade in North Staffordshire 1660–1760*, Manchester: University Press.

Webb, S. (1982), 'Gender and Authority in the Workplace', paper presented at BSA Annual Conference.

Weber, M. (1964), *The Theory of Social and Economic Organisation*, London: Macmillan.

Wertheimer, B. (1977), *We Were There*, New York: Pantheon Books.

Westwood, S. (1984), *All Day Every Day*, London: Pluto.

Whitaker, W. (1973), *Victorian and Edwardian Shopworkers*, Newton Abbot: David and Charles.

Widdowson, F. (1983), *Going up into the Next Class*, London: Hutchinson.

Wiesner, M. (1986), 'Early Modern Midwifery: A Case Study' in Hanawalt, B. (ed.), *Women and Work in Preindustrial Europe*, Bloomington: Indiana University Press.

Wild, R. and Hill, A. (1970), *Women in the Factory*, Institute of Personnel Management.

Williams, G., Blackstone, T. and Metcalf, D. (1974), *The Academic Labour Market*, Amsterdam: Elsevier Scientific Publishing.

Williams, K. (1980), 'From Sarah Gamp to Florence Nightingale: A Critical Study of Hospital Nursing Systems from 1840 to 1897' in Davies, C. (ed.), *Rewriting Nursing History*, London: Croom Helm.

Williamson, B. (1982), *Class, Culture and Community*, London: Routledge and Kegan Paul.

Willis, P. (1977), *Learning to Labour*, Aldershot: Gower.

Willmott, P. and Young, M. (1973), *The Symmetrical Family*, London: Routledge and Kegan Paul.

Wills, R. (1861), *Lays of Lowly Life*, London: Simpkin, Marshall and Co.

Wilson, A. (1978), *Finding a Voice*, London: Virago.

Wilson, V. (1971), 'An Analysis of Femininity in Nursing' in Fidell, L. and Delamater, J. (eds), *Women in the Professions*, London: Sage.

Wise, S. and Stanley, L. (1987), *Georgie Porgie*, London: Pandora.

Wolf, M. (1985), *Revolution Postponed*, London: Methuen.

Wright, S. (1985), '"Churmaids, Huswyfes and Hucksters": The Employment of Women in Tudor and Stuart Salisbury' in Charles, L. and Duffin, L. (eds), *Women and Work in Pre-Industrial England*, London: Croom Helm.

Yeandle, S. (1984), *Women's Working Lives*, London: Tavistock.

Young, I. (1981), 'Beyond the Happy Marriage: A Critique of the Dual Systems Theory' in Sargent, L. (ed.), *Women and Revolution: The Unhappy Marriage of Marxism and Feminism*, London: Pluto.

Zaretsky, E. (1976), *Capitalism, The Family and Personal Life*, London: Pluto.

Zemon Davis, N. (1986), 'Women in the Crafts in Sixteenth-Century Lyon' in Hanawalt, B. (ed.), *Women and Work in Preindustrial Europe*, Bloomington: University of Indiana Press.

Zihlman, A. (1981), 'Women as Shapers of Human Adaptation' in Dahlberg, F. (ed.), *Woman the Gatherer*, New Haven: Yale University Press.

Zimmeck, M. (1986), 'Jobs for the Girls: The Expansion of Clerical Work for Women 1850–1914' in John, A. (ed.), *Unequal Opportunities*, Oxford: Basil Blackwell.

Parliamentary Papers and Official Publications

1816 iii Children's Employment Commission

1842 xv Children's Employment Commission (Mines): First Report.

1842 xvi Children's Employment Commission (Mines): Appendix Pt I.

1842 xvii Children's Employment Commission (Mines): Appendix Pt II.

1843 xii Poor Law Commission: Report on Employment of Women and Children in Agriculture.

1843 xiii Children's Employment Commission.

1843 xiv Children's Employment Commission.

1845 xv Royal Commission on the Condition of the Framework Knitters.
1851 xxiii Commissioners' Reports: Report on Mining Districts.
1852–3 lxxxviii Pt I Census of Population.
1845–5 xiv Report of the Select Committee on the Stoppage of Wages (hosiery).
1860 xxii Select Committee on Masters and Operatives.
1863 xviii Children's Employment Commission: First Report.
1864 xxii Children's Employment Commission: Second Report.
1865 xx Children's Employment Commission: Fourth Report.
1867–8 xvii Report on Agriculture (Employment of Women and Children).
1867–8 xxxix Royal Commission on Trade Unions: Tenth Report.
1875 xvi Reports on Inspectors of Factories.
1876 xxx Factory and Workshops Act (Minutes of Evidence).
1888 xx Sweating Commission: First Report.
1888 xxi Sweating Commission: Second Report.
1892 xxxvi Pt 2 Royal Commission on Labour.
1893–4 xxxv The Agricultural Labourer: Vol. I (England).
1893–4 xxxvi The Agricultural Labourer: Vol. II (Wales), Vol. III (Scotland).
1893–4 xxxvii Royal Commission on Labour: Report on the Employment of Women.
1894 lxxxi Pt II Report on Statistics on the Employment of Women.
1899 lxxv Report on Education.
1908 lix Report of the Truck Commission.
1919 xxxi Report of the War Cabinet on Women in Industry.
1929–30 xvii Report on Distribution of Women in Industry.
1945–6 Royal Commission on Equal Pay.
1970–87 New Earnings Survey.
1981 Census: Economic Activity.
1983 General Household Survey.
1984, 1988 United States Bureau of the Census, Statistical Abstract of the United States.
1985 Labour Force Survey.
1985 Statistics of Education: Teachers in Service.
1988 Eurostat, Employment and Unemployment.

INDEX